200 + VEGETARIAN PASTA RECIPES

200 +
VEGETARIAN PASTA
RECIPES

MARLENA SPIELER

Thorsons

An Imprint of HarperCollins*Publishers*

For Leah Matisse
And for Bachi

Thorsons
An Imprint of HarperCollins*Publishers*
77–85 Fulham Palace Road,
Hammersmith, London W6 8JB
1160 Battery Street,
San Francisco, California 94111–1213

First published by Thorsons 1993
1 3 5 7 9 10 8 6 4 2

© Marlena Spieler 1993

Marlena Spieler asserts the moral right to
be identified as the author of this work

Illustrations by Dandi Palmer

A catalogue record for this book
is available from the British Library

ISBN 0 7225 2797 7

Phototypeset by Harper Phototypesetters Limited,
Northampton, England
Printed in Great Britain by
The Bath Press, Avon

CONTENTS

Acknowledgments
7

Introduction
8

A World Guide to Pasta
13

Soups and Stews
18

Cold Pasta Dishes
44

Very Quick Pasta
64

Pasta with Sauces of Vegetables, Cheeses and Beans
99

Far Eastern Pasta
189

Baked Pasta
216

Stuffed Pasta and Dumplings
233

Basic Recipes
252

Index
265

ACKNOWLEDGMENTS

For every cookbook that is written there are background eaters, dutifully tasting and chewing their way through the failures as well as the successes.

THANK YOU

Leah for her gastronomical stamina when the subject was pasta for dinner.

Alan McLaughlan, for his quirky shopping trips to Berwick Street and Portobello Road, not to mention Chrisp Street.

Christine Smith, who complained only politely when for months at a time everything we ate was *al dente*.

The family Wight: Rachel and Jim, Jenny and Jo Ann, for friendship, often accompanied by pasta.

Paul Richardson for his sense of humour and friendship whichever country we meet up in; Leslie Forbes for her generosity, encouragement and wonderful food ideas.

Paula Levine and Richard Hudd; Fred and Mary Barclay; Kathleen Griffen; Gretchen Spieler, who ate transcontinentally; Amanda and Tim Hamilton-Hemmeter for tales of Nigel the horse, as well as a recipe for very good tomato sauce; to Melissa and Steven Opper, who love pasta as much as I do; Kaye Loveridge for her computer expertise.

Freud, our garlic-smelling kitty, who sat on our laps at the dinner table and fought us for every forkful.

Thank you Sarah Sutton, always patient, always enthusiastic editor.

Deepest thanks to Executive Food Editor Michael Bauer of the *San Francisco Chronicle*, from whom I have learned much.

I'd like to acknowledge that several of the recipes in this book have been adapted from the *San Francisco Chronicle*, *Bon Appetit Magazine* (USA), *Taste Magazine* (UK), and books: *From Pantry to Table* (Addison Wesley USA), *Sun-Drenched Cuisine* (Ebury, U.K, Tarcher USA), *Hot & Spicy* (Grafton UK, Tarcher USA), and *The Flavour of California* (Thorsons, UK).

INTRODUCTION

From teething toddler to senior citizen, everyone loves pasta. The Chinese serve noodles on birthdays to signify long life; Eastern Europeans eat noodles sauced with peppery goulash or with sweet spices and gentle cheese; the French serve delicate pasta dishes with sauces of subtlety and grace; Southeast Asians with spicy, tart, and delightfully startling toppings. But it is the Italians who, rich or poor, humble or grand, eat pasta every day, with a passion. Pasta is central to the Italian drama of the dinner table, where everyday life is transcended and the little stories and happenings of the day are related, amplified, and chewed over.

Indeed, is there any other dish that one could eat every day of the week and not grow bored with? Pasta is consummately versatile and can be served with whatever the garden or market has to offer. The most delicious of pasta dishes are often the simple ones born of necessity, made from the frugal ingredients a cook might have on hand. Then there is the other delicious extreme: pasta splashed with rich cream or rare ingredients such as wild mushrooms or truffles.

And the pasta itself comes in an endless variety of shapes and sizes: ranging from supple strands to flat, wide noodles, from chunky, chewy tubes to curly worm-like shapes, tiny nuggets the size and shape of rice or letters of the alphabet, to even smaller ones the size of peppercorns, and so on, *ad infinitum*. I've seen heart-shaped pasta for Valentine's day, stars for national holidays, Christmas trees, and funny faces or little people-shapes for children to amuse themselves with.

While pasta is usually prepared from wheat flour, it may also be made from a wide variety of other grains and flavoured with a near endless selection of vegetables, herbs, etc. Wholewheat, buckwheat, rice, mung beans, yam flour, ground corn, vegetable powders such as artichoke, tomato, beetroot (beets), the list goes on and on. Natural foods shops often have a good selection, as do ethnic markets. Recently I made a delightful discovery in London's Chinatown of flat dried rice noodles tinted various pastel hues with vegetable mixtures.

Pasta can be prepared in a wide variety of ways, too: floating in broth, tossed with savoury vegetables, cloaked in silken cream, stir-fried into chow mein.

High carbohydrate, low-fat and inexpensive, pasta is as healthfully sustaining and as economical as the ingredients it shares the pot with.

A SHORT HISTORY OF PASTA

Though some claim that Marco Polo brought pasta from China to Italy, and hence Europe, we know that this is not true: he returned from his Asian travels in 1292 and records of pasta-eating in Italy date from much earlier than that.

Indeed, it is likely that pasta originated in the Middle East and spread from there. The first pasta was a pounded paste of toasted grains eaten in Neolithic times; eventually this paste was boiled into dumpling shapes, much like modern pasta.

From the Middle East it spread east and west, north and south. One of the first records we have of pasta-eating in Italy is a 4th-century bas-relief from a tomb outside Rome, showing pasta-making tools which look remarkably like the ones used today.

By the 15th century a huge variety of pasta existed in Italy, and the popularity of noodles and dumplings was spreading throughout Europe.

In the 18th century Thomas Jefferson brought pasta to the New World after having fallen in love with it in Italy. He took a pasta machine and some Parmesan cheese back to Washington so that his cook could prepare his favourite food.

Waves of Italian immigrants, as well as German and Swedish ones, brought their pasta dishes to America's culinary melting pot, until today pasta is one of the national dishes of the United States.

Pasta is universally loved in Britain, where the one-time national dish of 'spag bol' has given way to a wide range of pastas, tossed together with fresh vegetables, savoury oils and seasonings.

Pasta can be a humble dish for everyday nurturing, or an elegant dish of great sophistication. In this collection of recipes I have tried to include a little of everything, from rich to lean, simple to complex, traditional to innovative. The array of luscious meals one can prepare with pasta is virtually endless.

NOTES ON THE RECIPES

Measurements are given in metric, imperial and American. While American measurements are usually given in volume measures (i.e. cups) rather than weights, I have indicated amounts of uncooked pasta by weight because that is how it is sold. Since most dried pasta is sold in one pound packages, 4 oz of pasta roughly indicates a quarter of the package; if the package is of a different weight, adjust accordingly. When a small amount of uncooked pasta or any amount of cooked pasta is called for, it is given in cups rather than weight measurements.

In the **American equivalents** I've also taken a few liberties on behalf of ease of preparation.

For the soups, I call for 1 quart of stock or water in the U.S. ingredient lists, 1 litre/1¾ pints in the British. While the amounts are not exactly equal, they are close enough that there should be no problems. If any soup seems too dry or watery, adjust the liquid to suit your own taste.

Similarly, there are recipes in which the British amounts and American amounts might not appear to match. This is because some ingredients vary significantly in size or composition between the two countries, and I have included the one that will work the best in the country concerned.

All **garlic** means large cloves as I firmly believe one can never have too much garlic. I do admit, however, that the amounts of garlic in many of my recipes could be too much for some readers' taste – for those who don't share my passion feel free to reduce the amount to suit your own palate.

All **olive oil** is extra virgin or as full-flavoured an oil as you can find.

Vegetable stock, in a perfect world, means homemade and very flavourful (see page 260). In my less-than-perfect world, vegetable stock often means hot water mixed with a stock cube or two, unless otherwise noted.

Do not use ready-grated **Parmesan cheese**, use a chunk and grate it yourself or have it grated for you. If you cannot get a whole chunk of Parmesan, better to use a humbler cheese than a pre-grated one. A number of cheeses are delicious for grating and much less expensive than Parmesan. There are also various less expensive Parmesans, such as a very nice one from South America.

Serving portions are indicated in the recipes but are highly subjective: when it comes to pasta, what constitutes a meal-sized portion for one eater might be no more than a snack for someone else, and vice versa. It also depends on what else is on your menu, and whether the pasta is to be a first course, soup or main dish. When in doubt, use your own judgement about your own and your fellow eaters' appetites.

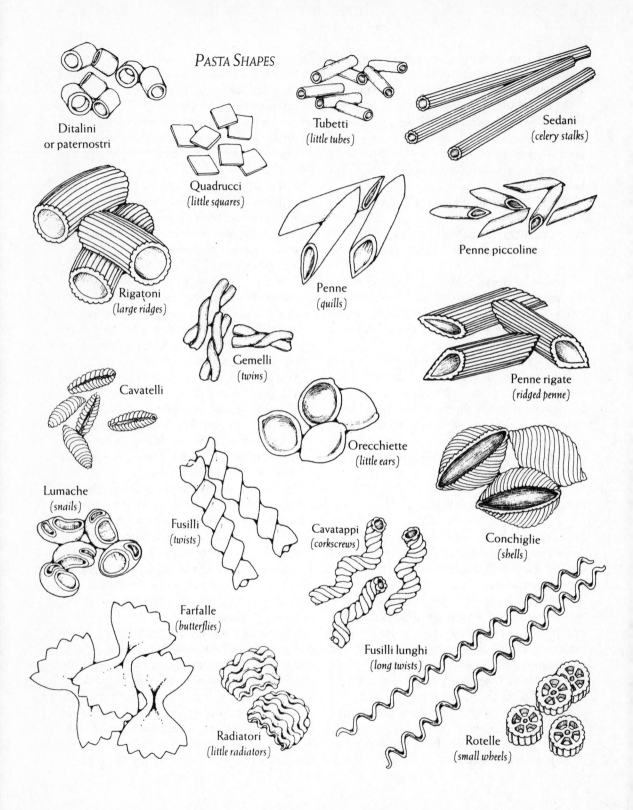

PASTA SHAPES

Ditalini
or paternostri

Quadrucci
(little squares)

Tubetti
(little tubes)

Sedani
(celery stalks)

Rigatoni
(large ridges)

Penne
(quills)

Penne piccoline

Gemelli
(twins)

Penne rigate
(ridged penne)

Cavatelli

Orecchiette
(little ears)

Lumache
(snails)

Fusilli
(twists)

Cavatappi
(corkscrews)

Conchiglie
(shells)

Farfalle
(butterflies)

Radiatori
(little radiators)

Fusilli lunghi
(long twists)

Rotelle
(small wheels)

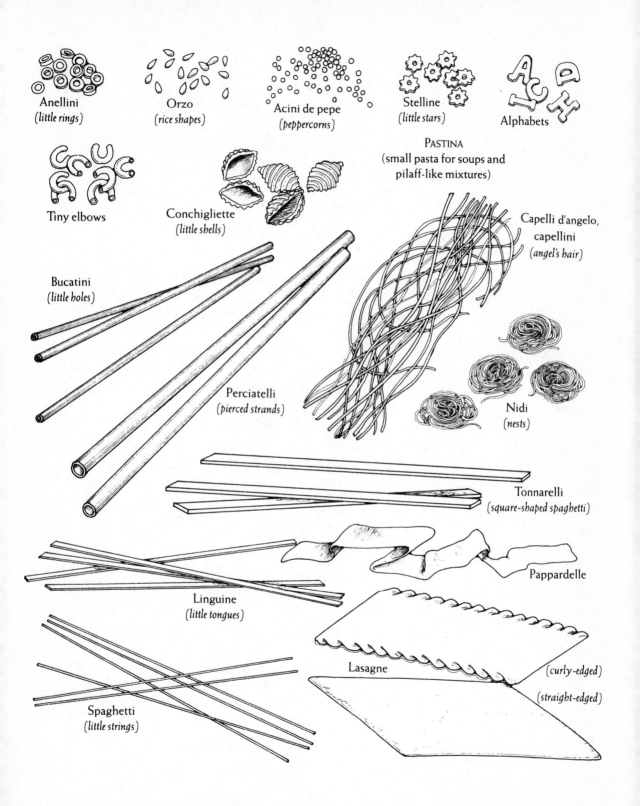

Anellini
(*little rings*)

Orzo
(*rice shapes*)

Acini de pepe
(*peppercorns*)

Stelline
(*little stars*)

Alphabets

PASTINA
(small pasta for soups and
pilaff-like mixtures)

Tiny elbows

Conchigliette
(*little shells*)

Capelli d'angelo,
capellini
(*angel's hair*)

Bucatini
(*little holes*)

Nidi
(*nests*)

Perciatelli
(*pierced strands*)

Tonnarelli
(*square-shaped spaghetti*)

Pappardelle

Linguine
(*little tongues*)

Lasagne

(*curly-edged*)

(*straight-edged*)

Spaghetti
(*little strings*)

A WORLD GUIDE TO PASTA

ITALIAN PASTA

Italian pasta, a simple mixture of flour and water, is pounded, rolled and extruded into a wide assortment of shapes with melodic-sounding names, and usually whimsical and playful meanings: radiatori (little radiators), vermicelli (little worms), farfalle (butterflies), to name a few. The differing shapes all lend themselves in different ways to the wide variety of sauces and toppings: thin strands of pasta such as spaghetti, vermicelli, etc. taste best with lively, vivacious sauces, while flat pasta is good with almost everything, especially richer sauces that can settle on them, and pastina (tiny pasta shapes) are best in soup or pilaf-type mixtures. Thick pasta tastes best with robust, feisty sauces, while thinner, more delicate pasta is good with light, subtle sauces. And stuffed pasta is best sauced simply, as its filling is like an inside-out sauce, giving its flavour and texture from the inside rather than as a topping. Such a diversity of shapes gives variety to the table of people who have often lived in poverty.

Fresh Pasta

Fresh pasta at its best is tender and silky, yet also supple and yielding to the teeth. It is quite different from pasta asciutta (dried pasta) which should be cooked al dente, that is, so that it is somewhat resistant to the teeth. That hearty, chewy quality is a result of using semolina flour, and extruding the pasta through a specially created machine. But when you make pasta at home you want to produce a smooth, tender noodle, the sort that is expensive or difficult to come by in the shops. This can be achieved by using plain flour and lots of eggs and rolling the dough rather than extruding it (although a number of pasta machines for domestic use are based on extruding). Rolling the dough may be done either by hand with a heavy roller – hard, hard work – or run through the classic hand-rolling pasta machine. I recommend the latter.

When making your own pasta you can use a number of vegetable or herb colourings and flavourings: pesto, saffron, hot peppers, and so on.

450g/1 lb plain flour, preferably unbleached	2 cups all-purpose flour, preferably unbleached
3 size-3 eggs	3 medium-sized eggs
½ teaspoon salt	½ teaspoon salt

1. Place the flour in a mound on a large flour-sprinkled board or in a large bowl, then make a hollow in the centre large enough to hold the eggs. I do this by placing my fist in the top of the mound and moving it until it forms a generous well.

2. Crack open the eggs into the well, add the salt, and beat the eggs with a fork, incorporating a small amount of flour as you go along. Use your free hand to keep the walls of flour upright and keep the eggs from dribbling out. Gradually all the flour will be incorporated. Towards the end you can just use your hands to mix it.

3. Knead the dough by hand for about 5–10 minutes, or in a food processor for about 20 seconds. It should be elastic and smooth and not break apart sharply when pulled. Place in a bowl or plastic bag, lightly oiled with olive oil, cover or seal, and leave for at least 30 minutes to tenderize the dough. You can store this in the refrigerator for up to 2 days.

4. Roll the pasta by breaking off a walnut-sized piece of dough, and flattening it enough to fit in the large size of the roller on your pasta machine. Roll it through once, then fold it and roll it through again. Gradually reduce the size of the roller until you achieve the desired thinness.

5. Use the pasta in whole sheets, or cut to the width desired, either using the cutters on the machine or by hand. Toss with flour then place on a board; alternatively you may dry the pasta over a chair or pole. It does not need to dry long; it should retain its moist freshness.

6. To cook: boil in rapidly boiling salted water until tender, only about 2–3 minutes.

Variations

White Wine Pasta: In place of one of the eggs, add 2–3 tablespoons dry white wine and

1 tablespoon olive oil. This makes a silky, suave pasta.

Pesto Pasta: In place of one of the eggs use 1 tablespoon pesto; alternatively, use 3 eggs and incorporate powdered pesto (available in America) into the flour.

Ginger Pasta: Add 3 tablespoons freshly grated ginger root along with the eggs.

Hot Red Pepper Pasta: Mix 3 tablespoons cayenne pepper or red chilli powder into the flour mixture.

Saffron: Add ½ teaspoon saffron to the eggs.

Corn Pasta: Substitute 4 ounces (½ cup) cornmeal for an equal amount of flour and add 4 ounces (½ cup) pureed sweetcorn with the eggs.

Rosemary Pasta: Add several tablespoons chopped fresh rosemary with the eggs.

Chive Pasta: Add a handful of chopped chives with the eggs.

DRIED PASTA

Dried Pasta, or pasta secca made from semolina and water, is chewy and supple, utterly satisfying. It should swell up as it absorbs the hot water it is cooked in, and remain firm to the teeth, or *al dente*, never sink to flabby. Choose pasta imported from Italy, though pasta from Greece can also be very good, too.

How to Cook Dried Pasta

Dried pasta may be cooked either by boiling for the whole cooking time or by boiling for a short while, then steeping. The most important thing to remember is not to overcook it. As the pasta continues to cook in its own heat while you transfer it to the colander to drain, remove it from the stove just before it reaches the state you want. Do not rinse drained pasta with cold water, unless it is to be used later. Instead, toss the drained pasta back into the pot with a drizzle of olive oil. I often add a clove of chopped garlic, too, and find that pasta seasoned with garlic and olive oil adds another dimension to any sauce that goes over it, especially a tomato and vegetable one.

An old wives' tale claims that the way to test pasta is to fling a few strands at the wall: if it sticks, the pasta is done. This was recently debunked by aficionados who said that if the pasta stuck to the wall it was overcooked. But it actually does work pretty well; just make sure that once you check the pasta by flinging the rest doesn't get a chance to overcook as it sits on the cooker. To fling or not to fling is up to you; for accuracy, however, I recommend tasting a piece or two of pasta as you go along, and judging the doneness with your teeth. But for fun, I recommend throwing that pasta at the wall.

Method one: Add the pasta to a large pot of rapidly boiling, salted water and boil until *al dente*. Add the salt to the water after it has boiled for a fresher taste. I don't recommend adding oil to the water as it sits on the top of the water during cooking and has no effect on the pasta beneath. The cooking time will depend upon the size and type of pasta. Use the package directions as a guide, but I find that the recommended times are usually too long, resulting in overcooked pasta. You must check every so often to be sure, then drain just when the pasta approaches firm-to-the tooth but no longer hard and crunchy inside.

Method two: This method results in a particularly toothsome, plump but firm pasta and is suited to sturdier shapes, such as spaghetti or penne, rather than thin, delicate ones, such as capellini or fresh pasta. First, add the pasta to a large pot filled with rapidly boiling salted water and boil for 2 minutes.

Then turn off the heat, cover, and leave to steep. Spaghetti takes about 6–8 minutes of steeping, other shapes vary. You will have to taste occasionally to ascertain the exact moment it is ready. Pasta can overcook by the steeping method as easily as it can by boiling, and it is equally nasty, so be vigilant.

RAGTAG PASTA

With a large selection of pasta, it is inevitable that at some point you will have only a small amount left in each bag. Soon you end up with a handful of small and chunky shapes, a handful of spaghetti, broken into short strands, a smattering of curly fusilli, etc. In the frugal Italian kitchen these ragtag ends of pasta are combined for minestrone, hearty bean soups, and the like. The combination of differing types of pasta adds textural and visual variety to even the simplest of soups, and transforms what otherwise might be tossed out or left to languish on the cupboard shelves into a useful and creative ingredient. In addition, if you pile the ever-changing variety of shapes into a large jar it makes a visual delight.

Serve Ragtag Pasta:
Cooked with vegetables such as peas and green beans, dressed with butter and cheese

In hearty minestrone-type soups or stews

With assorted beans, Calabrian style

Cooked with a variety of green summer vegetables: young beans, diced courgettes (zucchini), spinach, peas, etc., then sauced with a simple garlicky tomato sauce and a sprinkling of herbs.

FAR EASTERN PASTA

Cellophane noodles: these Chinese transparent noodles may be made from either mung beans (when they are called bean threads) or potato starch. Japanese transparent noodles are called shirataki and are made of yam flour.

Both need to be soaked before cooking: soak the Chinese ones for about 10 minutes in hot but not boiling water, then boil for about 3 minutes. The Japanese noodles will need about 20 to 25 minutes' soaking before boiling for 3 minutes.

Look for these in Chinese and other Far Eastern groceries.

Chinese egg noodles (mein): most supermarkets stock several types of dried Chinese noodles. They cook in a very short time, depending on their thickness, so check for doneness after about 3 minutes.

Chinese grocers usually stock fresh mein, and often in a wide variety of thicknesses. Fresh ones cook even quicker – 1 minute will do for the thinner ones.

Udon: these thick fresh Japanese noodles are usually available in vacuum packs from shops specializing in Japanese ingredients. They are often packed in one-portion snack-sized parcels. Udon may be wholewheat or white, with cooking times and directions given on the package.

Soba: these are thin, dried Japanese buckwheat noodles that cook very quickly. They may be thread thin or flat and almost fettuccine-like in shape. I prefer the latter.

Somen: these are thin Japanese noodles that cook very quickly and are most suitable for soups.

Ramen: the dried noodles in a packet with powdered broth are ramen. They come with a wide variety of fillings and make a savoury snack or light meal when garnished with a handful of something fresh: a few beansprouts, fresh coriander leaves (cilantro) or spring onions (green onions). Browned in a little butter or oil they make a delicious basis for a salad (see Auntie Estelle's Chinese Leaf Salad with Crunchy Noodles and Nuts, page 60).

Rice sticks: thin dried rice noodles, also called rice vermicelli or py mei fun. They are wiry and twig-like, and may be either boiled until fluffy and soft or deep-fried into crisp, puffy, serpent shapes.

To boil, soak in cold water for 10 minutes or follow the directions on the packet.

To fry to a crispy cloudlike shape, deep-fry at about 375° F until they puff up. Remove from the hot oil immediately after they have puffed up, before they even hint at browning or turning golden, as that detracts from their delicate taste and light, crisp texture.

Rice noodles: available dried and fresh from Chinese grocers. When fresh they are called chow fun. They are bland and soft, tasting of rice, and pleasingly tender to the teeth. Since they are quite delicate, they should be cooked – usually stir-fried – on the day of purchase, or at least within two days. To make chow fun with vegetables, first stir-fry them in a very hot wok then remove; stir-fry your vegetables, then combine the two mixtures along with a small amount of seasoning sauce.

Dried rice noodles are flat and thin and usually imported from Vietnam or Thailand. These are sometimes also called rice vermicelli, and sometimes rice sticks, but they are much wider. Soak in cold water for about 15 minutes, then boil until just tender, only a few minutes.

SOUPS AND STEWS

Pasta is traditionally served in soups the world over, whether floating in broths of sparkling clarity or simmered in savoury vegetable-filled potages. Often a handful of pasta is added to the soup at the last minute to cook in the broth and absorb its flavours, or the soup might be served ladled over cooked pasta.

Stuffed pasta is traditionally served in broth in various cultures: Italian style, with a finish of freshly grated Parmesan cheese, or Chinese style, with wonton as the pasta of choice and a final fillip of sesame oil and soy sauce. But plain pasta is delicious in broth too, or added to nearly any light soup to give it body.

Green Vegetable Soup with Pesto

SERVES 4

Short thick pasta bubbles in the pot along with a selection of green vegetables, the broth enriched by the last-minute addition of that intensely flavoured basil and garlic paste, pesto. Don't be tempted to add everything from the garden to the soup: it is at its best when only green vegetables are used. Take care also not to cook or overheat the pesto once added – cooking it dilutes and dulls its fresh, sassy flavour.

100g/4 oz ditalini or other short fat pasta
2 cloves garlic, coarsely chopped
2 tablespoons olive oil
2 tablespoons flour
1 litre/1¾ pints vegetable stock
4–5 cabbage leaves, blanched and thinly sliced (optional)
100–150g/4–5 oz cooked chopped fresh or frozen spinach (weight after cooking)
75–100g/3–4 oz fresh and blanched or frozen peas
4 heaped tablespoons pesto, or to taste

About ½ to ¾ cup ditalini
2 cloves garlic, coarsely chopped
2 tablespoons olive oil
2 tablespoons flour
1 quart vegetable stock
4–5 outer cabbage leaves (or other winter greens), blanched and thinly sliced
½ to ⅔ cup cooked chopped spinach (fresh or frozen)
½ cup fresh and blanched or frozen peas
¼ cup pesto, or to taste

1. Cook the pasta in rapidly boiling salted water until *al dente*. Drain and set aside.
2. Lightly sauté the garlic in the olive oil until just gilded, then sprinkle in the flour and cook out its rawness for just a few moments.
3. Off the heat stir in the stock, then return to the heat and cook for several minutes until slightly thickened. Add the cabbage leaves (if using), spinach and peas and cook through.
4. Just before serving add the cooked pasta and heat through. Serve each bowlful with a spoonful of fragrant pesto stirred in.

Mediterranean Roasted Vegetable Soup-Stew

SERVES 4–6

I devised this robust full-of-Mediterranean-flavour soup-stew during a winter holiday in the mountains of Ibiza. With the weather cold and grim, our main activity was going not to the beach, as we had envisioned beforehand, but to the market, and cooking and eating ourselves into delicious oblivion.

This soup resulted from a casserole full of leftover vegetables; in fact this is an ideal way of using up such leftovers, and steps 1–3 can be carried out a day ahead of the rest of the recipe. Our vegetables had been grilled over an open fire, and the smoky nuances gave it added depth, but if outdoor grilling is impossible, grill the vegetables indoors under a high heat until lightly charred.

For the grilled vegetables:
1–2 potatoes, unpeeled and whole
1 red pepper, cut into thick slices or chunks
1 aubergine, sliced
2–3 courgettes, thickly sliced lengthwise
Juice from 1–2 lemons
Olive oil as desired
3 cloves garlic, chopped
½–1 teaspoon thyme
Salt and pepper

For the soup:
5 cloves garlic, coarsely chopped
2 tablespoons olive oil
200g/7 oz cooked or tinned chickpeas, drained
10–12 cm/4–5 inch sprig fresh rosemary
325g/12 oz ripe fresh or tinned tomatoes, coarsely diced
1 litre/1¾ pints vegetable stock
175g/6 oz orzo or similar-shaped pasta
2–3 tablespoons pesto
50g/2 oz Parmesan cheese, freshly grated
Olive oil, for drizzling, if desired

For the grilled vegetables:
1–2 potatoes, whole and unpeeled
1 red bell pepper, cut into chunks or wedges
1 eggplant, thickly sliced
2–3 zucchini, thickly sliced lengthwise
Juice of 1–2 lemons
Olive oil as desired
3 cloves garlic, chopped
½–1 teaspoon thyme
Salt and pepper

For the soup:
5 cloves garlic, coarsely chopped
2 tablespoons olive oil
1 cup cooked garbanzo beans
4–5 inch sprig fresh rosemary
1½ cups coarsely diced fresh or canned tomatoes
1 quart vegetable stock
6 oz orzo or similar-shaped pasta
2–3 tablespoons pesto
¼ cup freshly grated Parmesan cheese

1. Prepare the vegetables: boil the potatoes until *al dente*, or not quite tender. Drain, and when just cool enough to handle, slice thickly. Drizzle the hot potato slices in about one third the lemon juice, olive oil, garlic and thyme and let marinate for at least 30 minutes.

2. In a separate shallow flat pan or dish, place the red (bell) pepper, aubergine (eggplant), and courgettes (zucchini) and drizzle with remaining lemon juice, olive oil, garlic and thyme. Season with salt and pepper and leave to marinate for at least 30 minutes (potatoes and vegetables can marinate nicely for up to 12 hours or overnight).

3. Remove vegetables from their marinade, reserving the lemon and olive oil mixture, and grill the vegetables over an open flame or under a high heat until lightly charred. Remove from heat and return to marinade. Leave in the marinade while you prepare the rest of the soup. (This can all be done a day ahead of points 4–6.)

4. Lightly sauté the garlic in the olive oil until just golden, then stir in the chickpeas (garbanzos) and cook for a minute or two.

5. Add the rosemary sprig, tomatoes, stock, orzo and grilled vegetables, and cook until the pastina is *al dente*. The soup will become very thick.

6. Stir the pesto into the soup and serve each bowlful sprinkled with the Parmesan cheese. Drizzle with a little extra olive oil if liked.

Goan Ginger-Scented Tomato and Cabbage Soup with Small Pasta and Fresh Mint

SERVES 4

This fragrant soup is satisfying but not heavy and hails from Goa, where Indian spicing such as ginger is often combined with Portuguese seasoning such as fresh mint. It makes an excellent first course.

100g/4 oz small pasta such as alphabets, or short thick-cut pasta
2 onions, coarsely chopped
3–5 cloves garlic, coarsely chopped
25g/1 oz butter
2 teaspoons ground ginger
1 small carrot, diced
400g/14 oz diced fresh or tinned tomatoes
1.5 litres/2½ pints vegetable stock
½ white cabbage, very thinly sliced
10–15 fresh mint leaves, very thinly sliced
Salt and freshly ground black and/or cayenne pepper, to taste

½ cup small soup pasta such as alphabets
2 medium onions, coarsely chopped
3–5 cloves garlic, coarsely chopped
2 tablespoons butter
1 small carrot, diced
2 teaspoons ground ginger
1¾–2 cups diced fresh or canned tomatoes
6 cups vegetable stock
½ white cabbage, very thinly sliced
10–15 fresh mint leaves, very thinly sliced
Salt and freshly ground black and/or cayenne pepper, to taste

1. Cook the pasta until *al dente*; drain and set aside.
2. Lightly sauté the onion and garlic in the butter until softened.
3. Stir in the ginger and carrot and cook for a few moments, then add the tomatoes, vegetable stock and cabbage. Cook over medium heat until the vegetables are tender, about 15–20 minutes. Adjust the seasoning with salt and black or cayenne pepper, adding more ginger if needed.
4. Ladle the soup over several spoonfuls of pasta per person. Season each portion with a sprinkling of fresh mint and serve immediately.

Cream of Garlic Soup with Tri-Coloured Pasta

SERVES 4–6

100g/4 oz multicoloured pasta such as shells, elbows, etc.

15–20 whole cloves of garlic, peeled but left whole, plus 1 clove, finely chopped

900ml/1½ pints vegetable stock

5 medium sized fresh or tinned tomatoes, coarsely chopped

Large pinch of thyme leaves, fresh or dried, crushed

350ml/12 fl oz single cream

25–50g/1–2 oz Parmesan cheese, freshly grated

Salt and freshly ground black pepper, to taste

4 oz multicoloured pasta such as shells, elbows, etc.

15–20 whole cloves garlic, peeled but left whole, plus 1 clove, finely chopped

3½ cups vegetable stock

5 fresh or canned diced tomatoes

Large pinch of fresh or dried thyme leaves, crushed

1½ cups half and half or light cream

¼–½ cup Parmesan cheese, freshly grated

Salt and freshly ground black pepper, to taste

1. Cook the pasta until _al dente_. Drain and rinse with cold water.
2. Meanwhile, simmer the whole, peeled cloves of garlic in the vegetable stock until tender. Add the tomatoes and cook for a few minutes longer, then season with the thyme.
3. Add the cream, heat until almost boiling (do not let it boil as the cream might curdle) then remove from the heat and add the cooked pasta. Return to the heat and warm through, then stir in the Parmesan cheese and the finely chopped garlic clove, and season with salt and black pepper. Serve immediately.

Broccoli and Pastina in Garlic Broth

SERVES 4–6

A light and zesty soup, fragrant with sweetly simmered garlic, studded with crunchy-tender broccoli and soothing tiny pasta shapes. It makes a lovely first course or midnight feast for alliophiles.

2 large heads garlic, cloves separated and peeled
1 litre/1¾ pints vegetable stock
225g/8 oz pastina, such as stelline, alphabets, orzo, acini de pepe, etc.
1 large bunch broccoli, cut into bite-sized florets and chunks of peeled stem
Salt and freshly ground black pepper, to taste
Freshly grated Parmesan cheese to serve
Olive oil to serve

2 large heads garlic, cloves separated and peeled
1 quart vegetable stock
8 oz pastina such as stelline, alphabets, orzo, acini de pepe, etc.
1 large bunch broccoli, cut into bite-sized florets and chunks of peeled stem
Salt and freshly ground black pepper, to taste
Freshly grated Parmesan cheese to serve
Olive oil to serve

1. Simmer the whole garlic cloves in the stock until tender, about 20 minutes.
2. Add the pastina and cook for 2 minutes or so, then add the broccoli and continue cooking until both pasta and broccoli are *al dente*.
3. Serve hot, each portion sprinkled with Parmesan cheese and/or olive oil, and salt and freshly ground black pepper.

Spicy Pumpkin Soup with Thin Pasta

SERVES 4–6

This French soup has an overlay of Latin American flavours.

4 cloves garlic, chopped
5 spring onions or shallots, chopped
25g/1 oz butter
1 tablespoon flour
1 red pepper, diced
450g/1 lb pumpkin, peeled and diced
1 tablespoon mild chilli powder
2 teaspoons paprika
½ teaspoon cumin
¼ teaspoon dried oregano leaves, crushed
250ml/8 fl oz tomato passata, or
   8 diced ripe fresh tomatoes, *or*
   400g/14 oz tin chopped tomatoes
900ml/1½ pints vegetable stock
250 ml/8 fl oz milk
100g/4 oz thin pasta such as
   spaghettini, capellini, etc.
400g/14 oz cooked or drained tinned
   white cannellini beans
Salt and cayenne pepper, to taste
Freshly grated Parmesan or other hard
   cheese to serve
Thinly sliced spring onions or fresh
   coriander leaves to serve (optional)

4 cloves garlic, chopped
5 green onions or shallots, chopped
2 tablespoons butter
1 tablespoon flour
1 red bell pepper, diced
2½–3 cups fresh pumpkin, peeled and
   diced
1 tablespoon mild chilli powder
2 teaspoons paprika
½ teaspoon cumin
¼ teaspoon dried oregano leaves, crushed
1 cup tomato passata or sauce, or 1½
   cups diced fresh or canned tomatoes
3½ cups vegetable stock
1 cup milk
4 oz thin pasta such as spaghettini or
   capellini, etc.
1½ cups cooked or drained, canned,
   cannellini (white kidney) beans
Salt and cayenne pepper, to taste
Freshly grated Parmesan or other hard
   cheese to serve
Thinly sliced green onions or cilantro
   to serve (optional)

1. Lightly sauté the garlic and spring (green) onions or shallots in the butter until softened, then sprinkle in the flour and cook for a few minutes. Add the red (bell) pepper and pumpkin and cook for another few minutes, then sprinkle in the chilli powder, paprika, cumin and oregano and cook for just a few moments longer.
2. Add the tomato passata, sauce, or tomatoes and stock, bring to the boil, then cover and simmer until the pumpkin is tender. Purée half the mixture and return it to the pan, so that you have a mixed texture.
3. Add the pasta and cook until *al dente*. If using very thin pasta cook it directly in the soup; if using thicker pasta such as spaghettini or spaghetti, first cook it in boiling water until half done, then drain and add to the soup.
4. When the pasta is nearly tender add the milk and beans to the soup and heat through. Season to taste with salt and cayenne pepper and serve hot, sprinkled with cheese, and with thinly sliced spring (green) onions or coriander (cilantro), if liked.

Spicy Lemon-Scented Tomato and Onion Broth with Spaghetti

SERVES 4

This actually evolved from a rustic Italian soup, but as it simmered, the pot cried out for tart citrus, hot pepper, and before you know it, the soup tasted more Caribbean than Italian.

100g/4 oz spaghetti
2 onions, coarsely chopped
4 cloves garlic, chopped
2 tablespoons olive oil
4–5 ripe fresh tomatoes, coarsely
    chopped
1 litre/1¾ pints vegetable stock
1 tablespoon tomato paste
Cayenne pepper to taste
Juice of ½ lemon
Several tablespoons of grated Cheddar,
    Lancashire, Wensleydale, or similar
    cheese
Large pinch of dried oregano

4 oz spaghetti (use one quarter of a
    1 lb package)
2 onions, coarsely chopped
4 cloves garlic, chopped
2 tablespoons olive oil
4–5 ripe fresh tomatoes, coarsely
    chopped
1 quart vegetable stock
1 tablespoon tomato paste
Cayenne pepper to taste
Juice of ½ lemon
Several tablespoons of grated Cheddar,
    Monterey Jack, medium asiago, or
    similar cheese
Large pinch of dried oregano

1. Cook the spaghetti until *al dente*. Drain and set aside.
2. Cook the onions and a quarter of the garlic slowly in the oil until the onions soften and become golden. Add the tomatoes and cook for a few minutes longer, then add the stock and tomato paste.
3. Cook over medium heat for 15–20 minutes or until the mixture is full flavoured and souplike. Season with cayenne pepper and the lemon juice.
4. Cut the cooked spaghetti into short lengths, mix with the remaining garlic and put a few spoonfuls into each serving bowl along with a spoonful of cheese.
5. Ladle the soup into the pasta-filled bowls, sprinkle with the oregano, crushing it between your fingers, and serve.

Provençal Garlic Soup

SERVES 4

Sweet garlic broth, scented with sage, simmered with a handful of thin pasta, then enriched with a mixture of egg and Parmesan cheese, makes an invigorating yet simply prepared soup.

2 heads garlic, cloves separated and peeled
1 litre/1¾ pints vegetable stock
1 teaspoon sage leaves, lightly crumbled if dry, chopped if fresh
Tiny pinch of cayenne pepper
4 nests (about 75–100g/3–4 oz) very thin pasta, broken up a little
2 eggs, lightly beaten
50g/2 oz Parmesan cheese, freshly grated

2 heads garlic, cloves separated and peeled
1 quart vegetable stock
1 teaspoon sage leaves, lightly crumbled if dry, chopped if fresh
Tiny pinch of cayenne pepper
4 nests (about 4 oz) very thin pasta, broken up a little
2 eggs, lightly beaten
¼ cup Parmesan cheese, freshly grated

1. Put the garlic cloves, vegetable stock, sage and cayenne in a pan and bring to the boil. Reduce the heat and simmer for about 20 minutes. Halfway through the cooking add the pasta, separating it into strands as it softens, and continue cooking until both pasta and garlic are tender.
2. Combine the eggs with the Parmesan cheese. Ladle a little hot broth into the egg mixture, stir well, then repeat. Off the heat, stir this mixture into the hot broth, letting the soup become creamy rather than letting the egg mixture cook. Return to the heat and cook, stirring, over low to medium heat until the soup thickens slightly. Serve immediately.

Tomato and Garlic Broth with Acini de Pepe, From an Italian Countryside Summer

SERVES 4

Acini de pepe means grains of black peppercorns. They are exactly the same size and have a delightful consistency, slithering down your throat as you swallow your soup. If acini de pepe are not available, use orzo, stelline, or other very small pasta.

1 onion, chopped
3 cloves garlic, chopped
2 teaspoons fresh thyme or
 ½ teaspoon dried thyme
1 carrot, diced
2–3 tablespoons olive oil
4–5 ripe fresh or tinned tomatoes,
 coarsely chopped
250 ml/8 fl oz tomato juice (or about
 half that amount of passata)
900ml/1½ pints vegetable stock
100–175 g/4–6 oz acini de pepe or
 other small, firm-textured pasta
Freshly grated Parmesan cheese to
 serve

1 onion, chopped
3 cloves garlic, chopped
2 teaspoons fresh thyme or
 ½ teaspoon dried thyme
1 medium sized carrot, diced
2–3 tablespoons olive oil
4–5 fresh or canned tomatoes, coarsely
 chopped
1 cup tomato juice
3½ cups vegetable stock
4–6 oz acini de pepe or other small
 firm textured pasta
Freshly grated Parmesan cheese to
 serve

1. Sauté the onion, garlic, thyme and carrot in the olive oil until softened and lightly golden. Add the tomatoes and continue cooking for 3–5 minutes.
2. Add the tomato juice, stock and pasta. Bring to the boil, then reduce the heat and simmer until the pasta is tender, about 10 minutes, depending on the pasta you choose. Be careful not to overcook the pasta.
3. Serve immediately, offering freshly grated Parmesan cheese separately.

Middle Eastern Cinnamon-Scented Egg and Lemon Soup with Courgettes (Zucchini) and Thin Pasta

SERVES 4–6

Thickening simple broths with a mixture of eggs beaten with lemon juice is a distinctively Middle Eastern technique, with variations throughout the region. Adding a little cinnamon is a culinary souvenir of Egypt, and its sweet scent is particularly nice with the tangy lemon and rich egg. Diced courgettes (zucchini) add a juicy, chunky vegetable texture to the soup.

1 litre/1¾ pints vegetable stock
450 g/1 lb courgettes, diced or sliced
4 cloves garlic, coarsely chopped
1 cinnamon stick
Handful of thin pasta strands (spaghetti, capellini, etc.), broken into short lengths
Salt and cayenne pepper, to taste
2 eggs, lightly beaten
Juice of 1–2 lemons, to taste
Fresh coriander leaves for garnish

1 quart vegetable stock
3–4 zucchini, diced or sliced
4 cloves garlic, coarsely chopped
1 cinnamon stick
Handful of thin pasta strands (spaghetti, capellini, etc.), broken into short lengths
Salt and cayenne pepper, to taste
2 eggs, lightly beaten
Juice of 1–2 lemons, to taste
Fresh cilantro leaves for garnish

1. Combine the stock, courgettes (zucchini), garlic, cinnamon, and pasta in a pan. Bring to the boil and cook until the pasta is *al dente* and the courgettes (zucchini) are tender. Season with salt and cayenne pepper.
2. Mix the beaten eggs with the lemon juice, then add a ladleful of hot soup and stir well to combine. Add another ladleful of soup, stirring well to make a creamy mixture rather than scrambled egg.
3. Off the heat stir the egg and lemon mixture into the hot soup, then return the pan to the stove and cook over medium heat until it begins to thicken.
4. Serve immediately, garnished with coriander (cilantro) leaves.

Italian-Inspired Soup of Tomatoes, Vegetables and Farfalle

SERVES 4–6

2 onions, chopped
5 cloves garlic, chopped
2 celery stalks, chopped
2 small to medium carrots, diced
2 tablespoons chopped fresh parsley
1 teaspoon fennel seeds
2 tablespoons olive oil
1 green pepper, diced
250ml/8 fl oz dry red wine
1 litre /1¾ pints vegetable stock
900g/2 lb ripe fresh tomatoes,
  chopped, or 2 400g/14-oz tins
  chopped tomatoes
1 tablespoon dried mixed herbs
2 courgettes, sliced
175g/6 oz farfalle (pasta butterflies)
Salt and freshly ground black pepper,
  to taste
Freshly grated Parmesan cheese to
  serve (optional)

2 onions, chopped
5 cloves garlic, chopped
2 celery stalks, chopped
2 small to medium carrots, diced
2 tablespoons chopped fresh parsley
1 teaspoon fennel seeds
2 tablespoons olive oil
1 green bell pepper, diced
1 cup dry red wine
1 quart vegetable stock
3 cups chopped tomatoes, fresh or
  canned
1 tablespoon dried mixed herbs
2 zucchini, sliced
6 oz farfalle (pasta butterflies or
  bowties)
Salt and freshly ground black pepper,
  to taste
Freshly grated Parmesan cheese to
  serve (optional)

1. Lightly sauté the onions, garlic, celery, carrots, parsley and fennel seeds in the olive oil until the onions are softened, then add the green (bell) pepper and cook for a few minutes.
2. Pour in the red wine and cook over high heat for about 5 minutes or until the alcohol evaporates and the wine reduces in volume, then add the stock, tomatoes, herbs, courgettes (zucchini) and pasta.
3. Cook over medium to high heat, stirring every so often, until the pasta and courgettes (zucchini) are tender. Taste for seasoning, adding salt and black pepper as needed.
4. Serve immediately, sprinkled with Parmesan cheese if liked.

Spicy Spanish Cabbage and Tomato Soup with Capellini

SERVES 6

Shredded cabbage bubbles away in a mildly chilli-flavoured tomato broth, enriched with a handful of thin capellini - such humble ingredients are transformed into an outstanding soup.

1 onion, coarsely chopped
6–8 cloves garlic, coarsely chopped
2 tablespoons olive oil
2–3 teaspoons paprika, to taste
2–3 teaspoons mild chilli powder
½ teaspoon cumin
½ green or white cabbage, very thinly sliced
1½ litres/1¾ to 2½ pints vegetable stock
675g/1½ lb ripe fresh tomatoes, peeled, seeded and diced or 1½–2 400g/14 oz tins chopped tomatoes
100g/4 oz capellini or similar very fine pasta
2–3 tablespoons coarsely chopped fresh coriander leaves
Lemon or lime wedges to serve

1 onion, coarsely chopped
6–8 cloves garlic, coarsely chopped
2 tablespoons olive oil
2–3 teaspoons paprika, to taste
2–3 teaspoons chilli powder, to taste (either a mild but flavourful chilli blend or pure New Mexico or ancho chilli)
½ teaspoon cumin
½ medium sized white or green cabbage, very thinly sliced
3–3½ cups vegetable stock
2 cups diced fresh or canned tomatoes
4 oz capellini or similar very fine noodles or pasta
2–3 tablespoons coarsely chopped cilantro leaves
Lemon or lime wedges to serve

1. Lightly sauté the onion and garlic in the olive oil until softened, then sprinkle in the paprika, chilli powder and cumin and cook for a moment or two.
2. Add the cabbage, about ⅔ of the stock and half the tomatoes. Bring to boil, then reduce heat and let simmer for an hour, adding extra stock if necessary to make up the liquid that boils away.
3. Add the remaining tomatoes and cook for another half hour or so. Meanwhile, cook the pasta until *al dente*, drain, and add to the soup.
4. Serve sprinkled with the coriander (cilantro) leaves and accompanied with wedges of lemon or lime to squeeze in.

Variation

Instead of capellini, serve the spicy cabbage and tomato soup with small chewy dumplings such as spätzle (see page 244).

Creamy Onion Soup with Tiny Pasta

SERVES 4–6

This rich soup begins like French onion soup: browned onions and stock, simmered for a long time until dark and sweetly fragrant. But here you add just enough cream to take the edge off the onions, and instead of serving the soup over a cheese-topped croûte, you serve it ladled over al dente orzo or other small pasta, then blanketed with grated cheese.

10 onions, coarsely chopped
25g/1 oz butter
1 litre/1¾ pints vegetable stock
100ml/4 fl oz single cream
1 egg, lightly beaten
225g/8 oz orzo or other small pasta, or thin pasta such as capellini, broken into short lengths
75g/3 oz Parmesan cheese, freshly grated

10 onions, coarsely chopped
2 tablespoons butter
1 quart vegetable stock
½ cup half and half or cream
1 egg, lightly beaten
8 oz orzo or other small pasta, or capellini broken into short lengths
3 oz Parmesan cheese, freshly grated

1. Lightly sauté the onions in the butter long and slowly, until they caramelize and turn first golden, then lightly brown. It will take about 30 minutes, at least, probably longer.
2. Add the stock and bring to the boil. Reduce the heat and simmer for at least an hour, preferably longer, or until the broth is richly flavoured.
3. Combine the cream and egg, then lighten the mixture by adding a ladleful or two of the broth. Stir this back into the onion soup and simmer for a few minutes over low to medium heat, but do not allow it to come to the boil.
4. Meanwhile, cook the pasta until *al dente*. Drain.
5. Serve the soup poured over the pasta, each portion sprinkled with a generous amount of Parmesan cheese.

Tomato and Pea Soup with Nidi

SERVES 4–6

A simple, nourishing soup that is delightful on a rainy summer evening – hearty yet not heavy at all. The tomato and pea broth is ladled over nidi – very thin pasta shaped into little nests, the tiny threads all rolled around each other in a nest-like circle. Capellini can also be used.

2 small to medium onions, chopped
4 cloves garlic, chopped
1 waxy potato, peeled and diced
2 tablespoons olive oil
3 tablespoons chopped fresh parsley
200g/7 oz peas (or use frozen petits pois)
Large pinch of fennel seeds
1 litre/1¾ pints vegetable stock
10 diced fresh ripe tomatoes or 1½ 400g/14 oz tins chopped tomatoes
Large pinch of dried mixed herbs
Salt and freshly ground black pepper, to taste
100g/4 oz nidi or very thin capellini
A few leaves of fresh basil, thinly sliced (optional)
Freshly grated cheese to serve

2 onions, chopped
4 cloves garlic, chopped
1 waxy potato, peeled and diced
2 tablespoons olive oil
3 tablespoons chopped fresh parsley
1 cup fresh or frozen peas
Large pinch of fennel seeds
1 quart vegetable stock
2 cups fresh or canned diced tomatoes
Large pinch of dried mixed herbs
Salt and freshly ground black pepper, to taste
4 oz nidi or capellini
A few leaves of fresh basil, thinly sliced (optional)
Freshly grated cheese to serve

1. Lightly sauté the onions, garlic, and potato in the olive oil. When the potato is lightly golden, add the parsley and cook until wilted and dark green.
2. Add the peas, fennel seeds, stock, tomatoes, mixed herbs and salt and black pepper. Bring to the boil and simmer for 5–10 minutes, slightly longer if using fresh tomatoes.
3. Meanwhile, cook the pasta until *al dente*. Drain and rinse with cold water. Set aside.
4. Place a clump of pasta in each soup bowl, then ladle the hot soup over. Sprinkle each portion with basil, if using, and offer grated cheese separately.

Roasted Tomato and Garlic Broth with Green Beans and Stelline (Tiny Stars)

SERVES 4

Clear and savoury tasting, this is a lovely soup: flavourful enough to satisfy yet light enough not to weigh you down.
The simple broth is created by sautéing garlic then adding diced roasted tomatoes and stock. That is all there is to it but it packs a deliciously strong flavour wallop. Tiny pasta such as stelline seems to taste best, and it looks delightful too, but if unavailable use thin pasta strands such as capellini or even broken spaghettini.

9 medium or 12 small tomatoes
3 cloves garlic, coarsely chopped
1–2 tablespoons olive oil
Handful of green beans, cut into bite-sized lengths
1 litre/1¾ pints vegetable stock
175g/6 oz stelline or other tiny pasta

9 medium or 12 small tomatoes
3 cloves garlic, coarsely chopped
1–2 tablespoons olive oil
Handful of green beans, cut into bite-sized lengths
1 quart vegetable stock
6 oz stelline or other tiny pasta

1. Roast the tomatoes as described on page 261.
2. Sauté the garlic in the olive oil until lightly gilded, add the green beans and cook for a minute or two, then add the tomatoes and their cooking juice. Pour in the vegetable stock and bring to the boil.
3. Meanwhile, cook the pasta until just tender. Drain.
4. Serve each bowl of soup with several spoonfuls of cooked pasta stirred in.

Variation

Chillied Roasted Tomato and Green Bean Broth: This Mexican variation has a spicy kick but is not uncomfortably hot. Add a teaspoon or so of mild chilli powder, to taste, when the soup is finished. Serve ladled over thin strands of cooked capellini instead of the star-shaped stelline.

African Spicy Peanut Soup-Stew with Noodles

SERVES 4–6

This African-inspired soup-stew is a version of one filled with vegetables, chillies and peanuts that I make at least once a month. I usually fling open the refrigerator to see what vegetables are languishing there, ready to be simmered in this spicy soup. But recently, when it was time to serve the soup, I added handfuls of cooked noodles – no doubt a result of testing recipes for this book. It was very good. I have since prepared this soup using couscous once, and thin rice noodles another time. They were good, too. The secret is to make the soup absolutely sing with high flavour, then whichever pasta you serve it with will taste right.

As a young friend from Ethiopia, Eyob, exclaimed as he lifted the first spoonful to his lips: 'It tastes, it actually tastes! Nothing I have eaten since I've been here could I taste!' There was a smile on his face.

4 shallots or 1 onion, chopped
3 cloves garlic, chopped
2 tablespoons vegetable oil
1 bay leaf
1 teaspoon paprika
½ teaspoon curry powder, or to taste
½ teaspoon cumin, or to taste
400g/14 oz ripe fresh or tinned tomatoes, diced
600ml/600ml vegetable stock
2–3 dried hot red chillies, left whole, or several generous shakes of dried red chilli flakes
½ carrot, diced
¼ small to medium white or green cabbage, thinly sliced or coarsely chopped
Handful of fresh or frozen green beans, cut into bite-sized lengths
50g/2 oz fresh or frozen spinach, chopped
4–6 heaped tablespoons peanut butter, preferably unsweetened and chunky
Juice of 1 lemon, or to taste
Several tablespoons of yogurt, or to taste

4 shallots or 1 onion, chopped
3 cloves garlic, chopped
2 tablespoons vegetable oil
1 bay leaf
1 teaspoon paprika
½ teaspoon curry powder, or to taste
½ teaspoon cumin, or to taste
1½ cups diced ripe or canned tomatoes
2½ cups vegetable stock
2–3 dried hot red chillies, left whole or several generous shakes of dried red chilli flakes
½ carrot, diced
½ small to medium white or green cabbage, thinly sliced or coarsely chopped
Handful of fresh or frozen green beans, cut into bite-sized lengths
¼ cup fresh or frozen spinach, chopped
4–6 heaped tablespoons peanut butter, preferably unsweetened and chunky
Juice of 1 lemon, or to taste
Several tablespoons of yogurt, to taste

Salt and freshly ground black pepper,
    to taste
125g/4 oz Chinese noodles (or rice
    noodles)
Garnishes
Celery leaves and/or fresh coriander
    leaves
4 tablespoons crushed peanuts
Hot pepper sauce
Lemon wedges

Salt and freshly ground black pepper,
    to taste
4 oz Chinese noodles (or rice noodles)
Garnishes
Celery leaves or cilantro
4 tablespoons crushed peanuts
Hot pepper sauce
Lemon wedges

1. Lightly sauté the shallots or onion and garlic in the vegetable oil until softened, then add the bay leaf, paprika, curry powder and cumin and cook for a moment. Add the tomatoes, vegetable stock, chillies, carrot and cabbage, then bring to the boil. Reduce the heat and simmer until the vegetables are very soft, at least 30 minutes.

2. Add the green beans and spinach and continue cooking at least 20 minutes longer, until all the vegetables are soft.

3. Stir in the peanut butter until melted, then add the lemon juice, yogurt and salt and black pepper. Add more curry powder or cumin if needed.

4. Meanwhile, cook the noodles until tender. Rinse with cold water and drain.

5. To serve, ladle the soup-stew over the noodles. Garnish with celery leaves and/or coriander leaves (cilantro), sprinkle with the crushed peanuts, and offer hot pepper sauce and lemon wedges separately.

SOUPS AND STEWS WITH BEANS

The combination of high-protein beans and starchy pasta is a good one, with the robust beans balancing the blander pasta. It is rustic rather than refined food, and seems to taste best with humble ingredients rather than delicate ones: onions, garlic, tomatoes, olive oil, hot pepper, leafy vegetables, etc. It is economical, too, as a potful of beans and pasta needs little in the way of embellishments. And it can last for days, evolving somewhat every day, depending upon what is in the market or larder, and growing richer in mingling flavours.

Pasta with beans makes nutritional sense, too. It is filled with complex carbohydrates and fibre, needing only a salad to make a complete, well-balanced meal.

Pasta e Fagioli a la Toscana
(Tuscan Soup of Puréed Beans with Pasta)

SERVES 4–6

Tuscany is known in Italy as the land of bean eaters because of their consumption of hearty legume dishes such as this one. It makes a good main-course, and leftovers just seem to get better for several days afterwards as you simmer in whatever is languishing in your refrigerator: courgettes (zucchini), spinach, etc., turning the potful into a minestrone. Since the pasta is apt to disintegrate when the leftover soup is reheated, you will probably want to add more, as you add more vegetables, stock and seasonings.

3–5 cloves garlic, chopped
1½ tablespoons olive oil
8 ripe fresh or tinned tomatoes, diced
2 teaspoons chopped fresh rosemary leaves
400g/14 oz cooked or drained tinned beans, either white cannellini or chickpeas
100ml/4 fl oz tomato passata or tomato juice
1 litre/1¾ pints vegetable stock
Pinch of red chilli flakes
Salt and freshly ground black pepper, to taste
75–100g/3–4 oz flat pasta ribbons or medium sized pasta shapes

3–5 cloves garlic, chopped
1½ tablespoons olive oil
1 cup diced fresh or canned tomatoes
2 teaspoons chopped fresh rosemary leaves
1⅔ cups cooked or drained, canned beans, either white kidney (cannellini) or garbonzo beans
½ cup tomato passata, tomato sauce, or tomato juice
1 quart vegetable stock
Pinch of red chilli flakes
Salt and freshly ground black pepper, to taste
3–4 oz flat pasta ribbons or medium sized pasta shapes

1. Lightly sauté the garlic in 1 tablespoon of the olive oil. When it begins to colour, add the tomatoes and rosemary and cook over a high heat for 5–10 minutes or until saucelike.
2. Mash the beans coarsely, leaving some whole. This may be done in a food processor or using a potato masher. Add the beans to the sauce, then add the tomato passata, stock, red chilli flakes, salt if needed, and black pepper, and pasta. Cook over medium heat until the pasta is tender; this will depend upon the type of pasta you choose.
3. Serve immediately, drizzling the remaining olive oil over each portion.

Variations

Serve at cool room temperature, with lemon wedges as accompaniment.

Pasta with Black-Eyed Peas: Follow the recipe above, but substitute an equal amount of cooked or drained tinned black-eyed peas for the beans. For the pasta, choose ditalini or a short elbow shape.

Macaroni with Red Beans and Tomatoes

SERVES 4–6

Robust and homy, this makes a sustaining supper dish. You could include other vegetables if you like, such as chard, cabbage, green beans, etc., but it is delicious as it is, with its small nuggets of onion, celery and carrot. The bean broth forms the cooking liquid for the pasta, and once it is all cooked together it is thick and soupy. Serve with a generous sprinkling of cheese. It needn't be Parmesan – any sharp cheese is lovely, even a humble Cheddar.

Dishes like this, based on beans and their cooking liquid, are great to have in your culinary repertoire as you cook your way through a big potful. Tinned beans are fine in many recipes, but in ones like this where you need the cooking liquid as well, the liquid from the tin is too salty and metallic-tasting, so use fresh.

225g/8 oz dried red kidney beans
1 onion, coarsely chopped
1 carrot, diced
2 celery stalks, chopped
3 cloves garlic, chopped
1 tablespoon chopped parsley (optional)
2 tablespoons olive oil
10 ripe fresh or tinned tomatoes, peeled and diced
250ml/8 fl oz tomato juice
½ vegetable stock cube
225g/8 oz shortcut macaroni
1 tablespoon tomato paste
1 teaspoon dried mixed herbs
Salt and freshly ground black pepper, to taste
100g/4 oz grated cheese, or to taste

1 cup dried red kidney beans
1 onion, coarsely chopped
1 medium sized carrot, diced
2 celery stalks, chopped
3 cloves garlic, chopped
1 tablespoon chopped parsley (optional)
2 tablespoons olive oil
10 ripe fresh or 1¼ cup diced canned tomatoes
1 cup tomato juice
½ vegetable bouillon cube
8 oz shortcut macaroni
1 tablespoon tomato paste
1 teaspoon dried mixed herbs
Salt and freshly ground black pepper, to taste
½ cup grated cheese, for sprinkling

1. Cook the beans until tender and leave to cool in their cooking liquid.
2. Lightly sauté the onion, carrot, celery, garlic and fresh parsley, if using, in the olive oil until softened and lightly browned.
3. Ladle in the beans and 500ml/16fl oz/2 cups of their cooking liquid, the tomatoes, tomato juice, stock (bouillon) cube and macaroni and bring to the boil. Cook over medium heat for about 5–7 minutes, stirring carefully so as not to break up pasta.
4. Cover and leave to stand for a few minutes to let the pasta absorb the liquid and plump up. If the mixture seems too dry, add more bean cooking liquid or tomato juice.
5. Stir in the tomato paste, mixed herbs, salt and black pepper, and serve immediately, each portion sprinkled with cheese.

Pasta Stew with White Beans and Black Olive Sauce

SERVES 4–6

Olive paste, oily, pungent and black, adds a touch of piquancy to this soup-stew of beans and pasta. If olive paste is unavailable, make your own by mincing pitted Mediterranean-style black olives in a food processor and adding enough olive oil to make a smooth paste.

175g/6 oz ditalini or other short macaroni
1 onion, thinly sliced
1 small to medium carrot, diced
2 cloves garlic, coarsely chopped
225g/8 oz cooked or drained tinned white beans
675g/1½ lb ripe fresh tomatoes, peeled and diced, or 1½ 400g/14oz tins chopped tomatoes
2 tablespoons chopped fresh parsley
500ml/16 fl oz vegetable stock
Salt and freshly ground black pepper, to taste

Olive Sauce
1 large clove garlic, chopped
1 teaspoon chopped fresh rosemary
1 tablespoon olive paste
3 tablespoons olive oil

6 oz ditalini or other short macaroni
1 onion, thinly sliced
1 small to medium carrot, diced
2 cloves garlic, coarsely chopped
1 cup cooked or drained canned white beans
1½–2 cups ripe fresh or canned tomatoes, peeled and diced
2 tablespoons chopped fresh parsley
2 cups vegetable stock
Salt and freshly ground black pepper, to taste

1. Cook the pasta until *al dente*. Drain and rinse with cold water then set aside.
2. Lightly sauté the onion, carrot and garlic until softened, then add the beans, tomatoes, parsley and stock and simmer for 5–10 minutes.
3. Meanwhile, mix all the ingredients for the olive sauce together. (This may be made in advance and stored in the refrigerator for up to a month.)
4. Add the pasta to the stew, reheat gently and serve each portion garnished with the olive sauce.

Variation

White Bean and Orzo Stew: Small, rice-shaped orzo are very good in this bean and pasta dish. Serve with a drizzle of lemon juice or wine vinegar, a sprinkling of oregano and raw chopped garlic, in place of the olive sauce.

Italian Soup of Pumpkin, Beans and Orzo

SERVES 4–6

Earthy pumpkin and red beans combine with small, tender orzo for a risotto-like pasta dish.

3 cloves garlic, chopped
1½ tablespoons olive oil
450g/1 lb winter squash or pumpkin, peeled and diced
900ml/1½ pints vegetable stock
250ml/8 fl oz tomato passata
100g/4 oz orzo or similar pasta
400g/14 oz cooked or drained tinned kidney beans
175–225g/6–8 oz chard or spinach, coarsely chopped or thinly sliced
Salt, freshly ground black pepper, and dried oregano, to taste
Freshly grated Parmesan cheese to serve

3 cloves garlic, chopped
1½ tablespoons olive oil
2½–3 cups peeled and diced pumpkin or other winter squash such as Hubbard
3½ cups vegetable stock
1 cup tomato sauce, passata or tomato juice
4 oz/¼ lb orzo or similar pasta
1¾ cups cooked or drained canned kidney beans
8 oz chard or spinach, coarsely chopped or thinly sliced (about half a bunch)
Salt, freshly ground black pepper, and dried oregano, to taste
Freshly grated Parmesan cheese to serve

1. Lightly sauté the garlic in the olive oil for just a moment; add the squash or pumpkin and turn in the garlic and oil to coat.
2. Pour in the stock and tomato passata, then cover and cook over medium heat until the squash or pumpkin is almost tender. Add the pasta and continue cooking for another 10–15 minutes until *al dente*.
3. Add the kidney beans and chard or spinach, and cook until chard or spinach is bright green and just tender.
4. Season with salt, black pepper, and oregano, and serve immediately, accompanied by grated Parmesan cheese.

Curried Yogurt Soup with Broccoli, Chickpeas (Garbanzos) and Lumachine

SERVES 4

Tangy with tart yogurt, this spicy bowlful is rich with the fresh bite of broccoli and nutty crunch of chickpeas. It makes a good main course for lunchtime or supper, along with a hearty salad, or as a first course for a more ambitious meal.

150g/5 oz lumachine or other small to medium shell-like pasta

1 large or 2 small stalks broccoli, cut into bite-sized florets and chunks of peeled stem

5 shallots, chopped

15g/½oz butter or 1 tablespoon vegetable oil

½ teaspoon curry powder, or to taste

1 tablespoon flour

1 litre/1¾ pints vegetable stock

250ml/8 fl oz/1 cup yogurt

1 egg, lightly beaten

400g/14 oz cooked or drained tinned chickpeas

1 clove garlic, finely chopped

Juice of ½ lemon, or to taste

Salt and red pepper flakes or cayenne pepper, to taste

5 oz lumachine or other small to medium shell-like pasta

1 large or 2 small bunches broccoli, cut into florets and bite-sized pieces of peeled stem

5 shallots, chopped

1 tablespoon butter or vegetable oil

½ teaspoon curry powder, or to taste

1 tablespoon flour

1 quart vegetable stock

1 cup yogurt

1 egg, lightly beaten

1⅔ cups cooked or drained canned garbanzos

1 clove garlic, finely chopped

Juice of ½ lemon, or to taste

Salt and red pepper flakes or cayenne pepper, to taste

1. Boil the pasta until half cooked, then add the broccoli and continue cooking until both are *al dente*. Drain and rinse with cold water. Set aside.

2. Lightly sauté the shallots in the butter or oil until softened and lightly gilded, then sprinkle in the curry powder and flour, stirring a few minutes to cook out the raw taste. Stir in the stock, bring to the boil, then reduce the heat and simmer for a few minutes until slightly thickened. Remove from the heat.

3. Mix the yogurt and beaten egg together then add a ladleful of hot soup, stirring to combine very well. Repeat several times. Add the egg mixture to the pot of hot soup and stir to combine well.

4. Add the chickpeas (garbanzos), pasta and broccoli, then heat through on low to medium heat, taking care not to curdle the mixture. Season with the garlic, lemon juice, salt, if needed, and red pepper flakes or cayenne pepper, and serve immediately.

Brown Lentil, Red Bean, Broccoli and Pasta Shell Stew

SERVES ABOUT 6

This is a hearty soup-stew in the robust minestrone style. For a main course, omit the grated cheese and serve each portion of soup-stew ladled over a slab of mild white cheese to melt in; as you eat the soup, each spoonful will yield a tiny bit of the rich cheese as well.

Leftovers are delicious reheated; I usually add a fresh lashing of chopped garlic, and sometimes give it a spicy shake of hot pepper sauce or cayenne pepper.

250g/9 oz Puy lentils, or other brown or green lentils
1 litre/1¾ pints vegetable stock
75g/3 oz tomato paste
225g/8 oz ripe fresh tomatoes, diced, or 400g/14oz tin chopped tomatoes
1 bunch broccoli or spinach, cut into bite-sized pieces
400g/14 oz cooked or drained tinned borlotti or red kidney beans
175g/6 oz pasta shells or other medium to large macaroni shapes
Large pinch each of dried thyme, sage, rosemary and mixed herbs
4 cloves garlic, chopped
225g/8 oz cheese of choice, grated
Salt and freshly ground black pepper, to taste
3 tablespoons olive oil, or to taste
3 tablespoons chopped fresh parsley

1 cup Puy lentils or other brown or green lentils
1 quart vegetable stock
3 oz/⅓ cup tomato paste
1 cup diced tomatoes, either fresh or canned
1 bunch broccoli or spinach, cut into bite-sized pieces
1½ cups cooked or drained canned borlotti or red kidney beans
6 oz pasta shells or other medium to large macaroni shapes
Large pinch each of dried thyme, sage, rosemary and mixed herbs
4 cloves garlic, chopped
8 oz cheese such as Monterey Jack, grated
Salt and freshly ground black pepper, to taste
3 tablespoons olive oil, or to taste
3 tablespoons chopped fresh parsley

1. Cook the lentils in the stock until just tender, about an hour.
2. Add the tomato paste, tomatoes, broccoli or spinach, beans, pasta, herbs, and half the garlic. Continue cooking until the pasta is *al dente*.
3. Gently stir in the remaining garlic, cheese, salt if needed, and black pepper.
4. Serve immediately, each portion sprinkled with olive oil and parsley.

Variation

Use an assortment of different types of beans, Calabrian style: combine borlotti, cannellini (white kidney), fava and chickpeas (garbanzos), and decrease the amount of lentils to a small handful, and substitute cabbage for the broccoli or spinach. Calabrians generally use spaghetti broken into thirds in place of macaroni and serve the hefty soup sprinkled with olive oil and parsley and omit the cheese stirred into the above recipe.

Chickpea and Tagliatelle Soup

SERVES 4

Simple fare from Italy's deep South, this soup is a broth filled with garlic-and-onion-sautéed chickpeas (garbanzos) and tender tagliatelle.

2 small to medium onions, chopped	2 small to medium onions, chopped
3 cloves garlic, chopped	3 cloves garlic, chopped
1 small carrot, chopped	1 small carrot, chopped
1 tablespoon chopped fresh parsley	1 tablespoon chopped fresh parsley
2 tablespoons olive oil	2 tablespoons olive oil
Salt and freshly ground black pepper	Salt and freshly ground black pepper
400g/14 oz cooked or drained tinned chickpeas	1½ cups cooked or drained canned garbanzos
1 litre/1¾ pints vegetable stock	1 quart vegetable stock
175g/6 oz fresh or dried tagliatelle	6 oz fresh or dried tagliatelle

1. Lightly sauté the onions, garlic, carrot and parsley in the olive oil until the onions are softened. Season with salt and black pepper, then add the chickpeas (garbanzos) and cook for a few minutes.
2. Add the stock and bring to the boil, then simmer for about 10 minutes or until well flavoured. Taste for seasoning.
3. Meanwhile, cook the pasta until *al dente*. Drain. Add to the soup and serve.

Variations

Chickpea and Tagliatelle Soup with Tomatoes and Rosemary: Add 450g/1 lb/2 cups ripe fresh chopped tomatoes, or 400g/14oz tin chopped tomatoes to the recipe above, along with 1½–2 teaspoons chopped fresh rosemary.

Pasta e Ceci alla Leccese: From Lecce (Apulia) comes this pasta and chickpea (garbanzo) soup which is strikingly different from others in that half the pasta is fried while the other half is boiled. It gives an unusual texture and richness to the soup.

Prepare the basic soup recipe but use fresh tagliatelle and increase the amount to 225g/8 oz/½ lb. Fry half of it until lightly golden, then drain on absorbent paper towels. Add the fried pasta to the soup at the end of its cooking time and cook for 1–3 minutes before serving. Season with hot red pepper flakes, and if the pasta has not been fried in olive oil, anoint the soup with a drizzle of olive oil before serving.

COLD PASTA DISHES

Cold pasta served with a raw or quickly cooked sauce and garnished with fresh vegetables can be one of the most refreshing dishes imaginable. The supple, cool noodles should contrast with the vivacious flavours and crisp textures they are paired with: strong-flavoured ingredients such as garlic, olive or sesame oil, onions, tomatoes, crisp vegetables, nuts, herbs and tangy cheeses. The important thing about cold pasta is that it retain its freshness – don't be tempted to turn it into the pasta-salad rubbish bin that some restaurants and recipes do.

Cold pasta should never be chilled to numbness, though a nicely chilled sauce can be an exciting counterpoint to freshly cooked hot pasta. Since many Far Eastern pasta dishes are enjoyed cold as well, do refer to that chapter (pp. 189–215) for additional recipes.

Garlic-and-Olive-Oil-Scented Macaroni Salad with Tomatoes, Goat Cheese and Basil

SERVES 4

8–10 ripe fresh tomatoes, diced
1 tablespoon balsamic or red wine vinegar, or to taste
Salt and freshly ground black pepper, to taste
325g/12 oz elbow pasta or lumachine (small shells)
3 tablespoons olive oil
3 cloves garlic, chopped
Handful of fresh basil leaves, coarsely chopped
100g/4 oz goat cheese, crumbled

8 to 10 ripe fresh tomatoes, diced
1 tablespoon balsamic or red wine vinegar, or to taste
Salt and freshly ground black pepper, to taste
12 oz elbow pasta or lumachine (small shells)
3 tablespoons olive oil
3 cloves garlic, chopped
¼ cup coarsely chopped fresh basil leaves
4 oz goat cheese, crumbled

1. Combine the tomatoes with the vinegar and salt to taste and leave to stand while you cook the pasta until _al dente_.
2. Drain the pasta and toss with the olive oil and garlic.
3. When the pasta is warm but not hot, combine with the tomato mixture. Leave to cool completely and toss with the basil. Serve each portion topped with the crumbled goat cheese and black pepper to taste.

Penne with Red (Bell) Peppers, Feta and Mint

SERVES 4

Like goat cheese, slightly creamy, pungent and salty feta cheese combines brilliantly with bland pasta. Red (Bell) peppers and garlic, lemon and mint, all amplify the Mediterranean flavour focus.

3 red peppers	3 red bell peppers
2 cloves garlic, chopped	2 cloves garlic, chopped
100g/4 oz feta cheese, crumbled	4 oz/¼ lb feta cheese, crumbled
3 tablespoons olive oil	3 tablespoons olive oil
325g/12 oz penne (pasta quills)	12 oz penne (pasta quills)
Juice of 1 lemon, or to taste	Juice of 1 lemon, or to taste
Coarsely ground black pepper to taste	Coarsely ground black pepper to taste
2 tablespoons finely chopped fresh mint leaves	2 tablespoons finely chopped fresh mint leaves

1. Roast the red (bell) peppers as described on page 262, then cut into bite-sized pieces.
2. Combine with the garlic, feta cheese, and olive oil.
3. Cook the pasta until *al dente*. Drain, then toss with the pepper and feta cheese mixture. Season with the lemon juice and black pepper, and serve either hot or cold, garnished with the chopped mint.

Variation

Penne with Black Olives, Feta, and Parsley: Substitute black Kalamata or oil-cured olives, pitted and quartered, for the grilled red (bell) peppers and use chopped parsley instead of, or in addition to, the mint. Proceed as above.

Spicy Fragrant East-West Noodles

SERVES 4

3 tablespoons fermented black beans, rinsed and drained
3 cloves garlic, chopped
Grated rind of ½ orange or 1 tangerine
2–3 dried hot red chillies, crumbled
75ml/3 fl oz vegetable oil
3 tablespoons toasted sesame oil
325g/12 oz Chinese egg noodles or Italian vermicelli
3–4 tablespoons chopped fresh coriander leaves
½ cucumber, diced or coarsely chopped
2 to 3 tablespoons crushed or coarsely chopped peanuts or toasted almonds
2–3 spring onions, thinly sliced
Soy sauce to taste

3 tablespoons fermented black beans, rinsed and drained
3 cloves garlic, chopped
Grated rind (zest) of ½ orange or 1 tangerine
2–3 dried hot red chillies, crumbled
⅓ cup bland vegetable oil
3 tablespoons toasted (Chinese) sesame oil
12 oz Chinese egg noodles or Italian vermicelli
¼ cup coarsely chopped fresh cilantro
½ cucumber, diced or coarsely chopped
¼ cup coarsely chopped or crushed peanuts or toasted almonds
2–3 green onions, thinly sliced
Soy sauce to taste

1. Gently heat the black beans, garlic, orange or tangerine rind and red chillies in the vegetable oil. Do not let the garlic brown or let the mixture boil. Leave to cool, then mix with the toasted sesame oil. This will make more oil than you need for this recipe, but it will keep for months in a well-sealed jar and makes a good flavouring addition for a variety of dishes, especially those with a Far-Eastern accent.

2. Cook the noodles until *al dente*, then drain and rinse with cold water, then drain again.
3. When ready to serve, toss the pasta with some of the flavoured oil, then garnish with coriander (cilantro) leaves, cucumber, peanuts or almonds, and spring (green) onions, and sprinkle with soy sauce.

Penne alla Malefemmina (Quill-Shaped Pasta with Spicy Tomatoes, Capers, Olives and Basil)

SERVES 4

Malefemmina means bad woman and, like the pasta served alla puttanesca, alla malefemmina refers to a spicy, lusty sauce of tomatoes, olives, capers, olive oil, basil, and a touch of hot pepper. There are so many differing tales about why these tasty dishes are called whore's pasta. Some say that it is because the dishes are so quick to prepare that they can be whipped up between customers; others say that only a loose woman would cook such a dish of strong flavours rather than the subtle aromas and wholesome dishes a good woman would serve.

325g/12 oz penne
50ml/2 fl oz olive oil
20 black Kalamata or other
    Mediterranean-type olives, pitted
    and halved
1 tablespoon capers
4–5 cloves garlic, chopped
225g/8 oz ripe fresh tomatoes, coarsely
    chopped and drained of excess juice,
    or 400g/14 oz tin tomatoes, drained
    and chopped (reserve juice for
    another use)
Handful of fresh basil leaves, some left
    whole, some torn in half
Salt and red chilli flakes, to taste

12 oz penne
¼ cup olive oil
20 black Kalamata or other
    Mediterranean-type olives, pitted
    and halved
1 tablespoon capers
4–5 cloves garlic, chopped
1 cup ripe fresh or canned tomatoes,
    drained (reserve the juice for
    another use) and coarsely chopped
¼ cup fresh basil leaves, some left
    whole, some torn in half
Salt and red chilli flakes, to taste

1. Cook the penne until *al dente*.
2. Meanwhile, combine the olive oil with the olives, capers, garlic, tomatoes and basil.
3. Drain the pasta and toss with the sauce; season with salt and red chilli flakes. Leave to cool and serve at room temperature or lightly chilled.

Variation

Use both black and pimiento-stuffed green olives for the sauce.

Pasta Shells and Broccoli with Spicy-Tangy Tahini Dressing

SERVES 4

Sesame-rich tahini makes a delicious and healthy dressing for this pasta and broccoli salad.

325g/12 oz pasta shells
1 large bunch broccoli, cut into bite-sized pieces
1 dried hot red chilli, crumbled
6 cloves garlic, coarsely chopped
3 tablespoons olive oil
100ml/4 fl oz tahini, mashed with a fork to smooth any lumps
1 teaspoon cumin
Juice of 1 lemon, plus extra lemon wedges to serve
Pinch of turmeric or curry powder
Salt and freshly ground black pepper, to taste

12 oz pasta shells
1 large bunch broccoli, cut into bite-sized pieces
1 hot dried red chilli, crumbled or red chlli flakes, to taste
6 cloves garlic, coarsely chopped
3 tablespoons olive oil
½ cup tahini, mashed with a fork to smooth any lumps
1 teaspoon cumin
Juice of 1 lemon, plus extra lemon wedges to serve
Pinch of turmeric or curry powder
Salt and freshly ground black pepper, to taste

1. Cook the pasta until half done, add the broccoli and continue cooking until the pasta and broccoli are both *al dente*. Drain.
2. Heat the chilli and half the garlic in the olive oil. Toss the pasta and broccoli in this mixture and set aside to cool.
3. Mix the remaining garlic with the tahini, cumin, lemon juice, turmeric or curry powder, salt and black pepper, and enough water to make a paste about the consistency of thick cream.
4. Just before serving, combine the pasta and broccoli with the tahini sauce. Serve with lemon wedges.

Fourth of July Macaroni Salad

SERVES 4

Before the advent of pasta salad, macaroni salad was the only cold pasta dish Americans knew. Seldom was there a community gathering without a big bowlful of macaroni salad; growing up I couldn't imagine a Fourth of July picnic without it. It consisted of macaroni bound together in a mayonnaise dressing, seasoned simply with such ingredients as onions, celery, hard-boiled egg, chopped sweet gherkins, diced tomato and/or beetroot, etc.

As tastes grew more sophisticated, macaroni salads began to disappear in favour of the new pasta salads, with pesto, sun-dried tomatoes, Kalamata olives, and so on. But macaroni salad can be really good, as witnessed by the following recipe, and it is delicious any day of the year, not just the Fourth of July.

325g/12 oz small to medium pasta shape of choice

75g-100g/3-4 oz fresh and blanched or frozen peas

4-6 heaped tablespoons mayonnaise, or to taste

1 tablespoon mustard of choice, or combination (such as wholegrain, Dijon, etc.)

1-2 celery stalks, plus leaves, chopped

½-1 small onion or 2 spring onions, chopped

1-2 hard-boiled eggs, diced

6-8 pimiento-stuffed green olives, coarsely chopped, or pickled cucumbers such as gherkins or the French cornichons, coarsely chopped

Few drops of vinegar or lemon juice

Salt, freshly ground black pepper and paprika, to taste

2 tablespoons chopped fresh parsley

12 oz small to medium pasta shape of choice

½ cup fresh and blanched or frozen peas

½ to ⅔ cup mayonnaise, or to taste

1 tablespoon mustard of choice, or combination (such as Tarragon, Dijon, Wholeseed, etc.)

1-2 stalks celery, plus leaves, chopped

½-1 small onion or 2 green onions, chopped

1-2 hard-boiled eggs, diced

6-8 pimiento-stuffed green olives, coarsely chopped, or 2 tablespoons chopped pickled cucumbers such as gherkins, French cornichons or bread and butter pickles

Few drops of vinegar or lemon juice

Salt, freshly ground black pepper and paprika, to taste

2 tablespoons chopped fresh parsley

1. Cook the pasta until *al dente*, adding the peas at the last minute to cook through; drain and rinse in cold water. Drain well again.
2. Combine the pasta and peas with all the remaining ingredients. Taste for seasoning.

Note: This is even better if it is left for a while for the flavours to blend. Be sure to store it in the refrigerator, however, as mayonnaise can quickly go off in warm temperatures, even room temperature.

Summer-Afternoon Pasta with Tomatoes, Mozzarella and Basil

SERVES 4

Cool and refreshing for a summer lunch on a terrace in Tuscany or in your own garden.

325g/12 oz large pasta shells, or gnocchi shapes

175g/6 oz jar peperoncini (Greek or Italian mildly spicy pickled peppers), drained

10–12 ripe sweet red tomatoes, diced, or use half fresh and half tinned

3 tablespoons olive oil, or to taste

1 tablespoon red wine vinegar or sherry vinegar

Large pinch of dried thyme, crumbled

Large pinch of dried mint, crumbled

Salt and cayenne pepper or red hot pepper flakes, to taste

100g/4 oz mozzarella cheese, diced

Handful of fresh basil leaves, thinly sliced

12 oz large pasta shells, or gnocchi shapes

½ cup peperoncini (Greek or Italian mildly spicy pickled peppers), drained

10–12 ripe sweet red tomatoes, diced, or use half fresh and half canned

3 tablespoons olive oil, or to taste

1 tablespoon red wine vinegar or sherry vinegar

Large pinch of dried thyme, crumbled

Large pinch of dried mint, crumbled

Salt and cayenne pepper or hot red pepper flakes, to taste

4 oz/¼ lb mozzarella cheese, diced

¼ cup fresh basil leaves, thinly sliced

1. Cook the pasta until *al dente*. Drain and combine with the peperoncini, tomatoes, olive oil, vinegar, thyme, and mint. Leave to cool.

2. When cool, season with salt and cayenne pepper or red pepper flakes, then add the cheese and basil and chill until ready to serve.

Noodles with Coriander (Cilantro)-Mint Raita and Cucumber

SERVES 4–6

A cool, green dressing that smells of sweet mint and spicy ginger, yet delivers a chilli pepper wallop. Serve topped with a handful of thinly sliced coriander (cilantro) and mint leaves, and a scattering of crunchy chopped cucumber.

2 cloves garlic, finely chopped
1 fresh green chilli pepper, or to taste, chopped
2 teaspoons chopped fresh ginger root
Large bunch of fresh mint leaves, thinly sliced
Large bunch of fresh coriander, thinly sliced
500ml/16 fl oz Greek yogurt
Salt to taste
325g/12 oz spaghetti or dried Chinese egg noodles
Several tablespoons of olive oil
Juice of ½ lemon, or to taste
¼–½ cucumber, coarsely chopped or finely diced, and drained of excess liquid

2 cloves garlic, finely chopped
1 fresh green chilli such as jalapeno, or to taste, finely chopped
2 teaspoons chopped fresh ginger root
Large bunch of fresh mint leaves, thinly sliced
Large bunch of cilantro, thinly sliced
2 cups yogurt, preferably whole milk
Salt to taste
12 oz spaghetti or dried Chinese egg noodles
Several tablespoons of olive oil
Juice of ½ lemon, or to taste
¼–½ cucumber, coarsely chopped or finely diced, and drained of excess liquid

1. Combine the garlic, chilli, ginger root, mint and coriander (cilantro) - reserving a small handful of mint and coriander (cilantro) for garnish - and blend in a liquidizer (blender) or food processor into a purée. Add the yogurt and blend into a pale green mixture. Season with salt and chill until ready to use (it may be made several days in advance).

2. Cook the spaghetti or noodles until *al dente*, then drain and toss with olive oil to taste.
3. Combine the pasta with the yogurt mixture, then season with the lemon juice.
4. Serve topped with a scattering of the reserved, chopped, coriander (cilantro) and mint, and the cucumber.

Cold Pasta with Broccoli, Sesame and Soy

SERVES 4

The combination of pasta, a crisp-tender vegetable such as broccoli, and a simple glistening of nutty sesame oil and salty soy sauce is far more delicious than any recipe this easy and uncomplicated deserves to be.

325g/12 oz pasta of choice: chunky elbows, seashells, fettuccine, Chinese pasta, lasagne, thin capellini, wonton wrappers, etc.
275–325g/10–12 oz broccoli, cut into bite-sized pieces
2–3 tablespoons toasted sesame oil, to taste
Soy sauce to taste
1 clove garlic, chopped (optional)
2 tablespoons toasted sesame seeds
1 tablespoon coarsely chopped fresh coriander leaves

12 oz pasta of choice (see above)
1–2 bunches broccoli, cut into bite-sized pieces, enough to make 3–4 cups
2–3 tablespoons toasted sesame oil, to taste
Soy sauce to taste
1 clove garlic, chopped (optional)
2 tablespoons toasted sesame seeds
1 tablespoon coarsely chopped fresh cilantro leaves

1. Boil the pasta until half cooked, then add the broccoli and continue cooking until the pasta is *al dente* and the broccoli is crisp-tender.
2. Drain and rinse in cold water. When cool, dress in sesame oil and soy sauce, add the garlic if using, and sprinkle with the sesame seeds and coriander (cilantro) leaves.

Variation

Spicy Penne with Green Beans, Chinese Style: Substitute thin green beans, cut into bite-sized pieces, for the broccoli. Add a shake of hot pepper sauce such as Tabasco for extra zest.

Fusilli Salad with Courgettes (Zucchini), Sun-Dried Tomatoes, and Rosemary

SERVES 4

325g/12 oz fusilli or other twisty pasta
4 small to medium courgettes, cut into bite-sized pieces
1–2 cloves garlic, chopped
2 teaspoons chopped fresh rosemary leaves
3 tablespoons olive oil
10 oil-marinated sun-dried tomatoes, drained and coarsely chopped
Salt and freshly ground black pepper, to taste
Dash of red wine vinegar (optional)

12 oz fusilli or other twisty pasta
4 small to medium zucchini, cut into bite-sized pieces
1–2 cloves garlic, chopped
2 teaspoons chopped fresh rosemary leaves
3 tablespons olive oil
10 oil-marinated sun-dried tomatoes, drained and coarsely chopped
Salt and freshly ground black pepper, to taste
Dash red wine vinegar (optional)

1. Boil the pasta until half cooked, then add the courgettes (zucchini) and continue cooking until both are *al dente*. Drain.
2. Toss with the garlic, rosemary, olive oil and sun-dried tomatoes then leave to cool. Season to taste before serving with salt, black pepper and the red wine vinegar if needed.

Farfalle with Multicoloured Tomato Salad

SERVES 4

Multicoloured tomatoes are a delight not only to the eye but to the tastebuds as well: each different shape and colour has its own flavour, sweetness and acidity. If you have a garden, grow as many types as you can; if not, seek out particularly tasty tomatoes and varied types. In addition to yellow and red ones, there are orange ones, variegated ones, and even a ripe green tomato that tastes luscious and sweet rather than overly tart, as unripe green tomatoes do.

In the following recipe, if multicoloured tomatoes are not available, use ordinary red ones.

325g/12 oz farfalle
3 cloves garlic, chopped
3 tablespoons olive oil
5–6 ripe, sweet fresh tomatoes,
    preferably a combination of red and
    yellow tomatoes, or a handful of
    tiny yellow and red cherry tomatoes
Salt and freshly ground black pepper,
    to taste
Pinch of sugar
Balsamic vinegar to taste
Several fresh basil leaves, rolled up and
    cut into thin strips

12 oz farfalle
3 cloves garlic, chopped
3 tablespoons olive oil
5–6 ripe tomatoes, either multicoloured
    or ordinary red ones
Salt and freshly ground black pepper,
    to taste
Pinch of sugar
Balsamic vinegar to taste
Several fresh basil leaves, rolled up and
    cut into thin strips

1. Cook the pasta until *al dente*. Drain and toss with the garlic and olive oil. Leave to cool.
2. Dice the tomatoes and season with salt and black pepper, sugar and balsamic vinegar.
3. Combine the cool pasta with the seasoned tomatoes and serve, sprinkled generously with basil.

Roasted Garlic with Cumin-Aubergine (Eggplant) and Capellini

SERVES 4

This recipe appears in The Flavour of California *(Thorsons), but I thought it was worth including it in this collection for its distinctive and unusual character. With Middle Eastern rather than Italian flavours and perfumes, it is unexpectedly delicious.*

3 heads garlic, broken into cloves but left unpeeled, plus 2 cloves raw garlic, peeled and chopped
3–4 tablespoons olive oil
Salt and cayenne pepper, to taste
1 aubergine, thinly sliced lengthwise
1–2 teaspoons cumin, or to taste
325g/12 oz capellini
Juice of ½ lemon
2 teaspoons chopped fresh coriander leaves or parsley

3 heads garlic, broken into cloves but left unpeeled, plus 2 cloves raw garlic, peeled and chopped
3–4 tablespoons olive oil
Salt and cayenne pepper, to taste
1 eggplant, thinly sliced lengthwise
1–2 teaspoons cumin, or to taste
12 oz capellini
Juice of ½ lemon
2 teaspoons chopped fresh cilantro leaves or parsley

1. Place the whole unpeeled garlic cloves on a baking sheet in a single layer and sprinkle with 2 tablespoons of the olive oil and salt to taste. Roast in the oven at 180°C/350°F/gas mark 4 for 30 minutes, then raise the heat to 200°C/400°F/gas mark 6 for another 10 minutes.
2. Remove from the oven and, when cool enough to handle, remove the skins. Toss the cooked garlic flesh with the oil they have cooked in, if any remains. Set aside.
3. Brush the aubergine slices (eggplant) with the remaining olive oil and sprinkle with about 1 teaspoon cumin. Grill (broil) until browned in spots and tender, then cut into matchstick pieces.
4. Cook the pasta until *al dente*, then drain.
5. Toss with the remaining olive oil and cumin, the roasted garlic flesh and the aubergine (eggplant). Season with salt, cayenne pepper, and the lemon juice. Add extra olive oil and cumin, if needed, and serve at room temperature, garnished with the coriander (cilantro) or parsley.

Pasta Shells with Courgettes (Zucchini) and Tomato-Olive Relish

SERVES 4

6–8 ripe fresh or tinned tomatoes, chopped

10–15 oil-cured black Mediterranean olives such as Kalamata or Niçoise, pitted and diced

2 tablespoons olive oil

2 teaspoons red wine vinegar

325g/12 oz pasta shells (or use elbows, ditalini, or other shortcut macaroni)

2 courgettes, diced

Salt and freshly ground black pepper, to taste

2 tablespoons chopped fresh parsley

6–8 ripe fresh or canned tomatoes, chopped

10–15 Mediterranean-type black olives, pitted and diced

2 tablespoons olive oil

2 teaspoons red wine vinegar

12 oz pasta shells (or use elbows, ditalini, penne, or other macaroni shape)

2 zucchini, diced

Salt and freshly ground black pepper, to taste

2 tablespoons chopped fresh parsley

1. Combine the tomatoes, olives, olive oil and vinegar. Set aside.
2. Cook the pasta until almost *al dente*, then add the courgettes (zucchini). Continue cooking until both are *al dente*. Drain.
3. Toss the hot pasta and courgettes (zucchini) with the cool tomato mixture. Add salt and black pepper, sprinkle with the chopped parsley, and serve at room temperature.

Pasta with Roasted Tomatoes and Red (Bell) Peppers

SERVES 4–6

Roasted ripe red tomatoes intensify in flavour as they bake and their juices ooze out, slightly caramelizing the sugars to balance their acidity. In this dish they are combined with slightly smoky roasted red (bell) peppers, and seasoned with garlic, olive oil and vinegar. Toss with tiny cooked orzo or with nearly any sort of larger pasta: rigatoni, capellini, ditalini, rotelle, penne, lumache are all very good.

20 small ripe red tomatoes (they must be fresh; tinned will not work)
4 red peppers
4–6 cloves garlic, chopped
3–5 tablespoons olive oil
2 teaspoons red wine vinegar, or to taste
Pinch of oregano or mixed herbs such as herbes de Provence
Salt and freshly ground black pepper
Several tablespoons of capers, to taste (optional)
450g/1 lb pasta of choice

20 small ripe red tomatoes (they must be fresh; canned will not work)
4 red bell peppers
4–6 cloves garlic, chopped
¼ (approximately) cup olive oil
2 teaspoons red wine vinegar, or to taste
Pinch of oregano or mixed herbs such as herbes de Provence
Salt and freshly ground black pepper
Several tablespoons of capers, to taste (optional)
1 lb pasta of choice

1. Roast the tomatoes as described on page 261.
2. Roast red (bell) peppers as described on page 262, then dice.
3. Combine the diced tomatoes and (bell) peppers with garlic, olive oil, vinegar, herbs,

salt and black pepper, and capers, if using. Leave to marinate for at least 15 minutes.
4. Cook the pasta until *al dente*. Drain and toss with the marinated tomatoes and red (bell) peppers, adding extra olive oil and vinegar, if needed, to keep it all moist and interesting.

Capellini with Beetroot (Beets) Relish, Broccoli and Blue Cheese

SERVES 4

4 medium to large beetroot, cooked but unvinegared
1 small to medium onion, chopped
1 tablespoon wine vinegar
Sugar, salt, freshly ground black pepper, and dried mixed herbs, to taste
2 tablespoons oil of choice
325g/12 oz capellini
2 bunches broccoli, cut into florets, the stalks peeled and sliced
1 tablespoon olive oil
125g/4½ oz blue cheese, such as a very ripe Danish blue, Roquefort, or Gorgonzola, crumbled into large pieces

4 medium to large beets, cooked
1 small to medium onion, chopped
1 tablespoon wine vinegar
Sugar, salt, freshly ground black pepper, and dried mixed herbs, to taste
2 tablespoons oil of choice
12 oz capellini
2 bunches broccoli, cut into florets, the stalks peeled and sliced
1 tablespoon olive oil
4–5 oz sharp blue cheese such as Danish blue, Maytag blue, Roquefort or Gorgonzola, crumbled into large pieces

1. Prepare the relish by dicing the beetroot (beets) and combining with the onion. Dress with the vinegar, a generous sprinkling of sugar, salt, black pepper and mixed herbs, and the oil. Set aside for at least 15 minutes.
2. Cook the capellini until half done, then add the broccoli and continue cooking until capellini and broccoli are both tender. Drain and dress with the olive oil, salt and black pepper. Cool to room temperature or slightly warmer.
3. Serve each portion of pasta and broccoli topped with a spoonful or two of the relish, including some of the marinade, and the nuggets of cheese.

Auntie Estelle's Chinese Leaf Salad with Crunchy Noodles and Nuts

SERVES 4

This unusual salad is prepared from Ramen-type noodles, the near-instant noodles that come in individual portions with their own soup and are quickly boiled for a light lunch or snack. Here, however, they are browned until crisp rather than boiled. The crunchy noodles are then tossed along with nuts into a salad of Chinese leaves with a sweet and savoury dressing.

The recipe is courtesy of my Auntie Estelle, who is more glamorous than kitchen-bound but nonetheless often amazes me by waltzing into her kitchen and effortlessly whipping up something unusual and outstanding. The salad needs to be served immediately upon assembling, but the various components can be prepared up to two days in advance and put together when ready to be served.

1 large head Chinese leaves, including stalks and core, base trimmed, leaves coarsely chopped

6 spring onions, thinly sliced

1 packet ramen-type noodles, coarsely crushed while still in the packet (be sure to reserve the little packet of seasoning)

50g/2 oz butter

3 tablespoons sesame seeds

50g/2 oz slivered almonds or roasted peanuts, coarsely chopped

2 tablespoons chopped fresh ginger root

3 tablespoons soy sauce

75g/3 fl oz vegetable oil

2 tablespoons sesame oil

50ml/2 fl oz rice vinegar

75g/3 oz sugar

Salt and freshly ground black pepper, to taste

2–3 tablespoons fresh coriander leaves

1 large head Chinese (Napa) Cabbage, coarsely chopped

6 green onions, thinly sliced

1 package ramen-type nodles, coarsely crushed while still in the package (be sure to reserve the little packet of seasoning)

3–4 tablespoons butter

3 tablespoons sesame seeds

¼ cup slivered almonds or roasted peanuts, coarsely chopped

2 tablespoons chopped fresh ginger root

3 tablespoons soy sauce

⅓ cup vegetable oil

2 tablespoons dark (toasted) sesame oil

¼ cup rice vinegar

⅓ cup sugar

Salt and freshly ground black pepper, to taste

2–3 tablespoons coarsely chopped cilantro leaves

1. Mix together the Chinese leaves (Napa cabbage) and spring (green) onions and set aside.
2. Brown the noodles in the butter, together with sesame seeds and seasoning powder from packet. When crunchy and deliciously browned, about 5–8 minutes, remove from the heat.
3. Make the dressing by combining the ginger root, soy sauce, vegetable oil, sesame oil, rice vinegar and sugar. Mix well, then season with salt and black pepper. The dressing will seem sweet but it works well with the other ingredients.
4. Just before serving, toss the Chinese leaves (Napa cabbage) and spring (green) onions with the dressing then top with a generous sprinkling of seeds, nuts, crispy noodles, and fresh coriander leaves (cilantro).

Tender Rice Noodles with Tomato, Black Olive and Herb Relish

SERVES 4–6

Far Eastern noodles are given the Mediterranean treatment here by being tossed with a mixture of sun-drenched ingredients: tomatoes, black olive paste, fresh rosemary or basil, and of course, lots of garlic. The dish itself takes about five minutes to throw together; as such it is invaluable for quick summer suppers or for solitary midnight feasts.

1 packet (about 375g/13 oz) rice noodles, about 3 mm/⅛ inch wide
3–4 cloves garlic, chopped
10 ripe, flavourful, fresh tomatoes, diced
3 tablespoons chopped fresh basil or 2 teaspoons chopped fresh rosemary
3 tablespoons black olive paste or about 20 black Mediterranean-type olives, pitted and diced
Pinch of red pepper flakes or dash of Tabasco sauce

1 package (about 13 oz) rice noodles, ⅛ to ¼ inch wide
3–4 cloves garlic, chopped
10 ripe, flavourful, fresh tomatoes, diced
3 tablespoons chopped fresh basil or 2 teaspoons chopped fresh rosemary
3 tablespoons black olive paste (olivada) or about 20 black Mediterranean-type olives, pitted and diced
Pinch of red pepper flakes or dash of Tabasco sauce

1. Cook the pasta until *al dente*. Drain, rinse, and drain well again.
2. Toss with the remaining ingredients and taste for seasoning.

Pacific Rim Pasta: Rice Noodles with Tomato-Chilli Salsa

SERVES 4–6

Tender rice noodles from the Far East, served cool with a spicy South of the Border tomato and chilli salsa, then drizzled with olive oil and ground cumin. A refreshing and sprightly dish for a sultry afternoon or evening.

1 packet (about 375g/13 oz) rice noodles, about 3mm/⅛ inch wide
325g/12 oz ripe fresh or tinned tomatoes, diced
3 tablespoons coarsely chopped fresh coriander leaves
3 cloves garlic, chopped
1–3 fresh green chillies, to taste, thinly sliced or chopped
½ teaspoon mild red chilli powder, or to taste
Salt to taste
1 tablespoon olive oil
Squeeze of lemon juice
½ teaspoon cumin, or to taste

1 package (about 13 oz) rice noodles, about ⅛ to ¼ inch wide
1½ cups diced ripe fresh or canned tomatoes
3 tablespoons coarsely chopped fresh cilantro leaves
3 cloves garlic, chopped
1–3 fresh green chillies such as jalapenoes, thinly sliced or chopped
½ teaspoon chilli powder (either supermarket mix or individual chilli powders such as New Mexico or ancho)
Salt to taste
1 tablespoon olive oil
Squeeze of lemon juice
½ teaspoon cumin, or to taste

1. Cook the rice noodles until just tender; drain and rinse in cold water.
2. To make the salsa: combine the tomatoes with 2 tablespoons of the coriander (cilantro), garlic, chillies and chilli powder. Leave to marinate for at least 30 minutes.
3. Just before serving, combine the rice noodles with the salsa. Season with salt, and serve drizzled with the olive oil and lemon juice, and sprinkled with the cumin and remaining coriander leaves (cilantro).

Chinese Peanut Butter-Dressed Noodle Salad with Red Cabbage and Bean Sprouts

SERVES 4–6

Red cabbage, cucumber, carrot, bean sprouts and cucumber, all provide the fresh crunch, chillied peanut sauce the spicy counterpoint, and bland Chinese noodles the base for the dish. Perfect for an informal summer lunch or buffet and nice for a picnic, too.

3 cloves garlic, finely chopped
4 heaped tablespoons peanut butter
1–2 teaspoons chopped fresh ginger root
½ fresh hot chilli, chopped, or
  cayenne pepper, to taste
2 tablespoons lemon juice
2 tablespoons sugar
1–2 tablespoons soy sauce, plus a little
  more to toss with the noodles
1 tablespoon sesame oil, plus a little
  more to toss with the noodles
50ml/2 fl oz water
450g/1 lb fresh Chinese noodles or
  325g/12 oz dried
1 bunch spring onions, thinly sliced
100g/4 oz bean sprouts
½ cucumber, diced
¼ red cabbage, diced or shredded
1 carrot, grated
2–3 tablespoons coarsely chopped fresh
  coriander leaves

3 cloves garlic, finely chopped
⅓ cup peanut butter
1–2 teaspoons chopped fresh ginger root
½ fresh chilli such as jalapeno, serrano,
  Thai, or cayenne pepper, to taste
2 tablespoons lemon juice
2 tablespoons sugar
1–2 tablespoons soy sauce, plus a little
  more to toss with the noodles
1 tablespoon sesame oil, plus a little
  more to toss with the noodles
¼ cup water
1 lb fresh Chinese noodles or 12 oz
  dried
1 bunch green onions, thinly sliced
4 oz bean sprouts
½ cucumber, diced
¼ red cabbage, diced or shredded
1 carrot, grated
2–3 tablespoons coarsely chopped fresh
  cilantro leaves

1. Combine the garlic, peanut butter, ginger root, chilli or cayenne pepper, lemon juice, sugar, soy sauce and sesame oil in a liquidizer, blender or food processor and process until smooth and thick, then add the water slowly as the machine whirls, letting the mixture form a thickish sauce. Taste for seasoning; it should be sweet, tart, nutty and quite spicy. Set aside.

2. Cook the noodles until *al dente*. Drain and rinse with cold water, then drain well again. Toss with a little sesame oil and soy sauce, then leave to cool.

3. Combine the cool noodles with the spring (green) onions, bean sprouts, cucumber, red cabbage and carrot, then top with the peanut sauce. Serve sprinkled with the coriander leaves (cilantro).

VERY QUICK PASTA

A good part of the joy of pasta is the fact that a welcoming plateful can be yours in a very short time, providing you have a few basic ingredients on hand: olive oil, garlic, and something – almost anything – fresh.

Fresh vegetables and herbs are the stars in the quick pasta kitchen – a handful of blanched vegetables or fragrant herbs tossed in hot garlicky oil or butter makes an almost instant and immensely satisfying dish. Purée it and you have a different savoury dish; lash it with cream, yet another. The variety is endless.

Storecupboard specialities such as pesto, olive paste, sun-dried tomatoes, etc. multiply the variety of flavours and recipes you have at your fingertips. These condiments add intense, concentrated flavour to quickly prepared dishes, and can sit on your kitchen shelf almost indefinitely awaiting the pleasures of your table.

Pasta Aglio e Olio

PASTA WITH GARLIC AND OLIVE OIL, TWO WAYS

SERVES 4–6

At its very simplest, Pasta Aglio e Olio is no more than al dente pasta tossed with chopped garlic and good olive oil. From here on, the versions become numerous, with additions of fresh herbs and/or hot peppers, as well as the option of heating the garlic in the oil: raw it will be pungent, hot and strong, while cooked it will be toastier and mellow.

While Pasta Aglio e Olio is not traditionally served with Parmesan cheese, I find that the occasional shake is delicious and adds even more variety.

3–6 cloves garlic, to taste
100ml/4 fl oz olive oil, or less if preferred
450g/1 lb spaghetti
Salt and coarsely ground black pepper,
   to taste

3–6 cloves garlic, to taste
½ cup olive oil, or less if preferred
1 lb spaghetti
Salt and coarsely ground black pepper,
   to taste

1. **Version 1**: With Raw Garlic: Combine the garlic with the olive oil. Cook the pasta until *al dente*, then drain and toss with the garlic and oil. Season with salt and black pepper, and serve immediately.
2. **Version 2**: With Lightly Toasted Golden Garlic: Heat the garlic in the olive oil until golden. Remove from the heat and set aside. Cook the pasta until *al dente*, then drain and toss with the garlic and oil. Season with salt and black pepper and serve immediately.

Variations Using Version 2

With Hot Pepper and Parsley: Add a generous pinch of hot red pepper flakes as you heat the garlic in the oil. Toss with the cooked pasta and a handful or two of chopped fresh parsley, preferably the flat-leaf Italian type.

With Cayenne Pepper, Parsley, and Lime: Prepare the basic recipe, adding parsley as above. Season forcefully with lots of cayenne pepper, and toss with the finely grated rind of 1 lime and the juice of 1–2 limes, or to taste. Also good with lemon.

With Capers: Add several teaspoons of capers to the hot pepper and parsley variation. A short squeeze or two of lemon juice is good, too.

With Basil Leaves: Add a small handful of torn or coarsely chopped fresh basil leaves to the oil as you heat the garlic.

With Cabbage, Italian style: A favourite dish of mine, this is an excellent example of *cucina povera*, the cooking of the poor. In Italy one of the more unusual cabbage varieties such as black cabbage might be used, but I find that ordinary white or green cabbage works just fine.

Coarsely chop half a head or so of white or green cabbage and add to the pan along with the garlic and hot red pepper flakes (see first variation). Sauté until tender and lightly browned, adding more oil, garlic, or pepper flakes if needed, season with salt, then serve with pasta of choice.

Tiny Elbow Pasta With Basil, Parsley and Lime

SERVES 4

The sweetness of basil pairs with fresh parsley and the jolt of sour lime in this invigorating, simple dish.

The very tiny elbow pasta is my favourite here - especially the brand Federici which is marked simply: quick-cooking macaroni. Do not be misled into thinking that this is an inauthentic product. It is the tiniest, sweetest, most succulent elbow macaroni you can imagine. And, yes, it is quick cooking: about 2–3 minutes.

4 cloves garlic, coarsely chopped
3–4 tablespoons olive oil
15–20 basil leaves, torn up coarsely
325g/12 oz small elbow-shaped macaroni
Handful of parsley, coarsely chopped
Grated rind and juice of ½–1 lime, to taste
Salt and freshly ground black pepper or cayenne pepper, to taste

4 cloves garlic, coarsely chopped
3–4 tablespoons olive oil
¼ cup coarsely chopped fresh basil
12 oz small elbow-shaped macaroni
¼ cup coarsely chopped parsley
Grated rind and juice of ½–1 lime, to taste
Salt and freshly ground black pepper or cayenne pepper, to taste

1. Heat the garlic in the olive oil until golden, then remove from the heat and add the basil. The basil should wilt in the hot oil and go bright green and glossy.
2. Cook the pasta until *al dente*, then drain.
3. Toss the drained pasta in the basil and garlic oil, together with the parsley and grated lime rind and juice. Season with salt and black or cayenne pepper, and serve immediately.

Garlicky Pasta with Fresh Green Herbs

SERVES 4–6

This is an excellent dish to throw together during spring and summer when herbs are abundant. Cheese would only interfere with all the herby flavours, but be sure to add enough salt and pepper.

The flavour and character of the dish depends completely on the choice and quantity of herbs you use. Use larger amounts of milder herbs such as parsley and smaller amounts of pungent ones such as fresh oregano or sage.

450g/1 lb spaghettti
8 cloves garlic, coarsely chopped
50–75ml/2–3 fl oz olive oil
Selection of chopped fresh herbs: 1 oz fresh parsley and/or basil, several tablespoons each chives, marjoram, thyme, sage, oregano, rosemary, tarragon, etc.
Salt and freshly ground black pepper, to taste

1 lb spaghetti
8 cloves garlic, coarsely chopped
¼ to ⅓ cup olive oil
Selection of chopped fresh herbs: ¼–½ cup fresh parsley and/or basil, ¼ cup chives, several tablespoons each of marjoram, oregano, thyme, sage, rosemary, tarragon, etc.
Salt and freshly ground black pepper, to taste

1. Cook spaghetti until *al dente*.
2. Meanwhile, heat the garlic in olive oil until it smells fragrant, just a few moments.
3. Toss the herbs in the garlicky hot oil. Remove from the heat.
4. Drain the pasta and toss in the pan with the garlicky oil and herbs. Season generously with salt and black pepper.

Fettuccine with A Confetti of Vegetables and Garlic-Mint Sauce

2 celery stalks, cut into matchsticks
2 carrots, cut into matchsticks
325g/12 oz fresh fettucine
8 cloves garlic, coarsely chopped
125ml/4 fl oz olive oil
3–4 tablespoons coarsely chopped fresh
    mint leaves
Salt and freshly ground black pepper,
    to taste

2 celery stalks, cut into matchsticks
2 carrots, cut into matchsticks
12 oz fresh fettuccine
8 cloves garlic, coarsely chopped
¼ cup olive oil
3–4 tablespoons coarsely chopped fresh
    mint leaves
Salt and freshly ground black pepper,
    to taste

1. Place the celery and carrots in a large pan of water, bring to the boil, then add the fettuccine and salt. Cook until *al dente*, 3–4 minutes. Drain.
2. Meanwhile, warm the garlic in the olive oil until fragrant and slightly golden, then remove from the heat and add the mint leaves, pepper and extra salt to taste.
3. Toss the pasta and vegetables with the garlic-mint sauce and serve immediately.

Wholewheat Spaghetti with Tomatoes, Green Beans, Pesto and Goat Cheese

SERVES 4–6

Chewy and nutty-tasting wholewheat spaghetti partners exuberantly with garlicky tomatoes, green beans, pesto and goat cheese. This makes a complex dish, far more flavourful than its simple preparation would indicate.

3 cloves garlic, finely chopped
3 tablespoons olive oil
2 ripe fresh or drained tinned tomatoes, diced and seeded
450g/1 lb wholewheat spaghetti, preferably an Italian brand
100g/4 oz green beans, cut into bite-sized lengths
3 heaped tablespoons pesto, or to taste
50–75g/2–3 oz goat cheese, preferably a fresh, light garlic- or chive-flavoured one, crumbled

3 cloves garlic, finely chopped
3 tablespoons olive oil
2 ripe fresh or drained canned tomatoes, diced and seeded
1 lb wholewheat spaghetti, preferably an Italian brand
4 oz green beans, cut into bite-sized lengths
¼ cup pesto, or to taste
2–3 oz goat cheese, preferably a garlic- or chive-flavoured one, crumbled

1. Heat the garlic in the olive oil just until it smells wonderful but is not yet turning golden. Add the tomatoes and cook for a minute or two, then remove from the heat.
2. Meanwhile, cook the spaghetti until half done then add the green beans and continue to cook until the beans are crisp-tender and bright green and the pasta is *al dente*.
3. Drain and toss in the garlicky-tomato mixture. Serve immediately, each portion topped with pesto and goat cheese.

Variations

Whole Wheat Spaghetti with Green Beans, Black Olive Paste, and Goat Cheese: Spoon black olive paste on to each portion instead of pesto, together with a sprinkling of chopped fresh basil or parsley and a dollop of goat cheese.

Wholewheat Spaghetti with Green Beans and Pesto: Choose either Pesto Genovese (page 255) or Basil and Parsley Pesto (page 255). Cook the spaghetti with the beans as in the basic recipe. Drain and toss with several large tablespoons of pesto. Serve sprinkled with Parmesan cheese or Pecorino Sardo.

Spaghetti with Sautéed Curly Endive and Balsamic Vinegar

SERVES 4–6

Young curly endive, or frisée, is my favourite for this recipe, as it is just bitter enough to be interesting but not so bitter as to commandeer the entire dish unpleasantly.

450g/1 lb spaghetti
4 cloves garlic, coarsely chopped
3 tablespoons olive oil
1 head frisée or curly endive, trimmed of its core, the leaves cut into bite-sized pieces
1 tablespoon balsamic vinegar (or use red wine vinegar), or to taste
Salt and freshly ground black pepper, to taste

1 lb spaghetti
4 cloves garlic, coarsely chopped
3 tablespoons olive oil
1 head frisée or escarole, trimmed of its core and the leaves cut into bite-sized pieces
1 tablespoon red wine vinegar or several teaspoons balsamic vinegar, or to taste
Salt and freshly ground black pepper, to taste

1. Cook the spaghetti until *al dente*.
2. Meanwhile, sauté 3 cloves of the garlic in about 2 tablespoons of the olive oil then quickly sauté the curly endive (frisée) in this mixture. Add the vinegar, cook for a moment, then remove from the heat. Season with salt and black pepper.
3. Drain the pasta and toss with the remaining garlic and olive oil, then serve each portion topped with a big spoonful of the sautéed curly endive (frisée), adding extra vinegar if needed.

Variations

Pasta with Cannellini (White Kidney) Beans and Curly Endive: White beans are the perfect classic pairing for sautéed curly endive. Add 100–175g/4–6 oz drained beans when you sauté the curly endive, and season with a sprinkling of red chilli flakes if desired.

Pasta with Radicchio: Instead of curly endive, use 2 heads of red radicchio or green and red striated Treviso lettuce. Follow the basic recipe above.

Fettuccine with Mascarpone, Pine Nuts and Basil

SERVES 4–6

This is very rich, with fresh, fragrant basil to lighten and enliven it. The mixture of basil and cheese should coat the pasta rather than drown it. Lightly toasted pine nuts add texture to this plateful of classic flavours.

Serve as a first course, followed by something savoury and strongly flavoured such as a tomato-braised vegetable casserole.

50g/2 oz pine nuts

325–450g/12–16 oz fresh fettuccine, the most delicate you can find

25g/1 oz butter, preferably unsalted, softened

Several large tablespoons mascarpone cheese, softened and at room temperature

Salt and freshly ground black pepper, to taste

4 tablespoons freshly grated Parmesan cheese, plus extra to serve

Handful of fresh basil leaves, torn or coarsely chopped

⅓ cup pine nuts

12–16 oz fresh fettuccine, the most delicate you can fine

2–3 tablespoons butter, preferably unsalted, softened

Several large tablespoons mascarpone cheese, softened and at room temperature

Salt and freshly ground black pepper, to taste

¼ cup freshly grated Parmesan cheese, plus extra to serve

¼ cup fresh basil leaves, torn or coarsely chopped

1. Toast the pine nuts in an ungreased heavy frying pan (skillet) over medium heat until flecked lightly brown, tossing them as they turn for even browning. Set aside.
2. Cook the pasta until *al dente*.
3. Drain and toss first with the butter, then with the mascarpone cheese, then with the toasted pine nuts, salt and black pepper and Parmesan cheese. Sprinkle with the basil and serve immediately, offering extra Parmesan cheese separately.

Fazzoletti di Seta (Handkerchiefs) of Pasta with Pesto

SERVES 4–6

Delicate squares of homemade pasta, fazzoletti, are served tumbled artlessly into small piles on each plate to look like a dropped handkerchief. This simple dish is from the region of Liguria, where the basil scent of pesto wafts through every alleyway, shop and window.

In Liguria the pasta is prepared from a dough made with white wine for added delicacy; I substitute shopbought pasta squares such as wonton noodles or other fresh pasta.

As with other simple dishes, all of the ingredients must be of the highest quality: tender, fresh-tasting pasta, homemade pesto (see pages 255–56) or a freshly made one from a delicatessen, freshly grated Pecorino Romano or Parmesan cheese.

325–450g/12–16 oz flat wide fresh pasta such as wonton noodles or other pasta sheets, about 7.5 cm/3 inches square
40g/1½ oz butter
225g/8 oz pesto
Freshly grated Pecorino Romano or Parmesan cheese, about 2–3 tablespoons per person

12–16 oz flat wide pastas, about 3 inches square such as wonton wrappers
3 tablespoons butter
1 cup pesto
Freshly grated Pecorino Romano or Parmesan cheese, about 2–3 tablespoons per person

1. Boil the pasta until *al dente*; this will only take 2–3 minutes. Drain well and carefully, as delicate pasta tends to fall apart easily.
2. Toss the cooked pasta with the butter, then serve each portion immediately, topped with a generous helping of pesto and the grated cheese.

Variations

Pasta with Pesto and Mascarpone: Follow the recipe above, with the addition of a tablespoon or two of mascarpone on each portion of pasta. As you eat the pasta, the mascarpone dissolves into a creamy sauce that makes this delicious dish even better and a worthy beginning to any special meal.

Pasta with Pesto and Goat Cheese: Spoon a small amount of a tangy fresh goat cheese on to each pesto-topped pasta portion.

Ditalini with Flageolets and Pesto

SERVES 4

Chunky pasta tossed with delicate greenish flageolet beans and pesto makes an outstanding, quickly prepared dish. The beans have a delicate heartiness that blends particularly well with the pasta and pesto. If flageolets are unavailable, use cannellini (white kidney) beans instead.

325g/12 oz ditalini (short, round macaroni), or small elbow or shell pasta
25g/1 oz butter
400g/14 oz cooked or drained tinned flageolet beans
1 clove garlic, chopped
190g/6½ oz jar of pesto, or homemade (see page 255)

12 oz ditalini or other short, round macaroni
2 tablespoons butter
1½ cups cooked or drained canned flageolet beans
1 clove garlic, chopped
¾ cup pesto, either shop-bought or homemade (see page 255)

1. Cook the pasta until *al dente*.
2. Drain, return to the pan, and toss and over a low heat with the butter, flageolet beans, and garlic, to warm through.
3. Remove from the heat and stir in the pesto. Serve immediately.

Variation

Pasta with Flageolets and Green Beans: Instead of ditalini, choose a flat pasta such as fettuccine, and add a handful of green beans, cut into bite-sized pieces, to the boiling water when the pasta is about half cooked. (If yellow wax beans are available, add them as well.) Toss with butter, garlic and pesto as in the recipe above.

Rosemary-and-Garlic-Buttered Pasta

SERVES 4

Rosemary and garlic butter is delicious melted on to any pasta, especially fresh pasta. Try it on wonton noodles, or cheese-filled ravioli, or wide egg noodles, topped with a handful of coarsely grated Parmesan cheese.

325g/12 oz pasta of choice
25–40g/1–1½ oz butter, preferably
   unsalted, softened
2 cloves garlic, or to taste, finely
   chopped
2–4 tablespoons finely chopped fresh
   rosemary
Salt and coarsely ground black pepper,
   to taste

12 oz pasta of choice
2–3 tablespoons butter, preferably
   unsalted, softened
2 cloves garlic, or to taste, finely
   chopped
2–4 tablespoons finely chopped fresh
   rosemary
Salt and coarsely ground black pepper,
   to taste

1. Cook the pasta until *al dente*. Drain.
2. Toss with the butter, garlic and rosemary, and season with salt and black pepper. Serve at once.

Lockshen and Cheese

SERVES 4

Lockshen is the Yiddish word for noodles, and this is the dish I grew up eating, the dish I end up cooking whenever I'm in the mood for a little comfort, pasta-style.

Cottage cheese is eaten with pasta in a variety of ways throughout Europe. In Eastern Europe, interestingly, the dish might be sweet, with sugar and cinnamon replacing the salt and pepper. And in Italy, it is fresh ricotta, cottage cheese's Mediterranean cousin, that pairs with pasta for this comforting and wholesome dish.

I like lockshen with garlic, and lots of it (see Variation).

325g/12 oz pasta of choice, preferably
   short, chubby shapes or curly twists
40g/1½ oz butter, or to taste
325g/12 oz plain cottage cheese
Salt and freshly ground black pepper,
   to taste

12 oz pasta of choice
3 tablespoons butter, or to taste
12 oz cottage cheese
Salt and freshly ground black pepper,
   to taste

1. Cook the pasta until *al dente*. Drain.
2. Mix in the butter well, then serve each portion topped with a dollop of cottage cheese and sprinkled with salt and pepper. Alternatively, you can toss it all together, then serve.

Variation

Marlena's Cottage Cheese and Pasta: My favourite deviation from the above involves tossing the pasta with olive oil rather than butter and sprinkling the cottage cheese with a generous amount of raw, chopped garlic, before serving. Sometimes I add a sprinkling of fresh herbs such as basil, oregano, etc. This dish invigorates as it comforts, and my two daughters have become addicted to it, as has our cat.

Wholewheat Spaghetti with Toasted Garlic, Hot Pepper and Broccoli

SERVES 4–6

Midnight-feast stuff, this, as long as you don't have to be anywhere polite the next morning.

325–450g/12–16 oz wholewheat
   spaghetti
1 large bunch broccoli, cut into small
   florets
8–10 cloves garlic, coarsely chopped
4 tablespoons olive oil
1 dried hot red chilli, broken into
   several pieces
Salt and freshly ground black pepper,
   to taste

12–16 oz wholewheat spaghetti
1 large bunch broccoli, cut into small
   florets
8–10 cloves garlic, coarsely chopped
¼ cup olive oil
1 dried hot red chilli, broken into
   several pieces
Salt and freshly ground black pepper,
   to taste

1. Cook the spaghetti until half done; add the broccoli and continue cooking until both pasta and broccoli are *al dente*.
2. Meanwhile, heat the garlic in the olive oil with the red chilli. When the garlic is golden, remove the pan from the heat and remove the bits of chilli. Discard the chilli and set the oil aside.
3. Drain the pasta and broccoli and toss with the reserved garlic and olive oil mixture. Season with salt and black pepper to taste.

Spaghetti with Garlic-Buttered Breadcrumbs

SERVES 4–6

Breadcrumbs browned with olive oil into a state of golden crispness then tossed with chopped raw garlic is the topping that makes this otherwise plain buttered pasta into something special. The crumbs take on the same role as grated Parmesan cheese in similar dishes: they provide a contrast of texture against the benignly buttered pasta. The garlic may be omitted, if preferred, and the dish will still be very nice.

175g/6 oz stale country-style bread
3 tablespoons olive oil
Salt and freshly ground black pepper,
   to taste
3 cloves garlic, chopped
450g/1 lb spaghetti
25g/1 oz butter, or to taste

6 oz stale country-style bread
3 tablespoons olive oil
Salt and freshly ground black pepper,
   to taste
3 cloves garlic, chopped
1 lb spaghetti
2–3 tablespoons butter, or to taste

1. Make breadcrumbs by grating the bread on the large holes of a grater. This works better than a liquidizer (blender) or food processor.
2. Lightly sauté the crumbs in the olive oil first in a heavy frying pan (skillet), then put into a moderate oven, 180°C/350°F/gas mark 4, for 10–15 minutes or until golden. Remove from the oven, toss with salt, black pepper and the garlic and set aside.
3. Cook the spaghetti until *al dente* then drain (reserving a few spoonfuls of the cooking water) and toss in the butter. Add a tablespoon or two of the cooking liquid back to the buttered pasta and toss well. This helps make a slightly creamy mixure. Season with salt and black pepper.
4. Serve the pasta immediately, topped with the toasted crumbs.

Wide Noodles with Garlic Butter, Fresh Sage and Black Wrinkled Olives

SERVES 4

Nuggets of salty black olives punctuate the delicacy of garlic-buttered wide noodles, while fresh sage adds its savour to this simple summer dish.

Serve accompanied by sliced, sweet, ripe tomatoes sprinkled with basil or marjoram, sea salt and olive oil.

325g/12 oz wide egg pasta ribbons
25g/1 oz unsalted butter, softened
1 tablespoon olive oil
3–4 cloves garlic, chopped
1–2 tablespoons coarsely chopped fresh sage leaves
About 15 wrinkled black (oil- or salt-cured) olives, pitted and halved
3 tablespoons freshly grated Parmesan cheese, or to taste
Salt and freshly ground black pepper, to taste

12 oz wide egg noodles
2 tablespoons unsalted butter, softened
1 tablespoon olive oil
3–4 cloves garlic, chopped
1–2 tablespoons coarsely chopped fresh sage leaves
About 15 wrinkled black olives (oil- or salt-cured), pitted and halved
3 tablespoons freshly grated Parmesan cheese, or to taste
Salt and freshly ground black pepper, to taste

1. Cook the pasta until *al dente*.
2. Meanwhile, mix the butter, olive oil and garlic together.
3. Drain the pasta, then return to the pan and toss with the butter mixture, sage and olives over a low to medium heat so that the pasta stays nice and hot and the butter melts evenly throughout the noodles.
4. Serve immediately, seasoned with salt and black pepper and sprinkled with Parmesan cheese.

Broccoli Carbonara

PASTA AND BROCCOLI TOSSED WITH BEATEN EGG AND CHEESE

SERVES 4

Adding a small amount of butter at the end gives the pasta a certain glossiness and richness. As always, when you are preparing a dish in which eggs are only lightly cooked, seek out a reliable source of free range, salmonella-free specimens.

325g/12 oz lumachine (small shells) or elbow shapes
275–325g/10–12 oz broccoli, cut into bite-sized florets, the stems peeled and sliced
1 egg, lightly beaten
2 tablespoons milk
75g/3 oz Parmesan cheese, freshly grated
Salt and freshly ground black pepper, to taste
15–25g/½–1 oz unsalted butter, at room temperature

12 oz lumachine (small shells) or elbow shapes
1 large bunch or 2 small bunches broccoli, cut into bite-sized florets, the stems peeled and sliced
1 egg, lightly beaten
2 tablespoons milk
⅓ cup freshly grated Parmesan cheese
Salt and freshly ground black pepper, to taste
1–2 tablespoons unsalted butter, at room temperature

1. Cook the pasta in boiling water until half-done, about 4 minutes. Add the broccoli and continue cooking until the pasta is *al dente* and the broccoli bright green and just cooked through. Drain.
2. Mix the egg with the milk and half the cheese, then toss the hot drained pasta and broccoli with this mixture, letting the heat cook the egg as it tosses. Add the remaining Parmesan cheese, salt if needed, black pepper, and the butter, tossing to mix well. Serve immediately.

Leslie Forbes' Last-Minute Spicy Pasta with Red Pesto and Asparagus

SERVES 4–6

*Leslie cooks the sort of strongly flavoured, simple yet imaginative food that I adore.
Once she put saffron in her corn muffins: it was a moment of culinary inspiration.
She's always adding this and that ingredient that one might think would clash yet
they combine harmoniously like so much gastronomical jazz improvisation.*

*Such is the case with this pasta recipe, thrown together with what was on hand in the
Forbes kitchen.*

450g/1 lb penne
225g/8 oz asparagus, tough ends
  broken off and saved for another
  use (peel, dice, and use as the basis
  for a soup), the stalks cut into bite-
  sized pieces
2–3 tablespoons chillied olive oil (see
  page 257)
190g/6½ oz jar red pesto, or use
  homemade (see page 256)
50g/2 oz Parmesan cheese, shaved
  rather than grated

1 lb penne
½ lb asparagus, tough ends broken off,
  stalks cut into bite-sized pieces
2–3 tablespoons chillied olive oil (see
  page 257)
⅔ cup shop-bought red pesto, or use
  homemade (see page 256)
2 oz Parmesan cheese, shaved rather
  than grated (about ½ cup shaved
  cheese)

1. Boil the pasta until about half cooked, then add the asparagus and continue cooking until the pasta is *al dente* and the asparagus is crisp-tender. Drain.

2. Toss with the chillied olive oil, then the red pesto and serve immediately, topped with the Parmesan cheese.

Buckwheat Soba with Peas and Cream

SERVES 4

Japanese flat buckwheat pasta, also known as soba, tastes of the grain it is ground from: earthy, wholemeal, and almost sweet. It is traditionally served with clear soup in Japan and Korea, and is also popular served cold, sometimes with a poached egg, and with spicy condiments such as chilli oil, wasabi (strong horseradish) paste, spring (green) onion, and even chips of ice for a refreshing summer snack.

The following recipe, however, uses the soba in a distinctly Western way: tossed with peas, cream and Parmesan cheese. It is a rich and Alfredo-like mixture, but unusual for its buckwheat flavour.

225g/8 oz buckwheat soba, preferably the flat fettuccine-like noodles
50g/2 oz butter
2 cloves garlic, chopped
175–225g/6–8 oz fresh and blanched or frozen peas
250ml/8 fl oz single cream
100g/4 oz Parmesan cheese, freshly grated
Freshly ground black pepper, to taste

8 oz/½ lb buckwheat soba, preferably the flat fettuccine-like noodles
4 tablespoons butter
2 cloves garlic, chopped
1 cup fresh and blanched or frozen peas
1 cup whipping cream
1 cup freshly grated Parmesan cheese
Freshly ground black pepper, to taste

1. Cook the buckwheat soba in boiling water until *al dente*. Drain.
2. Melt the butter with the garlic, then add the peas and cook until the peas are cooked through if-fresh, or heated through if frozen.
3. Pour in the cream and heat until bubbles form around the edge of the pan.
4. Toss with the hot drained pasta and Parmesan cheese, then serve immediately seasoned with black pepper (it will most likely not need salt as the Parmesan cheese is salty).

Broth-Cooked Pasta Tossed with Olives and Parsley

SERVES 4–6

Cooking pasta in stock, then seasoning it with olive oil, fresh herbs and something very pungent, makes a delicious and straightforward dish. The pasta absorbs the flavours of the stock, and the simple saucing seems to have its flavours amplified.

You may use any sort of pasta you like: strands such as spaghetti or short, fat shapes such as ditalini or penne, and, whatever you do, be sure to save the stock for another dish.

450g/1 lb pasta of choice
1 litre/1¾ pints vegetable stock
3–4 tablespoons olive oil
About 25 Kalamata olives, pitted and diced, or several tablespoons black olive paste
Handful of coarsely chopped fresh parsley

1 lb pasta of choice
1 quart vegetable stock
3–4 tablespoons olive oil
About 25 Kalamata olives, pitted and diced, or several tablespoons black olive paste
¼ cup coarsely chopped fresh parsley

1. Cook the pasta in the boiling stock until *al dente*. Drain and reserve the stock for another use.

2. Toss the hot drained pasta with the remaining ingredients and serve immediately.

Pasta with Black Olive and Rosemary Cream

SERVES 4

This silken sauce is simple: a purée of inky black olives and a whiff of rosemary with rich cream. A sprinkling of Parmesan cheese pulls it all together.

325g/12 oz fettuccine
3 tablespoons black olive paste
2 teaspoons chopped fresh rosemary, or to taste
250ml/8 fl oz single cream
25g/1oz butter, preferably unsalted
Salt and freshly ground black pepper, to taste
Freshly grated Parmesan cheese, to taste

12 oz fettucine
3 tablespoons black olive paste
2 teaspoons chopped fresh rosemary, or to taste
1 cup whipping cream
2 tablespoons butter, preferably unsalted
Salt and freshly ground black pepper, to taste
Freshly grated Parmesan cheese, to taste

1. Cook the pasta until *al dente*.
2. Meanwhile, combine the olive paste and rosemary, then stir in the cream. Set aside.
3. Drain the pasta and toss first with the butter, then with the sauce. Season with salt and black pepper, and add Parmesan cheese to taste.

Variation

With Goat Cheese or Feta Cheese: Instead of Parmesan, toss the dressed pasta with mild creamy goat cheese or tangy feta cheese, crumbled, and let it melt in. Include a clove of chopped garlic in the olive paste mixture.

Lumachine with Sun-Dried Tomatoes

SERVES 4

Strips of sun-dried tomato soften in the boiling water as the pasta cooks; simply buttered and seasoned with garlic and thyme, this makes a pleasant and easy bowlful.

325g/12 oz lumachine (shells), farfalle (butterflies) or elbow-shaped pasta
10–15 sun-dried tomatoes, the dry, unmarinated type, cut into strips
25–40g/1–1½ oz butter
1 clove garlic, chopped
Salt, freshly ground black pepper and thyme, to taste

12 oz lumachine (shells), farfalle (butterflies) or elbow-shaped pasta
10–15 sun-dried tomatoes, the dry, unmarinated type, cut into strips
2–3 tablespoons butter
1 clove garlic, chopped
Salt, freshly ground black pepper and thyme, to taste

1. Cook the pasta and sun-dried tomatoes in boiling water until the pasta is tender. Drain (the water may be reserved for soup, etc. since it will have some flavour from the tomatoes).
2. Toss in the butter, garlic, salt, black pepper and thyme.

Variation

Lumachine with Sun-Dried Tomatoes and Yellow Squash: Tender, sweet summer squash adds a sunny note to this simple pasta: add 1 or 2 diced yellow summer squash – either yellow crookneck or golden courgettes (zucchini) – to the cooking water with the pasta and sun-dried tomatoes. If yellow squash is not available, use courgettes (zucchini). Mangetout (snow peas) or sugar snap peas are sweetly delicious cooked along with the squash and pasta.

Spaghetti or Penne with Sun-Dried Tomatoes and Goat Cheese

SERVES 4–6

325–450g/12–16 oz spaghetti or penne
20 sun-dried tomatoes, either dry or
  marinated in oil, cut into strips
3–4 cloves garlic, chopped
3 tablespoons olive oil, or to taste
Salt, freshly ground black pepper, and
  thyme or crumbled dried mixed
  herbs, to taste
150g/5 oz fresh, tangy goat cheese,
  coarsely crumbled

12–16 oz spaghetti or penne
20 sun-dried tomatoes, either dry or
  marinated in oil, cut into strips
3–4 cloves garlic, chopped
3 tablespoons olive oil, or to taste
Salt, freshly ground black pepper, and
  thyme or crumbled dried mixed
  herbs, to taste
5 oz fresh, tangy goat cheese, coarsely
  crumbled

1. Cook the pasta in boiling water until *al dente*. If using dry sun-dried tomatoes, cook them with the pasta; if using marinated, add to the cooked pasta with the other ingredients.
2. Drain the pasta and toss with the garlic, olive oil, salt, black pepper, herbs, and sun-dried tomatoes if using marinated ones.
3. Toss with the goat cheese then serve immediately.

Tarragon and Lemon Pasta with Sharp Cheese

SERVES 4

Admittedly it sounds unlikely, but the combination is delicious, all the more so for its unexpected flavours. The tarragon and lemon lighten up the cloak of melting cheese.

325g/12 oz short pasta of choice
40g/1½ oz unsalted butter
Juice of ½ lemon, or to taste
½ teaspoon dried tarragon, or to taste, crumbled between the fingers
175-225g/6-8 oz mature Cheddar cheese, coarsely grated
Salt and freshly ground black pepper, to taste

12 oz short pasta of choice
3 tablespoons unsalted butter
Juice of ½ lemon, or to taste
½ teaspoon dried tarragon, or to taste, crumbled between the fingers
⅔-1 cup coarsely grated sharp cheese, such as medium (unaged) asiago or aged Pecorino, or a mature Cheddar
Salt and freshly ground black pepper, to taste

1. Cook the pasta until *al dente*; drain.
2. Toss with the butter, lemon juice, tarragon, cheese, salt if needed and black pepper. Serve immediately.

Spaghetti al Zenzero

SPAGHETTI WITH GARLIC, GINGER, HOT PEPPER, MINT AND BASIL

SERVES **4**

An unusual variation on the ubiquitous Roman dish of pasta with olive oil and garlic. The fresh ginger and hot pepper give a spicy kick, while the mint and basil are leafy, sweet and fresh.

325–450g/12–16 oz spaghetti
6–10 cloves garlic, coarsely chopped
5cm/2 inch piece fresh ginger root,
    unpeeled, cut into 4–5 thin slices
Pinch of red pepper flakes
75ml/3 fl oz olive oil
Salt to taste
2 tablespoons thinly sliced or coarsely
    chopped fresh basil leaves
2 tablespoons thinly sliced or coarsely
    chopped fresh mint leaves

12–16 oz spaghetti
6–10 cloves garlic, coarsely chopped
2 inch piece fresh ginger root,
    unpeeled, cut into 4–5 thin slices
Pinch of red pepper flakes
¼–⅓ cup olive oil
Salt to taste
2 tablespoons thinly sliced or coarsely
    chopped fresh basil leaves
2 tablespoons thinly sliced or coarsely
    chopped fresh mint leaves

1. Cook the spaghetti until *al dente*.
2. Meanwhile, heat the garlic, ginger and red pepper flakes in the olive oil, cooking until the garlic becomes golden around the edges. Do not brown. Remove and discard the ginger slices.
3. Drain the spaghetti, then toss with the flavoured oil. Add salt to taste.
4. Serve immediately, tossed with the basil and mint.

Variation

For Roman-style spaghetti with garlic, mint, and a whiff of lemon, follow the above recipe but omit the ginger and basil. Increase the amount of red pepper to taste, and serve the pasta either hot or at room temperature, with lemon wedges or a dash of balsamic vinegar.

Wholewheat Spaghetti with Goat Cheese, Fresh Tomatoes, and Olives

SERVES 4

For this dish of exuberant and vivid flavours be sure to use wholewheat pasta imported from Italy (such as the de Cecco brand). It has a nutty flavour and supple texture, whereas other wholewheat pasta cooks up to a slightly gummy consistency, with a taste that is heavy and almost sweet.

325–450g/12–16 oz Italian wholewheat spaghetti
About 15 Italian or Greek black olives, pitted and coarsely chopped
About 15 green olives, pitted and coarsely chopped
3 cloves garlic, chopped
4 ripe fresh tomatoes, peeled, seeded and diced
100ml/4 fl oz olive oil, or more to taste
150g/5 oz goat cheese, coarsely crumbled
25g/1 oz fresh basil leaves, torn or coarsely cut up
Freshly ground black pepper to taste

12–16 oz Italian wholewheat spaghetti
About 15 Italian or Greek black olives, pitted and coarsely chopped
About 15 green olives, pitted and coarsely chopped
3 cloves garlic, chopped
4 ripe fresh tomatoes, peeled, seeded and diced
¼ cup olive oil, or more to taste
5 oz goat cheese, coarsely crumbled
½ cup fresh basil leaves, torn or coarsely cut up
Freshly ground black pepper to taste

1. Cook the pasta until *al dente*.
2. Meanwhile, combine the black and green olives with the garlic, tomatoes and olive oil.
3. Drain the pasta and toss with the olive mixture, then toss in the goat cheese, basil and black pepper. Serve immediately.

Fettuccine with Green Olives, Goat Cheese, and Thyme

SERVES 4

Goat cheese and green olives make a tangy yet lightly creamy sauce for pasta.

325–450g/12–16 oz fettuccine or other
  pasta of choice
2–3 cloves garlic, chopped
3–4 tablespoons chopped green olives
  or green olive paste
½ teaspoon fresh thyme or
  ¼ teaspoon dried thyme
3 tablespoons olive oil
150g/5 oz goat cheese, crumbled
Red chilli flakes or coarsely ground
  black pepper, to taste

12–16 oz fettuccine or other pasta of
  choice
2–3 cloves garlic, chopped
3–4 tablespoons chopped green olives
  or green olive paste
½ teaspoon fresh thyme or
  ¼ teaspoon dried thyme
3 tablespoons olive oil
5 oz goat cheese, crumbled
Red chilli flakes or coarsely ground
  black pepper, to taste

1. Cook the pasta until *al dente*.
2. Meanwhile, warm the garlic, olives and thyme gently in the olive oil; do not brown.
3. Drain the pasta and toss with the garlic and olive mixture and the goat cheese, warming it over low heat so that the cheese melts into a clinging, creamy sauce.
4. Season with red chilli flakes or black pepper and serve immediately.

Fusilli Verde with Broccoli and Red (Bell) Pepper in Spicy Tomato Sauce

SERVES 4

4–6 cloves garlic, chopped
½–1 red pepper, thinly sliced or coarsely chopped
2 tablespoons olive oil
1 bunch broccoli, cut into florets, stems peeled and diced
Handful of fresh and blanched or frozen peas
225g/8 oz ripe fresh or tinned tomatoes, chopped
Cayenne pepper to taste (start with about ¼ teaspoon)
Generous pinch of thyme
275–325g/10–12 oz fusilli verde, or other green pasta
Salt to taste
Grated cheese (optional)

4–6 cloves garlic, chopped
½–1 red bell pepper, thinly sliced or coarsely chopped
2 tablespoons olive oil
1 bunch broccoli, cut into florets, stems peeled and diced
¼ cup fresh and blanched or frozen peas
1 cup chopped fresh or canned tomatoes
Cayenne pepper to taste (start with about ¼ teaspoon)
Generous pinch of thyme
12–16 oz fusilli verde, or other green pasta
Salt to taste
Grated cheese (optional)

1. Lightly sauté the garlic and red (bell) pepper in the olive oil, then add the broccoli and a few tablespoons of water. Cover and cook over high heat for a minute or two until just tender. Add the peas and tomatoes, season with cayenne pepper and thyme, cover and cook for another 5–10 minutes.
2. Meanwhile, cook the pasta until *al dente*; drain and toss with the sauce. Season with salt, if needed, and serve with grated cheese if liked.

Spaghetti o Cavatieddi with Tomatoes and Rocket (Arugula)

SERVES 4–6

From the deep south of Italy, this dish is usually prepared with older, strongly flavoured specimens of rocket, or arugula. For those who have only eaten rocket in salads, this dish is a revelation. And it couldn't be simpler or quicker to prepare; take care, though, that you cut the rocket into small enough lengths, as it can become stringy and hard to chew.

If you come across the delightfully twisted pasta shapes such as cavatieddi or gemelli, or even the flat, ear-shaped orecchiette, do try them with this lively sauce.

450g/1 lb spaghetti or cavatieddi or similar pasta shape
100–175g/4–6 oz coarsely chopped rocket
6–8 shallots or 3–4 cloves garlic, chopped
2 tablespoons olive oil
450g/1 lb ripe fresh or tinned tomatoes, chopped
Salt and red pepper flakes or cayenne pepper, to taste

1 lb spaghetti or cavatieddi or similar pasta shape
2 cups coarsely chopped arugula
6–8 shallots or 3–4 cloves garlic, chopped
2 tablespoons olive oil
2 cups ripe fresh or canned tomatoes, chopped
Salt and red pepper flakes or cayenne pepper, to taste

1. Cook the pasta until almost *al dente;* add the rocket (arugula), cook for a few moments longer, then drain.
2. Meanwhile, lightly sauté the shallots or garlic in the olive oil, then add the tomatoes. Cook over high heat until the sauce thickens, then season with salt and hot pepper flakes or cayenne pepper.
3. Toss the pasta and rocket (arugula) with the tomato sauce and serve immediately.

Variations

Add rocket (arugula) to the tomato sauce rather than the pasta. This works well when the rocket is on the older, spicier side.

Wholewheat Pasta with Broccoli Tops (Broccoli Rabe): Prepare the recipe above, using wholewheat pasta instead of the spaghetti or cavatieddi, and broccoli tops (broccoli rabe) instead of the rocket (arugula). This needs rather more hot pepper flakes or cayenne pepper than the preceding recipe. Finish with a sprinkling of fresh herbs such as basil and oregano, and freshly grated Parmesan, Pecorino, or similar cheese.

Hot Pepper and Garlic Spaghetti

SERVES 4–6

If you flavour the cooking water with hot peppers and garlic, the pasta itself becomes spicy. It needs no more than a glistening of olive oil and a sprinkling of parsley and fresh garlic. Despite its robust flavouring, the dish itself is light.

Any pasta, except the tiny shapes, could be used instead of spaghetti; I happen to like farfalle, the little butterfly shapes.

3 hot dried or fresh chilli peppers, chopped
9 cloves garlic, chopped
100ml/4 fl oz water
450g/1 lb spaghetti or other pasta of choice
3–4 tablespoons olive oil
3–4 tablespoons chopped fresh parsley
Salt to taste

3 hot dried or fresh chilli peppers, chopped
9 cloves garlic, chopped
½ cup water
1 lb spaghetti or other pasta of choice
¼ cup olive oil, or to taste
¼ cup chopped fresh parsley
Salt to taste

1. Process the chilli peppers, 6 of the garlic cloves and the water in a liquidizer (blender) or food processor until it makes a pungent soup-like mixture. Take care when opening up the top, as the fumes will be strong.
2. Bring a large pan of salted water to the boil. Pour the chilli and garlic mixture through a sieve into the boiling water; save or discard the solids as desired. Add the pasta to this seasoned boiling water and cook until _al dente_. Drain.
3. Toss the hot drained pasta with the olive oil, remaining garlic and the parsley. Season with salt.

Pasta with Creamy Pesto and Blue Cheese Sauce

SERVES 4

This rich dish is perfumed with basil and garlic, the pungent flavour of blue cheese smoothed over with cream. It has the flavours of torta basilica, that northern Italian concoction of Gorgonzola, basil, and mascarpone cheese.

A handful of toasted pine nuts gives the dish a crunchy texture, but if unavailable, simply omit, as it will be delicious regardless. And it is equally good hot or cold.

325g/12 oz fresh pasta, delicate dried
   fettuccine, or the sturdier penne
225g/8 oz blue cheese, crumbled
75ml/3 fl oz single cream
3 tablespoons pesto
2 cloves garlic, finely chopped
3 tablespoons pine nuts
Salt and freshly ground black pepper,
   to taste
Thinly sliced fresh basil leaves
   (optional)

12 oz fresh fettuccine or dried pasta
   such as fettuccine or penne
8 oz blue cheese, crumbled
⅓ cup whipping cream
¼ cup pesto
2 cloves garlic, finely chopped
3 tablespoons pine nuts
Salt and freshly ground black pepper,
   to taste
Thinly sliced fresh basil leaves
   (optional)

1. Cook the pasta until *al dente*.
2. Meanwhile, mix the blue cheese, cream, pesto and garlic together.
3. Toast the pine nuts in an ungreased heavy frying pan (skillet) until lightly browned.

4. Drain the pasta and toss with the sauce; season with salt, if needed, and black pepper. Serve immediately, sprinkled with the toasted pine nuts, and the fresh basil, if using.

Fettuccine with Truffle Sauce

SERVES 4–6

Because a dish takes under five minutes to prepare does not mean it is less than superb. Take this little concoction of buttered fettuccine tossed with chopped garlic and as much truffle as you can get your hands on. It is from the Italian province of Umbria; in Alba a similar dish is prepared with the heady white truffles instead of the black ones.

450g/1 lb fresh fettuccine
3 tablespoons olive oil or 40g/1½ oz butter
2 cloves garlic, finely chopped
25–50g/1–2 oz black truffle paste
Salt to taste

1 lb fresh fettuccine
3 tablespoons olive oil or butter
2 cloves garlic, finely chopped
2–4 tablespoons/1–2 oz black truffle paste
Salt to taste

1. Cook the pasta until *al dente*; fresh fettuccine takes only a few minutes.
2. Drain and toss with the olive oil or butter and the garlic, then with the truffle paste. Season with salt and serve.

Variations

Fettuccine with Truffle Sauce and Strands of Multicoloured Vegetables: Serve the pasta tossed with a selection of vegetables cut into matchsticks, then cooked in the water with the pasta: 1 carrot, 1 celery stalk, 1 courgette (zucchini), a handful of green beans.

Pasta with Truffle Cream: Toss in 75–100ml/ 3–4 fl oz double (heavy) cream (or ¼ cup whipping cream or Italian mascarpone cream cheese), or to taste.

Gnocchi with Truffle Sauce: Substitute chewy potato gnocchi (available in many delicatessens and supermarkets) for the fettuccine. These little potato dumplings are particularly good with the savoury truffle sauce.

Broth-Cooked Orzo with Lemon and Parsley

SERVES 4

Cooking pasta in stock gives extra flavour. The garlic is optional – it really is a nice dish without it, but I cannot resist its lure.

1 litre/1¾ pints vegetable stock
325g/12 oz orzo or other very small
  pasta
1 tablespoon olive oil
1–2 cloves garlic, finely chopped
Juice of 1–2 lemons, to taste
25g/1 oz fresh parsley, chopped
Salt and freshly ground black pepper,
  to taste

1 quart vegetable stock
12 oz orzo or other very small pasta
1 tablespoon olive oil
1–2 cloves garlic, finely chopped
Juice of 1–2 lemons, to taste
½ cup chopped fresh parsley
Salt and freshly ground black pepper,
  to taste

1. Bring the stock to the boil then add the pasta and cook until *al dente*. Drain and reserve the stock for another use.

2. Toss the orzo with the olive oil and garlic, then season with the lemon juice, parsley, salt and black pepper. Serve immediately.

Spaghetti with Double Tomato Relish and Fresh Mozzarella

SERVES 4–6

This fresh, salady mixture of sun-dried tomatoes, fresh tomatoes, masses of basil and garlic all bound up in olive oil makes a delicious sauce for hot pasta, especially with diced mozzarella cheese melting creamily in.

450g/1 lb spaghetti
6–8 very ripe fresh tomatoes, diced
  (and peeled if you prefer)
15 oil-marinated sun-dried tomatoes,
  coarsely chopped (or use sun-dried
  tomato paste)
Several large handfuls fresh basil,
  thinly sliced or coarsely chopped
3 cloves garlic, chopped
3–4 tablespoons olive oil
Salt and freshly ground black pepper,
  to taste
225g-325g/8–12 oz fresh mozzarella (the
  light, white milky cheese that comes
  in a watery brine rather than the
  drier, firmer, pizza-topping), diced

1 lb spaghetti
6–8 very ripe fresh tomatoes, diced
  (and peeled if you prefer)
15 oil-marinated sun-dried tomatoes,
  coarsely chopped (or use sun-dried
  tomato paste)
¼ cup thinly sliced or coarsely
  chopped fresh basil
3 cloves garlic, chopped
3–4 tablespoons olive oil
Salt and freshly ground black pepper,
  to taste
8–12 oz fresh, milky, mozzarella
  cheese, diced

1. Cook the spaghetti until *al dente*.
2. Meanwhile, mix the fresh and sun-dried tomatoes with the basil, garlic and olive oil. Taste for seasoning, adding salt and black pepper, and more garlic, if needed.
3. Drain the spaghetti, toss with the sauce and mozzarella cheese and serve immediately.

Spaghetti with Green Beans, Goat Cheese, Garlic and Basil

SERVES 4–6

450g/1 lb spaghetti
325g/12 oz green beans, cut into bite-
    sized lengths
5 cloves garlic, chopped
3 tablespoons olive oil
100g/4 oz goat cheese, crumbled
Salt and freshly ground black pepper,
    to taste
Handful of fresh basil leaves, torn or
    cut up

1 lb spaghetti
1½ cup bite-sized pieces of green
    beans
5 cloves garlic, chopped
3 tablespoons olive oil
4 oz goat cheese, crumbled
Salt and freshly ground black pepper,
    to taste
2–3 tablespoons fresh basil leaves, torn
    or cut up

1. Cook the spaghetti until half done, then add the green beans and continue cooking until both are *al dente*.
2. Meanwhile, combine the garlic and olive oil.
3. Drain the pasta, toss with the garlic and olive oil, then with the goat cheese. Season with salt and black pepper, add the basil, then serve.

Variations

Pasta with Broad (Fava) Beans and Goat Cheese: The combination of broad (fava) beans and goat cheese is very popular in many parts of Italy, such as the islands, where goat cheese is more common than cows'-milk cheese, as it is easier to raise goats in these mountainous regions.

Follow the recipe above but use peeled broad (fava) beans instead of green beans. If they are very young you do not need to peel their skin after you remove them from the pod, but seldom do shops sell such tender young beans, so use your own judgement.

Pasta with Broad (Fava) Beans, Goat Cheese and Black Olives: Add a handful of diced oil-cured black olives to the above recipe.

Spaghetti with Garlic Butter and Walnuts

SERVES 4–6

Golden sautéed garlic is combined with warm toasted nuts, then tossed with spaghetti, Parmesan cheese, and a small amount of mascarpone or cream, to gild this already rich dish.

325g/12 oz spaghetti
4–6 cloves garlic, coarsely chopped
50g/2 oz butter
100g/4 oz shelled walnuts, halved and coarsely chopped
100ml/4 fl oz mascarpone cheese or double cream
40g/1½ oz Parmesan cheese, freshly grated
Salt and freshly ground black pepper, to taste

12 oz spaghetti
4–6 cloves garlic, coarsely chopped
4 tablespoons butter
¾ cup shelled walnuts, halved and coarsely chopped
½ cup whipping cream or 2–3 heaping tablespoons Mascarpone (rich Italian cream cheese)
⅓ cup freshly grated Parmesan cheese
Salt and freshly ground black pepper, to taste

1. Cook the spaghetti until *al dente*.
2. Meanwhile, sauté the garlic in the butter until fragrant and lightly golden, then add the walnuts and swirl around in the garlic butter. Remove from the heat and stir in the mascarpone or double (whipping) cream. Set aside.
3. Drain the spaghetti, toss with the sauce, then with the Parmesan cheese. Season with salt and black pepper and serve immediately.

Variation

Ravioli con Salsa de Noci: For this Ligurian classic, use spinach- and cheese-stuffed ravioli instead of spaghetti, and do not fry the garlic and walnuts. Rather, increase the amount of walnuts to 200g/7 oz (1½ cups) then grind in a grinder or food processor until finely chopped. Combine the ground nuts with the garlic, butter, mascarpone or cream, and Parmesan cheese and mix well. Toss with the cooked ravioli and serve immediately, sprinkled with a handful of finely chopped fresh basil.

Buttered Bay-Scented Capellini

SERVES 4

Utterly simple with an elusive, subtle flavour. The bay leaves scent the thin strings of pasta, permeating each and every strand. While the quantity below makes enough to serve 4, I often make enough for only 1 or 2 as this is awfully good late-night snack food.

4–6 fresh or dried bay leaves
325g/12 oz capellini
Butter to taste
Salt and freshly ground black pepper,
  to taste

4–6 fresh or dried bay leaves
12 oz capellini
Butter to taste
Salt and freshly ground black pepper,
  to taste

1. Add the bay leaves to a large pot of salted water, then bring to the boil.
2. Add the capellini, cook until just tender then drain. Remove the bay leaves.
3. Toss the hot drained pasta in plenty of butter, then add salt and black pepper to taste. Serve immediately.

PASTA WITH SAUCES OF VEGETABLES, CHEESES AND BEANS

Pasta with a Sauce of Rustic Baked Tomatoes

SERVES 4–6

This recipe is courtesy of Amanda Hamilton-Hemmeter, who often prepares it as a late summer lunch at her Sonoma County vineyard when tomatoes are ripe and sweet.

The long-baked sauce remains fresh and strongly flavoured as the slow cooking intensifies the flavours of the tomatoes.

Besides being delicious, it is also very easy to prepare: put it in the oven, turn it on, and retrieve it 3 hours later. You must use a heavy pan, baking dish or pot so the temperature remains constant and the tomatoes don't scorch, and it must be enamelled so that there is no metal leaching into the sauce. As for the tomatoes: don't peel them, since the tangy bits of peel in the sauce add to its charm. If you don't like tomato skins, however, by all means peel the tomatoes before preparing the recipe.

Enough olive oil to cover the bottom of the baking dish or heavy pot by about 3–6mm/⅛–¼ inch
Enough ripe tomatoes, cut into quarters and uneven chunks, to fill up the baking dish or pot by about half to two-thirds.
450g/1 lb rigatoni or pasta of choice
A generous amount of red pepper flakes and chopped garlic, to taste
Freshly grated Parmesan cheese to serve
Herbs: dried oregano, fresh basil, marjoram or parsley, to taste

1. In a heavy enamelled casserole dish, toss the olive oil with the tomatoes.
2. Cover with a tightly fitting lid and place in the oven. Turn the heat on to 180°C/350°F/gas mark 4 and leave for 3 hours. The sauce may be made in advance and stored in the refrigerator for up to 5 days.
3. Cook the pasta until *al dente*, then drain.
4. Season the sauce with red pepper flakes and chopped garlic, then put the lid back on for just a moment. The seasonings will mellow into the sauce but not cook.
5. Spoon the tomato mixture over the pasta. Serve sprinkled with grated Parmesan cheese and herbs.

Variation

Pasta with Rustic Baked Tomatoes and Goat Cheese: Follow the recipe above but serve topped with about 150g/5 oz tangy fresh goat cheese or ewe's cheese, crumbled into bits. Delicious either hot or cool.

Penne alla Puttanesca

PASTA WITH OLIVES, CAPERS, AND TOMATOES, WHORE'S STYLE

SERVES 4–6

The lusty sauces made with garlic, tomatoes, olives and capers are often known as Whore's style (see Penne alla Malefemmina on page 48).

Don't serve cheese with this dish: just the last minute sprinkling of parsley, and perhaps a little extra hot pepper if desired.

4 tablespoons olive oil
4–6 cloves garlic, chopped
2 pickled peperoncini (Italian or Greek bottled spicy peppers), chopped
900g/2 lbs ripe fresh tomatoes, peeled, diced, and drained of excess juice or 1½ 400g/14 oz tins of chopped tomatoes
2 tablespoons tomato paste
Pinch of sugar (optional)
About 20 Kalamata olives, pitted and quartered
1–2 tablespoons capers
Salt to taste
450g/1 lb penne
2 tablespoons chopped fresh parsley and/or fresh basil

¼ cup olive oil
4–6 cloves garlic, chopped
2 pickled peperoncini (Italian or Greek bottled spicy pickled peppers), chopped
2 lbs ripe fresh tomatoes, peeled and diced, and drained of excess juice, or 2 large (1 lb) cans tomatoes
2 tablespoons tomato paste
Pinch of sugar (optional)
About 20 Kalamata olives, pitted and quartered
1–2 tablespoons capers
Salt to taste
1 lb penne
2 tablespoons chopped fresh parsley and/or fresh basil

1. Heat the olive oil, garlic and peperoncini together until the garlic is fragrant and beginning to colour.
2. Add the tomatoes, tomato paste, and the sugar if needed, and bring to the boil. Reduce the heat and simmer for 15 minutes.

Remove from the heat, add the olives and capers, then taste for salt. Set aside and keep warm.

3. Meanwhile, cook the pasta until *al dente*. Drain and toss with the sauce, then serve sprinkled with the parsley and/or basil.

Spaghetti with Orange-Scented Tomato Sauce

SERVES 4–6

A squeeze of orange juice in a simple sauce of garlic- and basil-seasoned tomatoes adds an unusual and delightfully subtle nuance.

3 tablespoons olive oil
2–3 cloves garlic, coarsely chopped
10–15 fresh basil leaves
900g/2 lb fresh ripe tomatoes, diced,
   or 1½ 400g/14 oz tins chopped
   tomatoes
Salt to taste
Juice of 1 orange
Small shake of Tabasco sauce
450g/1 lb spaghetti

3 tablespoons olive oil
2–3 cloves garlic, coarsely chopped
10–15 fresh basil leaves
2 lbs fresh ripe tomatoes, diced or
   2 large (1 lb) cans chopped tomatoes
Salt to taste
Juice of 1 orange
Small shake of Tabasco sauce
1 lb spaghetti

1. Heat 2 tablespoons of the olive oil with the garlic and half the basil leaves until the garlic colours, then add the tomatoes and salt. Cook over high heat until thickened, about 15–20 minutes.
2. Add the orange juice, season with the Tabasco, and continue to cook over high heat for about 5 more minutes. Taste for seasoning.
3. Cook the spaghetti until *al dente*. Drain.
4. Toss the hot drained spaghetti with the sauce, then serve with the remaining olive oil drizzled over, sprinkled with the remaining basil leaves.

Fettuccine with Spicy Tequila-Spiked Creamy Tomato Sauce

SERVES 4

A variation on the vodka-spiked sauces that were fashionable on the Via Veneto in Rome a few years ago, only here the vodka is replaced by a bit of tequila. When the tequila boils away it leaves in its wake a vague and pleasant vegetal quality.

4 cloves garlic, chopped
¼ teaspoon red pepper flakes or 1–2 dried red chillies, halved and seeds removed
2 tablespoons olive oil or 25g/1 oz butter
2 tablespoons tequila
8 ripe fresh tomatoes, diced or 400g/ 14 oz tin chopped tomatoes
75ml/3 fl oz single cream
Salt and freshly ground black pepper, to taste
325g/12 oz fresh fettuccine
Freshly grated Parmesan cheese to serve

4 cloves garlic, chopped
¼ teaspoon red pepper flakes or 1–2 dried red chillies, halved and seeds removed
2 tablespoons olive oil or butter
2 tablespoons tequila
8 ripe fresh tomatoes, diced or 1½ cups chopped tomatoes
⅓ cup whipping cream
Salt and freshly ground black pepper, to taste
12 oz fresh fettuccine
Freshly grated Parmesan cheese to serve

1. Sauté the garlic and hot pepper in the olive oil or butter. Remove from the heat and, keeping your face away from the pan, add the tequila. Do not pour it directly from the bottle as it is likely to burst into flames.
2. Return the pan to the heat and add the tomatoes, and cook over high heat, letting the mixture flame up then cook down until the flames die and the liquid is reduced by half.
3. Add the cream and cook for a few more minutes, then season with salt and black pepper.
4. Meanwhile, cook the pasta until *al dente*, then drain.
5. Serve with the sauce and a dusting of Parmesan cheese.

Pasta Arrabbiata
(Pasta with Chilli-Spiked Tomato Sauce)

SERVES 4

A good arrabbiata sauce can either grab your throat with its fiery heat or merely warm you gently, as you prefer. It should also, to my taste at least, fairly reek with garlic.

The spicy character of the sauce makes a delicious foil to other additions: sun-dried tomatoes, fresh basil leaves, goat cheese, slices of browned aubergine, chopped rocket (arugula) or spinach.

1–2 dried red chillies, crumbled, or
    cayenne pepper, to taste
4–6 cloves garlic, chopped
2–3 tablespoons olive oil
250ml/8 fl oz tomato passata
Salt and freshly ground black pepper,
    to taste
325g/12 oz pasta of choice: vermicelli,
    fettuccine, spaghetti, bucatini, etc.
3 tablespoons chopped fresh parsley
Freshly grated Parmesan cheese to
    serve (optional)

1–2 dried red chillies, crumbled, or
    cayenne pepper, to taste
4–6 cloves garlic, chopped
2–3 tablespoons olive oil
1 cup tomato passata or tomato sauce
Salt and freshly ground black pepper,
    to taste
12 oz pasta of choice: vermicelli,
    fettuccine, spaghetti, bucatini, etc.
3 tablespoons chopped fresh parsley
Freshly grated Parmesan cheese to
    serve (optional)

1. Warm the chillies or cayenne pepper and garlic in the olive oil until the garlic is fragrant. As always, when heating chillies in oil take care not to inhale the irritating fumes.
2. Add the tomato passata and salt and black pepper to taste. Cook the sauce 5–10 minutes longer, to meld the flavours.
3. Cook the pasta until *al dente*; drain.
4. Serve the pasta tossed with the sauce and sprinkled with the parsley, and offer Parmesan cheese separately.

Variations

Pasta Arrabbiata with Ginger-Garlic Butter, Lemon and Mint: Prepare as above, but serve topped with a nugget of ginger-garlic butter, sprinkled with 1–2 tablespoons each of chopped fresh mint and parsley, and accompanied by lemon wedges.

To make ginger-garlic butter, mix 50g/2 oz (4 tablespoons) softened unsalted butter with ½–1 teaspoon grated fresh ginger, 1 clove chopped garlic, and a pinch of salt.

Pasta Arrabbiata with Coriander (Cilantro) Pesto: Serve the sauced pasta with a generous dab of coriander (cilantro) pesto, made by mixing in a liquidizer (blender) or food processor 3 cloves chopped garlic, 1 bunch chopped fresh coriander leaves (cilantro), 50–75g/2–3 oz (¼–⅓ cup) Parmesan or other hard cheese, coarsely grated, and 2–3 tablespoons olive oil with salt and black pepper or cayenne pepper to taste.

Conchiglie Tricolore with Garlic and Tomato Sauce

SERVES 4–6

The multi-hued seashells – or any shape pasta you like – are lovely sauced with a simple sauté of garlic and tomatoes. It's a lusty, straightforward sauce that is good with plain pasta as well.

This is quintessential Italian summertime fare, or food for a Californian evening, or for a British afternoon when the rain just will not stop.

450g/1 lb multicoloured seashell pasta
6–8 cloves garlic, coarsely chopped
3 tablespoons olive oil
900g/2 lb ripe fresh tomatoes, diced, or 1½ 400g/14 oz tins tomatoes, well-drained (save the juice for another purpose)
Salt and freshly ground black pepper
Pinch of sugar
3–6 large fresh basil leaves, very thinly sliced
Freshly grated Parmesan cheese to serve (optional)

1 lb multicoloured seashell pasta
6–8 cloves garlic, coarsely chopped
3 tablespoons olive oil
2 lb ripe fresh tomatoes, diced, or 2 cups canned tomatoes, diced and drained (save the juice for another purpose)
Salt and freshly ground black pepper
Pinch of sugar
3–6 large fresh basil leaves, very thinly sliced
Freshly grated Parmesan cheese to serve (optional)

1. Cook the pasta until *al dente*.
2. Meanwhile, warm the garlic in the olive oil and when fragrant and just beginning to colour add the tomatoes and cook over medium to high heat for a few minutes.
3. Season with salt and black pepper and the sugar and set aside for a moment or two.
4. Drain the pasta and toss with the tomato sauce. Serve sprinkled with the basil and with Parmesan cheese if liked.

Variation

Ditalini, Spaghetti, Green Beans and Peas with Garlic and Tomato Sauce: The combination of tiny circles of ditalini and long strands of spaghetti, slashes of green bean and small dots of peas is whimsical and visually delightful. Vary the proportions of vegetables and pasta to taste.

Prepare the tomato sauce as above. Cook about 175g/6 oz ditalini, then after 3 or 4 minutes when it is nearly chewy but still has quite a bit of resistance to the teeth, add a large handful of fresh green beans cut into bite-sized lengths, and about 175g/6 oz spaghetti. Continue cooking for another few minutes, then add about 100g/4 oz (½ cup) fresh or frozen peas. Cook a minute or two more, until all the pasta is *al dente*, then drain and serve with the garlic and tomato sauce.

Pasta with Tomato Sauce, Beaten Egg, Cheese and Basil

SERVES 4–6

The addition of beaten egg and cheese makes a simple tomato sauce softer and smoother. I've tried it both ways: tossing the pasta with the sauce first, then with the beaten egg, and saucing the pasta with egg and cheese, Carbonara style, then adding the tomato sauce. Each gives a slightly different result.

2 onions, chopped
60g/2½ oz butter
4 cloves garlic, coarsely chopped
900g/2 lb very ripe fresh tomatoes, peeled, seeded and diced, or 1½ 400g/14 oz tins tomatoes, drained and sliced (reserve the juice)
Salt and freshly ground black pepper, to taste
Pinch of sugar
450g/1 lb pasta of choice: spaghetti, tiny shells, elbows, etc.
3 eggs, lightly beaten
75g/3 oz Parmesan cheese, freshly grated
100g/4 oz Mozzarella or similar cheese, grated
About 10 leaves fresh basil, cut into very thin strips

2 onions, chopped
5 tablespoons butter
4 cloves garlic, coarsely chopped
2 lb ripe fresh tomatoes, peeled, seeded and diced, or 2 cans (1 lb each) chopped tomatoes
Salt and freshly ground black pepper, to taste
Pinch of sugar
1 lb pasta of choice: spaghetti, tiny shells, elbows, etc.
3 eggs, lightly beaten
¾ cup freshly grated Parmesan cheese
4 oz Mozzarella or similar cheese, such as Monterey Jack, grated
About 10 fresh basil leaves, cut into very thin strips

1. In a wide frying pan (skillet), rather than a saucepan (the larger cooking surface will evaporate the liquids and intensify the sauce more quickly), lightly sauté the onions in 40g/1½oz (3 tablespoons) of the butter until softened, then add the garlic and continue to cook for a minute or so.

2. Add the tomatoes, salt and black pepper, and sugar, and cook over medium to high heat until the liquid is nearly evaporated. Add a little of the reserved juice, say

100 ml/4 fl oz (½ cup), taste for seasoning, and set aside to keep warm.

3. Meanwhile, cook the pasta until *al dente*. Combine the beaten eggs with the Parmesan and mozzarella (or Jack) cheeses.

4. Drain the pasta and mix with the remaining butter and black pepper to taste. Toss the buttered pasta with the egg and cheese mixture, taking care that it forms a creamy cloak rather than becoming scrambled.

5. Once the cheese has melted, add the tomato sauce and mix through. Serve immediately, garnished with the basil.

Variation

This is also delicious cool. Prepare as above, but use olive oil instead of butter, and equal amounts mozzarella (or Jack) and Parmesan cheeses.

Pasta with Asparagus and Creamy Light Pesto Sauce

SERVES 4–6

The creamy pale green sauce, subtly scented with basil, and the delicate asparagus go particularly well with fresh pasta in this dish.

325–450g/12–16 oz good-quality fresh flat ribbon pasta
325g/12 oz fresh asparagus, cut into 5cm/2 inch lengths
100g/4 oz pesto (see page 255) – bottled doesn't taste right here
40g/1½ oz unsalted butter, softened
125ml/4 fl oz single cream
1 clove garlic, finely chopped
Salt and freshly ground black pepper, to taste

12–16 oz good-quality fresh flat ribbon pasta
12 oz fresh asparagus, cut into 2 inch lengths
½ cup pesto (see page 255) or use frozen
3 tablespoons unsalted butter, softened
½ cup whipping cream
1 clove garlic, finely chopped
Salt and freshly ground black pepper, to taste

1. Cook the pasta and asparagus together in the boiling water until the pasta is *al dente* and the asparaugs crisp-tender, about 3 minutes. Drain.
2. Mix the pesto with the butter, cream, garlic, and salt and black pepper.
3. Toss the hot pasta and asparagus with the creamy pesto mixture and serve immediately.

Fettuccine alla Perugina (Fettuccine with Fresh Tomato and Asparagus Sauce)

SERVES 4–6

The medieval town of Perugia in Umbria is known for several culinary reasons: silken chocolate baci (kisses), of course, and black truffles nearly as good as those in France. But come the asparagus season, the thin green shoots are in abundant supply, fresh and grassy tasting and tossed into every dish imaginable,' especially this pasta dish.

Like many wonderful foods, its simplicity belies its superlative flavour. It is simply a zesty tomato sauce in which a generous amount of asparagus is simmered, ladled over pasta and sprinkled abundantly with fresh herbs. Any large pasta, especially the long, flat, ribbony shapes such as fettuccine, linguine and even spaghetti, is delicious with this sauce. Curly pasta such as fusilli lunghi are good too.

4 cloves garlic, chopped
2 tablespoons olive oil
12–15 small fresh tomatoes, preferably Italian, peeled, seeded and diced
3 tablespoons tomato paste
250ml/8 fl oz water
Salt and freshly ground black pepper, to taste
Pinch of sugar (optional)
325–450g/12–16 oz asparagus, cut into 3.5–5cm/1½–2 inch lengths
325g/12 oz fettuccine or pasta of choice
10–15 fresh basil leaves, coarsely chopped or torn (or chopped parsley, marjoram, etc.)
2–3 tablespoons freshly grated Parmesan cheese

4 cloves garlic, chopped
2 tablespoons olive oil
12–15 small fresh tomatoes, preferably Italian or Roma, peeled, seeded and diced
3 tablespoons tomato paste
1 cup water
Salt and freshly ground black pepper, to taste
Pinch of sugar (optional)
¾–1 lb asparagus, cut into 1½–2 inch lengths
12 fettuccine or pasta of choice
10–15 fresh basil leaves, coarsely chopped or torn (or chopped parsley, marjoram, etc.)
2–3 tablespoons freshly grated Parmesan or other grating cheese such as Asiago, Pecorino, etc.

1. Heat the garlic in the olive oil until just warmed and fragrant, then add the tomatoes and sauté until softened; this will take only a few minutes. Add the tomato paste and water, season with salt and freshly ground black pepper and the sugar, if needed, then add the asparagus.

2. Bring to the boil, then reduce the heat and cook until the asparagus is just tender.
3. Meanwhile, cook the pasta until *al dente*. Drain.
4. Toss the cooked pasta with the sauce and top with the basil and grated Parmesan cheese. Serve immediately.

Gnocchi with Artichokes, Porcini and Carrot

SERVES 4–6

While gnocchi usually refers to soft dumplings made from potatoes, it is also the name of a particularly chewy shell-shaped pasta, which is good with rich vegetable sauces such as this one. Here, the rich sauce is tempered by the grating of fresh carrot.

15g/½ oz dried porcini mushrooms
500ml/16 fl oz hot, but not quite boiling, water
1 onion, finely chopped
3 cloves garlic, chopped
2 tablespoons olive oil
3 fresh artichoke hearts, prepared as described on page 263, and cut into large dice or 8 drained tinned or thawed frozen artichoke hearts
1 carrot, coarsely grated
75ml/3 fl oz single cream
Salt and freshly ground black pepper
Small squeeze of lemon juice (unless using tinned artichokes; they are acidic enough)
350–450g/12–16 oz dried shell-shaped pasta gnocchi or other seashell pasta
25–50g/1–2 oz butter
Freshly grated Parmesan cheese to serve

½ oz dried porcini mushrooms
2 cups hot, but not quite boiling, water
1 onion, finely chopped
3 cloves garlic, chopped
2 tablespoons olive oil
3 fresh artichoke hearts, diced (see page 263) or 8 frozen and defrosted artichoke hearts, cut into large dice
1 carrot, coarsely grated
⅓ cup whipping cream
Salt and freshly ground black pepper
Small squeeze of lemon juice
12–16 oz dried shell-shaped gnocchi pasta or other seashell pasta
2–3 tablespoons butter
Freshly grated Parmesan cheese to serve

1. Rehydrate the mushrooms in the hot water as described on page 262, reserving the liquid, then set aside.
2. Sauté the onion and garlic in olive oil until softened, then add the artichoke hearts and mix together. Add the porcini and grated carrot and cook through for a few minutes.
3. Pour the mushroom soaking liquid into the pan and cook down until reduced by about half. Add the cream, swirl through, and season with salt and black pepper and a dash of lemon juice. Set aside.
4. Cook the pasta until *al dente*. Drain, toss with the butter, and serve with the sauce, offering Parmesan cheese separately.

Lemon-Scented Couscous with Artichokes, Olives and Sun-Dried Tomatoes

SERVES 4–6

Couscous is a tiny grain-like pasta made of hard semolina wheat, traditionally favoured throughout North Africa as well as in Sicily. In recent years it has made its way into French cuisine as well as Californian and British.

The little pellets of pasta are usually sold pre-steamed so that they need only to be steeped in a hot savoury sauce to plump them up into a luscious grain dish. In Morocco, Tunisia and Sicily, it is usually steamed over a spicy stew filled with vegetables, meat or fish. For my favourite vegetarian version, refer to another of my books, Hot & Spicy (Grafton Books).

Here we have a different sort of couscous, more Mediterranean and contemporary in flavour. It is cooked in the lemon-scented stock, then topped with the mixture of artichokes, sun-dried tomatoes and olives. There is no authenticity to this dish: it skips merrily throughout the Mediterranean, picking up flavours along the way.

2 large heads garlic, cloves separated and peeled	2 large heads garlic, cloves separated and peeled
2 tablespoons olive oil	2 tablespoons olive oil
6 artichokes, prepared as on page 263, blanched and sliced	6 artichokes, prepared as on page 263, blanched and sliced
250ml/8 fl oz dry white wine	1 cup dry white wine
¼ teaspoon dried thyme or herbes de Provence	¼ teaspoon dried thyme or herbes de Provence
600ml/1 pint vegetable stock, plus extra as needed	2½ cups vegetable stock, plus extra as needed
2 lemons, cut into quarters	2 lemons, cut into quarters
15–20 black Italian- or Greek-style olives	15–20 black Italian- or Greek-style olives
5–10 oil-marinated sun-dried tomatoes, quartered or sliced into strips	5–10 oil-marinated sun-dried tomatoes, quartered or sliced into strips
325g/12 oz instant couscous	12 oz instant couscous (1 package)
40g/1½ oz butter	3 tablespoons butter

1. Place the garlic cloves in a baking dish and toss with the olive oil. Bake in the oven at 190°C/375°F/gas mark 5 oven about 10 minutes, or until the garlic begins to brown lightly.
2. Add the blanched and sliced artichoke hearts, white wine, herbs, half the vegetable stock and half the lemon quarters. Bake for another 20–30 minutes until the liquid is reduced in volume and the artichokes are lightly browned.

3. Remove the lemon quarters. Add the olives and sun-dried tomatoes, plus the remaining stock and return to the oven to heat through. Remove from the oven and pour about half the liquid into a saucepan. Return the artichoke mixture to the oven.

4. Add enough extra stock to the saucepan to make it up to 600ml/1 pint (2½ cups). Heat until almost boiling, then squeeze the remaining lemon quarters into the pan. Pour this over the couscous, then dot with the butter, cover and leave to absorb the sauce and plump up, about 10 minutes.

5. Serve the hot couscous topped with the artichoke, olive, and sun-dried tomato mixture, plus the sauce it has cooked in.

Fettuccine with Creamy Diced Artichoke Sauce

SERVES 4

Rich and elegant, this is very quick and easy to make once the artichokes have been prepared and blanched. It really does need to be made with fresh artichokes to avoid the acidic flavours that often develop in tinned or frozen ones.

Almost any pasta shape can be used – spaghetti, penne, pappardelle – but the delicacy of good-quality fresh fettuccine makes this dish special.

4–5 medium to large artichokes, prepared as on page 263
1 small onion, chopped
1 clove garlic, chopped
25g/1 oz butter
125ml/4 fl oz vegetable stock
300ml/10 fl oz single cream
Pinch of cayenne pepper or freshly ground black pepper
450g/1 lb fresh fettuccine or 325g/12 oz dried fettuccine
Freshly grated Parmesan cheese to serve

4–5 fresh artichokes, prepared and blanched as on page 263
1 small onion, chopped
1 clove garlic, chopped
2 tablespoons butter
½ cup vegetable stock
1½ cup whipping cream
Pinch cayenne pepper or freshly ground black pepper
1 lb fresh fettuccine or 12 oz dried fettuccine
Freshly grated Parmesan cheese to serve

1. Dice the blanched artichokes, then set aside.

2. Lightly sauté the onion and garlic in the butter. When softened add the blanched artichokes and cook together for a few minutes.

3. Add the stock then bring to the boil and simmer for several minutes until the artichokes are quite tender. Add the cream, heat through, and season with cayenne or black pepper. Salt is unlikely to be needed as both the stock and the Parmesan cheese are salty. Cover and set aside while you cook the pasta.

4. Cook the pasta until just tender. Drain and toss with the sauce, then serve immediately, sprinkled with Parmesan cheese.

Spaghetti with Lusty Tomato and Pea Sauce

SERVES 4–6

Peas seasoned with fennel and Italian herbs such as thyme, marjoram, etc. make a robust tomato sauce that is good with nearly any hearty shape of pasta, such as penne, spaghetti, wheel-shapes, fusilli lunghi, and so on. I often grate very unItalian cheeses over this – Cheddar, Monterey Jack, or Cantal, for example – and they are delicious.

1 small onion, chopped
3 cloves garlic, chopped
2 tablespoons olive oil
900g/2 lb ripe fresh tomatoes, chopped, or 1½ 400g/14oz tins chopped tomatoes
2 tablespoons tomato paste (optional)
Pinch of sugar
325g/12 oz fresh or frozen peas
½ teaspoon dried mixed herbs or thyme, or to taste
¼ teaspoon fennel seeds, or to taste
Salt and freshly ground black pepper, to taste
325–450g/12–16 oz spaghetti
Handful of chopped fresh parsley or basil
Freshly grated Parmesan or other sharp grating cheese to serve

1 small onion, chopped
3 cloves garlic, chopped
2 tablespoons olive oil
2 lb ripe fresh tomatoes, chopped, or 2 1 lb cans chopped tomatoes
2 tablespoons tomato paste (optional)
Pinch of sugar
12 oz fresh or frozen peas
½ teaspoon dried mixed herbs or thyme, or to taste
¼ teaspoon fennel seeds, or to taste
Salt and freshly ground black pepper, to taste
12–16 oz spaghetti
¼ cup chopped fresh parsley or basil
Freshly grated Parmesan or other sharp grating cheese to serve

1. Lightly sauté the onion and garlic in the olive oil. When soft and translucent, add the tomatoes, crushing them as you add them, tomato paste, sugar, peas, dried herbs, and fennel seeds. Bring to the boil and cook over medium to high heat for about 10 minutes, or until the peas are tender and the tomato sauce has thickened. Season with salt and black pepper.
2. Meanwhile, cook the pasta until *al dente*. Drain and toss with the sauce. Serve immediately, sprinkled with parsley or basil and cheese.

Variations

Tricolour Spaghetti with Tomato and Pea Sauce: Serve the sauce ladled over tricolour spaghetti. The robust sauce is particularly good with the hearty quality of the multi-vegetable pasta.

Macaroni with Peas and Ricotta: Serve the sauce with short fat macaroni shapes, and top each portion with a dollop of creamy ricotta cheese and a flurry of coarsely grated Parmesan.

Radiatore with Tomato Sauce and Multicoloured (Bell) Peppers: Radiatore are small curly-edged pasta, delicious with hearty tomato sauces. Their name means little radiators but they are more than mere whimsy: the ruffled edges are a delicious trap for lashings of savoury sauce.

Make the tomato sauce, but omit the peas and include instead ½ each red, yellow and green (bell) peppers, diced and sautéed with the onion and garlic. Add a spoonful of capers, too, if you like.

Orzo with Peas in Saffron and Garlic Cream

SERVES 4

Tiny pasta in saffron- and garlic-scented cream makes a succulent first course or supper dish to spoon up any time when you are leaning towards indulgence.

325g/12 oz orzo or other small seed-
    shaped pasta
6 cloves garlic, chopped
40g/1½ oz butter
500ml/16 fl oz vegetable stock
175ml/6 fl oz single cream
100ml/4 fl oz Greek yogurt or *crème fraîche*
225g/8 oz peas, preferably petits pois,
    either fresh and blanched or frozen
Large pinch of saffron dissolved in
    1 tablespoon cold water
75g/3 oz Parmesan cheese, freshly grated

12 oz orzo or other small seed-shaped
    pasta
6 cloves garlic, chopped
3 tablespoons butter
2 cups vegetable stock
¾ cup whipping cream
½ cup *crème fraîche* or sour cream
1 cup peas, preferably petits pois,
    either fresh and blanched or frozen
Large pinch of saffron dissolved in
    1 tablespoon cold water
¾ cup freshly grated Parmesan cheese

1. Cook the orzo until *al dente*. Drain and set aside.
2. Lightly heat the garlic in the butter, then when gilded and aromatic, add the stock and the cooked orzo. Heat until bubbly around the edges.
3. Stir in the cream, then add Greek yogurt or *crème fraîche* (or sour cream), peas and saffron. Heat together, stirring well so that the sauce is smooth and creamy – it should be soupy, but thickened.
4. Serve immediately, each portion topped with Parmesan cheese.

Variations

Orzo with Asparagus and Saffron and Garlic Cream: Instead of the tiny peas, use asparagus tips, cut into bite-sized pieces. Cook the asparagus with the orzo, adding it when the pasta is half done. Proceed as above, omitting the peas.

Orzo with Courgette (Zucchini) Blossoms: This is a variation on the classic pairing of squash blossoms with pasta or Arborio rice. Clean about 15 courgette (zucchini) flowers or other squash blossoms, removing the stems and pistils. Cut into large pieces and add to the orzo instead of the peas.

Paglia e Fieno al Aurora

YELLOW AND GREEN PASTA IN A CREAMY TOMATO SAUCE WITH MUSHROOMS AND PEAS

SERVES 4–6

Paglia e fieno means straw and hay, and it is a whimsical term for yellow and green pasta, reminiscent of the yellow hay stacks and green piles of straw that are so much a part of the Tuscan landscape.

1 small onion, chopped
4 cloves garlic, chopped
225g/8 oz mushrooms, coarsely chopped
25g/1 oz butter
750g/1½ lb ripe fresh tomatoes, peeled and chopped or 1 400g/14 oz tin chopped tomatoes
50g/2 oz tomato paste
250ml/8 fl oz vegetable stock
250ml/8 fl oz single cream
225g/8 oz fresh and blanched or frozen peas
Salt and freshly ground black pepper, to taste
225g/8 oz yellow fettuccine
225g/8 oz green fettuccine
Freshly grated Parmesan cheese to serve
Handful of fresh basil leaves, cut into thin strips, or several tablespoons coarsely chopped fresh marjoram

1 small onion, chopped
4 cloves garlic, chopped
½ lb mushrooms, coarsely chopped
2 tablespoons butter
1½ lb ripe fresh tomatoes, peeled and coarsely chopped or 1½ cups canned chopped tomatoes
3–4 tablespoons tomato paste
1 cup vegetable stock
1 cup whipping cream
1 cup fresh and blanched or frozen peas
Salt and freshly ground black pepper, to taste
8 oz yellow fettuccine
8 oz green fettuccine
Freshly grated Parmesan cheese to serve
Handful of fresh basil leaves, cut into thin strips, or several tablespoons coarsely chopped fresh marjoram

1. Lightly sauté the onion, garlic and mushrooms in the butter. When softened, add the tomatoes, tomato paste, and stock then cook over medium heat until thick and saucelike, about 5–10 minutes.
2. Stir in the cream and cook for another 10 minutes or until the sauce is somewhat thickened and the flavours have combined. Add the peas, then season to taste with salt and black pepper.
3. Meanwhile, cook the pasta until *al dente*.

Drain and serve immediately, tossed with the sauce and sprinkled with the basil or marjoram. Offer Parmesan cheese separately.

Variation

Instead of peas add a handful of thin green beans, blanched and cut into bite-sized lengths. If yellow wax beans are available, include these as well.

Spaghetti with Green Beans, Tomatoes and Olives

SERVES 4–6

4–5 cloves garlic, coarsely chopped
50ml/2 fl oz olive oil ,
Handful of fresh basil leaves
225g/8 oz green beans, as tender and
fresh as possible
10–15 ripe fresh tomatoes, diced
Pinch of sugar
Salt and freshly ground black pepper,
to taste
450g/1 lb spaghetti
10 oil-cured black olives, pitted and
diced
Freshly grated Parmesan cheese or
other grating cheese, to serve

4–5 cloves garlic, coarsely chopped
¼ cup olive oil
¼ cup coarsely chopped or torn fresh
basil leaves
½ lb green beans, as tender and fresh
as possible
10–15 ripe fresh tomatoes, diced
Pinch of sugar
Salt and freshly ground black pepper,
to taste
1 lb spaghetti
10 oil-cured black olives, pitted and
diced
Freshly grated Parmesan cheese or
other grating cheese, to taste

1. Heat the garlic in the oil until fragrant and lightly golden, then add the basil and the beans. Cook for a few moments then add the tomatoes. Cook over medium heat, adding a little water if necessary, until the mixture is saucelike. Season with the sugar and salt and black pepper.
2. Cook the pasta until _al dente_. Drain and serve tossed with the sauce. Sprinkle with the diced black olives and pass the Parmesan cheese.

Variation

If yellow wax beans are available, add a handful along with the green beans.

Ditalini with Fennel-Scented Peas

SERVES 4

This sauce is very light, based on peas in a reduction of onion and garlic-scented broth, flavoured with fennel seed.

Leftovers are delicious spooned into a light tomato or mushroom broth, vegetable soup, or minestrone.

2 onions, chopped	2 onions, chopped
4 cloves garlic, chopped	4 cloves garlic, chopped
25g/1 oz butter or 2 tablespoons olive oil, or a mixture of the two	2 tablespoons butter, olive oil, or a combination of the two
2 tablespoons chopped fresh parsley	2 tablespoons chopped fresh parsley
225g/8 oz fresh or frozen peas	1 cup fresh blanched or frozen peas
500ml/16 fl oz vegetable stock	2 cups vegetable stock
Large pinch of each of mixed dried herbs and fennel seeds	Large pinch each of mixed dried herbs and fennel seeds
325g/12 oz ditalini, elbows, or other short pasta	12 oz ditalini, elbows, or other short pasta
Salt and freshly ground black pepper, to taste	Salt and freshly ground black pepper, to taste
Freshly grated Parmesan cheese to serve	Freshly grated Parmesan cheese to serve

1. Lightly sauté the onions and garlic in the butter and/or olive oil until softened.
2. Add the parsley and peas and cook for a minute or two until both are bright green, then add the stock. Raise the heat and cook over a very high heat until the liquid is reduced to only a few tablespoons and is very intensified in flavour.
3. Add the herbs and fennel seeds and set aside.
4. Meanwhile, cook the pasta until *al dente*. Drain and toss with the pea sauce, season with salt and black pepper, then serve sprinkled generously with Parmesan cheese.

Variation

Tomato Broth with Peas and Ditalini: Prepare this fragrant soup with any leftover peas and ditalini you might have. Sauté several cloves of chopped garlic in 1 tablespoon olive oil, then stir in 6–8 diced, ripe fresh tomatoes (1 cup) and 1 litre/1¾ pints (1 quart) vegetable stock. Bring to the boil, then add the leftover peas and ditalini and heat through. Season with salt, black pepper, herbs and freshly grated Parmesan or Pecorino cheese to taste.

Gingered Fusilli Lunghi with Corn, Courgettes (Zucchini) and Peppers

SERVES 4–6

This sauce is a lively melange of sautéed onions, garlic, hot and sweet (bell) peppers smoothed out with a glistening of Greek yogurt or sour cream. The thick winding twists of fusilli lunghi are very nice in this sauce, but rotelle (wagon wheels), cavatappi (hollow corkscrews) or any chunky pasta would be good, too.

2 onions, chopped	2 onions, chopped
3 cloves garlic, chopped	3 cloves garlic, chopped
1 green pepper, chopped	1 green bell pepper, diced
2 tablespoons olive oil	2 tablespoons olive oil
½–1 fresh red chilli, seeded and chopped	½–1 red jalapeno chilli, seeded and chopped
2 small courgettes, diced	2 zucchini, diced
250–375ml/8–12 fl oz vegetable stock	1–1½ cups vegetable stock
Kernels from 2–3 ears corn	2–3 cups corn kernels (kernels from 2–3 ears of corn)
225g/8 oz diced fresh or tinned tomatoes	1 cup chopped fresh or canned tomatoes
¼ teaspoon grated fresh ginger root, or to taste	¼ teaspoon grated fresh ginger root, or to taste
3–4 tablespoons Greek yogurt, *crème fraîche*, or sour cream	3–4 tablespoons Greek yoghurt, *crème fraîche*, or light sour cream
325g/12 oz fusilli lunghi or other pasta of choice	12 oz fusilli lunghi or other pasta of choice
100g/4 oz mild white cheese such as mozzarella, mild Cheddar, etc., diced	¼ lb/4 oz mild white cheese (Jack, mozzarella, etc.), diced
3–4 tablespoons chopped fresh coriander leaves	3–4 tablespoons chopped cilantro

1. Lightly sauté the onions, garlic and green (bell) pepper in olive oil until softened, then add chilli and courgettes (zucchini). Cook for 5 minutes or so, then add the stock and raise the heat, letting the stock evaporate to about half its original volume.
2. Add the corn and tomatoes and continue to cook over high heat for 5–10 minutes or until the corn is cooked through and the mixture has thickened and is saucelike, but remains thinner than most pasta sauces.
3. Season with ginger root and stir in the yogurt, *crème fraîche* or sour cream. Keep warm.
4. Cook pasta until *al dente*. Drain, then toss with sauce and cheese. Serve sprinkled with fresh coriander leaves (cilantro).

Pasta with Green Beans, Red (Bell) Peppers, Olives, Basil and Pine Nuts

SERVES 4–6

A gaily coloured dish with fresh and lively flavours. The amounts given need not be followed exactly.

2 red peppers, diced
6 cloves garlic, chopped
3 tablespoons olive oil
Salt and freshly ground black pepper,
    to taste
450g/1 lb spaghetti
225g/8 oz green beans, cut into bite-
    sized lengths
3 tablespoons toasted pine nuts
About 15 Kalamata or similar black
    Mediterranean-style olives, pitted
    and quartered
About 10 fresh basil leaves, thinly
    sliced

2 red bell peppers, diced
6 cloves garlic, chopped
3 tablespoons olive oil
Salt and freshly ground black pepper,
    to taste
1 lb spaghetti
1 cup green beans, cut into bite-sized
    lengths
3 tablespoons toasted pine nuts
About 15 Kalamata or similar black
    Mediterranean-style olives, pitted
    and quartered
About 10 fresh basil leaves, thinly
    sliced

1. Sauté the (bell) peppers with half the garlic in the olive oil until softened and lightly browned in places. Season with salt and black pepper. Set aside and keep warm.
2. Boil the spaghetti until half cooked, then add the green beans and continue cooking until both the beans and pasta are *al dente*. Drain.
3. Toss the spaghetti and green beans with the sautéed (bell) peppers, the remaining garlic, the pine nuts, olives and basil. Serve immediately or at warm room temperature.

Variation

Substitute 4 diced and well-drained tomatoes for the red (bell) peppers.

Spaghetti with Basil-Scented Courgette (Zucchini) Shreds and Cream

SERVES 4–6

This is a rich and succulent dish, perfect for a first course or in more generous portions as a main course or even a midnight feast.

6 courgettes
2 onions, chopped
2 cloves garlic, chopped
25g/1 oz butter
375ml/12 fl oz single cream
75g/3 oz Parmesan cheese, freshly grated
450g/1 lb spaghetti
1 egg, lightly beaten
Salt and freshly ground black pepper, as needed
Handful of fresh basil leaves, thinly sliced, or large pinch of dried basil or mixed herbs, crushed between the fingers

6 small to medium sized zucchini
2 onions, chopped
2 cloves garlic, chopped
2 tablespoons butter
1½ cups whipping cream
¾ cup freshly grated Parmesan cheese
1 lb spaghetti
1 egg, lightly beaten
Salt and freshly ground black pepper, as needed
2–3 tablespoons fresh basil leaves, thinly sliced, or large pinch of dried basil or mixed herbs, crushed between the fingers

1. Shred the courgettes (zucchini) on the large holes of a grater. Leave in a colander to drain for an hour if you have time. (Another trick for ridding them of excess water is to spin briefly in a salad spinner.)
2. Lightly sauté the onions and garlic in the butter until softened, then add the shredded courgettes (zucchini), and cook for a minute or so over medium to high heat until half tender, half crunchy. Add the cream, raise the heat and cook until slightly thickened, then stir in half the cheese. Set aside.
3. Meanwhile, cook the spaghetti until *al dente*. Drain. Stir the beaten egg into the sauce, then toss this mixture with the spaghetti, letting the heat of the spaghetti thicken the sauce. If the egg does not cook from the heat of the pasta alone, place it over medium heat for a few minutes, stirring all the time, until it thickens.
4. Season with salt if needed, black pepper, and the basil or herbs, then serve immediately, sprinkled with the remaining Parmesan cheese.

Pasta with Courgettes (Zucchini), Beaten Egg and Cheese

SERVES 4

This is typical southern Italian fare, based on what is at hand. In the summer this means lots of courgettes (zucchini) as anyone who has ever grown them in a sunny climate will tell you.

325g/12 oz tubular pasta such as ziti, penne, elbow pasta, etc.
2 medium sized courgettes, diced
6–10 cloves garlic, chopped
2 tablespoons olive oil
2 eggs, lightly beaten
50g/2 oz Parmesan cheese, freshly grated
Salt and freshly ground black pepper, to taste

12 oz tubular pasta such as ziti, penne, elbow pasta, etc.
2 medium sized zucchini, diced
6–10 cloves garlic, chopped
2 tablespoons olive oil
2 eggs, lightly beaten
½ cup freshly grated Parmesan cheese
Salt and freshly ground black pepper, to taste

1. Boil the pasta and courgettes (zucchini) together until *al dente*, adding the courgette (zucchini) when the pasta is half done. Drain.
2. Meanwhile, heat the garlic in the olive oil but do not brown.
3. Toss the drained pasta and courgettes (zucchini) in this garlic-olive oil mixture, then toss with the beaten eggs, then with the cheese.
4. Serve immediately, seasoned with black pepper and with salt, if needed.

Variation

Pasta with Sautéed Courgettes (Zucchini), Mozzarella Cheese and Egg: Slice rather than dice the courgettes (zucchini) and sauté them with the garlic in the olive oil instead of cooking with the pasta. Toss the sautéed courgettes (zucchini) with the cooked pasta, beaten eggs and Parmesan cheese, then add 225g/8 oz (about ⅔ cup) mozzarella cheese, diced (the firm kind, not the soft, fresh, milky kind) and toss together until the cheese becomes soft and melting.

Orzo Pilaff with Tomatoes and Diced Courgettes (Zucchini)

SERVES 4

Sautéed courgettes (zucchini) are simmered in tomato sauce and stock then cooked with tiny, rice-shaped orzo. Then diced white cheese is spooned in to melt into a rich, thick sauce.

Other vegetables may be used instead of the courgettes (zucchini): diced carrots, green beans, peas, fennel, asparagus, onion – whatever looks good either in the garden or at the grocers. I often use a combination of whatever is in season.

3 cloves garlic, chopped
2 courgettes, diced
2–3 tablespoons olive oil
675g/1½ lb ripe fresh tomatoes, diced, or 1 400g/14 oz tin chopped tomatoes
500ml/16 fl oz vegetable stock
Dried mixed herbs to taste
325g/12 oz orzo
175–225g/6–8 oz mild white cheese such as fontina or mozzarella, diced
Salt and freshly ground black pepper, to taste
1 tablespoon chopped fresh parsley or other fresh herbs

3 cloves garlic, chopped
2 zucchini, diced
2–3 tablespoons olive oil
1½ lb ripe fresh tomatoes, diced, or 2 cups canned chopped tomatoes
2 cups vegetable stock
Dried mixed herbs to taste
12 oz orzo
¾–1 cup diced or coarsely grated mild white cheese such as fontina or Monterey Jack
Salt and freshly ground black pepper, to taste
1 tablespoon chopped fresh parsley or other fresh herbs

1. Sauté the garlic and courgettes (zucchini) in the olive oil until lightly golden, then add the tomatoes, stock and dried herbs and bring to the boil.
2. Stir in the orzo, cover and reduce the heat. Cook for about 10 minutes or until the orzo has absorbed most of the liquid and is al dente. Taste halfway through and add more water or stock if needed. It should be fairly thick and soupy when cooked through.
3. Stir in the cheese and heat for a few minutes to melt. Season with salt and black pepper, then stir in the parsley or other herbs and serve immediately.

Pasta with Puréed Red (Bell) Pepper Sauce

SERVES 4–6

This is one of the easiest yet most elegant sauces I know. It takes two hours to cook, but the big plus is that most of that time it simply sits in the oven, slowly baking its way to strong and delicious flavour. However, if baking for a such long time is impractical, the vegetable mixture may be slowly sautéed on top of the stove instead.

6 red peppers, diced
2 yellow peppers, diced
3 onions, diced
3–4 ripe fresh tomatoes, diced
10–12 cloves garlic, coarsely chopped
Salt and freshly ground black pepper,
   to taste
2 tablespoons olive oil
75–150ml/3–5 fl oz single cream
450g/1 lb fettuccine or other pasta
Finely chopped fresh basil or marjoram
   leaves, to serve (optional)
Freshly grated Parmesan cheese, to
   serve

6 red bell peppers, diced
2 yellow bell peppers, diced
3 onions, diced
3–4 ripe fresh tomatoes, diced
10–12 cloves garlic, coarsely chopped
Salt and freshly ground black pepper,
   to taste
2 tablespoons olive oil
⅓–⅔ cup whipping cream
1 lb fettuccine or other pasta
2–3 tablespoons finely chopped fresh
   basil or marjoram leaves to serve
   (optional)
Freshly grated Parmesan cheese, to serve

1. Place the red and yellow (bell) peppers, onion, tomatoes and garlic in an earthenware casserole.
2. Sprinkle with salt and toss with the olive oil, then bake, uncovered, in the oven at 180°C/350°F/gas mark 4 for 2 hours, turning once or twice. (This may be done up to two days in advance if you like.)
3. Blend the vegetables in a liquidizer (blender) or food processor until puréed, then add enough cream to form a sauce and purée together until fairly smooth. Push through a sieve to rid the sauce of the stringy bits of skin. Season with salt and black pepper. Keep warm.

4. Cook the pasta until *al dente*. Drain and toss with the sauce. Garnish with herbs and Parmesan cheese.

Variation

Creamy Red (Bell) Pepper Bisque: This creamy purée makes the basis for a superb soup. Purée as above, using about three quarters of the vegetable mixture. Sieve, then combine this smooth purée with 350ml/12 fl oz (1½ cups) vegetable stock, a pinch of fennel seeds, and the reserved baked vegetables. Heat until bubbles form around the edge. Serve immediately, garnished with a thin sprinkling of fresh basil.

Pasta with Red, Yellow and Green (Bell) Peppers and Black Olives

SERVES 6

Slow-baked (bell) peppers with salty black olives and a splash of tomato is delicious tossed with thin spaghettini or capellini. Add a dash of balsamic vinegar at the end for a tangy accent and to help round out the flavours.

3 green peppers, diced
2 yellow peppers, diced
2 red peppers, diced
15 cloves garlic, chopped
Salt and freshly ground black pepper, to taste
3–4 tablespoons olive oil
4–6 ripe fresh tomatoes, diced or 115–180g/4–6 oz diced tinned tomatoes
10–15 Kalamata or other Greek-style black olives, pitted and halved
Dash of balsamic vinegar
Finely chopped fresh thyme, marjoram, basil, or other herb, to serve
450g/1 lb pasta of choice: either long strands such as fettuccine or chunky shapes such as seashells, penne, etc.
Coarsely grated or shaved Parmesan cheese to serve

3 green bell peppers, diced
2 yellow bell peppers, diced
2 red bell peppers, diced
15 cloves garlic, chopped
Salt and freshly ground black pepper, to taste
3–4 tablespoons olive oil
½–⅔ cup diced fresh or canned tomatoes
10–15 Kalamata or other Greek-style black olives, pitted and halved
Dash of balsamic vinegar
2–3 tablespoons finely chopped fresh thyme, basil, marjoram, oregano, parsley, etc.
1 lb pasta either long strands such as spaghetti or fettuccine, or chunky shapes such as seashells, penne, etc.
Coarsely grated or shaved Parmesan or similar cheese, to serve

1. Place the (bell) peppers and garlic in a flat earthenware dish. Toss with salt, black pepper and the olive oil then bake uncovered in the oven at 200°C/400°F/gas mark 6 for 1½ hours, tossing once or twice during this time. Add tomatoes and return to the oven for another 30 minutes.
2. Remove from the oven and add the olives and herbs. Season with a dash of balsamic vinegar, and keep warm.
3. Cook the pasta until *al dente*. Drain and toss with the (bell) pepper mixture, adding more herbs if you like. Serve sprinkled with the coarsely grated or shaved Parmesan cheese.

Variations

Serve the above pasta sprinkled with goat cheese instead of Parmesan cheese, and let it melt in seductively.

Piperade Pasta: Cook 450g/1 lb spaghetti until *al dente*, then toss with 2 lightly beaten eggs mixed with a generous amount of freshly grated Parmesan cheese. Combine with the above vegetable mixture, but omit the olives and sprinkle the finished dish with several tablespoons of chopped fresh basil.

Pasta with Provençal Flavours

SERVES 4–6

Once I wandered into a café in Arles in Provence and was virtually held captive by the owner, who was fixated, predictably enough, on Van Gogh. His rambling life story was as muddled as the poor artist's, but this artiste was of the kitchen rather than the canvas. And in what seemed like a reward for a nearly unendurable afternoon of listening on my part (I was young; my French was not brilliant; I could not figure out how to get up and leave) the café owner served me up portion upon portion of dishes he had invented. They were all related in some obscure way to Van Gogh, and they were all outstandingly delicious. This recipe is my version of the pasta dish he served, redolent with the orange, herb, fennel and saffron scents of Provence.

1 onion, chopped
1 red pepper, diced
3 cloves garlic, chopped
2 tablespoons olive oil
100ml/4 fl oz dry white wine
8 ripe fresh tomatoes, chopped, or 1
    400g/14 oz tin chopped tomatoes
100ml/4 fl oz tomato juice or passata
    (if using fresh tomatoes)
Pinch of sugar (optional)
1.25cm/½ inch piece orange rind
Generous pinch of fennel seeds or ½
    bulb fresh fennel, coarsely chopped
1 tablespoon tomato paste
Generous pinch of herbes de Provence
    or other dried mixed herbs
Pinch of saffron threads
Salt and freshly ground black pepper,
    to taste
325–450g/12–16 oz pasta such as
    spaghettini or capellini
Finely chopped fresh basil, to serve
Beetroot, Tomato and Onion Relish
    (optional; see below)

1 onion, chopped
1 red bell pepper, chopped
3 cloves garlic, chopped
2 tablespoons olive oil
½ cup dry white wine
8 ripe fresh tomatoes, diced, or 1 cup
    canned diced tomatoes
½ cup tomato juice, passata, or sauce
    (if using fresh tomatoes)
Pinch of sugar (optional)
½ inch piece orange zest
Generous pinch of fennel seeds or ½
    bulb fresh fennel, coarsely chopped
1 tablespoon tomato paste
Generous pinch of herbes de Provence
    or other dried mixed herbs
Pinch of saffron threads
Salt and freshly ground black pepper,
    to taste
12–16 oz pasta such as spaghettini or
    capellini
2–3 tablespoons chopped fresh basil, to
    serve
Beet, Tomato and Onion Relish
    (optional; see below)

1. Lightly sauté the onion, red (bell) pepper, and garlic in the olive oil until softened.
2. Add the white wine and boil until reduced

in volume by at least half. Add the tomatoes and juice, the sugar, if needed, orange rind (zest), fennel and tomato paste and simmer for about 10 minutes or until full flavoured.

3. Season the sauce with the mixed herbs (herbes de Provence). Toast the saffron in an ungreased frying pan (skillet) until it darkens slightly, crush into a powder with the back of a spoon or a mortar and pestle, then add to the sauce along with salt and black pepper.

4. Cook the pasta until *al dente*, drain. Toss with the sauce and serve sprinkled with basil.

Tomato, Beetroot (Beet), and Onion Relish: This tangy, simple-to-prepare relish makes a refreshing addition. Just combine 3 diced ripe fresh tomatoes with 2 diced small cooked beetroot (beets), and half a chopped onion. Season with 1 clove chopped garlic, if liked, and dress with olive oil and lemon juice or wine vinegar to taste.

Variation

Couscous Provençal: Prepare the sauce above but double the amount of saffron and add 500ml/16 fl oz (2 cups) hot vegetable stock. Pour this mixture over 325g/12 oz instant couscous, dot with a little butter, and cover. Leave for 10 minutes to absorb the liquid, then taste for seasoning. If it is too dry or uncooked, add a little more liquid and heat over a medium flame. Omit the beetroot relish.

Pasta with Tomato and Courgette (Zucchini) Sauce

SERVES 4–6

While courgettes (zucchini) are usually at their best when cooked only lightly, in this traditional sauce they are simmered until they softly fall apart.

3–5 cloves garlic, chopped
2 tablespoons olive oil
250ml/8 fl oz tomato passata
3–4 small to medium courgettes, cut into bite-sized chunks
325g/12 oz pasta of choice such as fettuccine, spaghetti, etc.
Freshly grated Parmesan cheese to serve
Chopped fresh parsley, basil, thyme or other herbs of choice, to serve

3–5 cloves garlic, chopped
2 tablespoons olive oil
1 cup tomato passata or tomato sauce
3–4 small to medium zucchini, cut into bite-sized chunks
12 oz pasta of choice such as fettuccine, spaghetti, etc.
Freshly grated Parmesan cheese to serve
2–3 tablespoons chopped fresh parsley, mixed with basil, thyme or other herbs of choice, to serve

1. Lightly sauté the garlic in the olive oil until fragrant but not browned. Add the tomato passata (or tomato sauce) and courgettes (zucchini). Cover and simmer until the courgettes (zucchini) are falling apart, adding water or stock if needed to keep a saucelike consistency.

2. Cook the pasta until *al dente*. Drain.

3. Serve the pasta tossed with the sauce and sprinkled with Parmesan cheese and herbs.

Fettuccine with Creamy Pumpkin and Red (Bell) Pepper Sauce

SERVES 4

This golden-hued sauce is suave and creamy, with sweet, earthy pumpkin (or other winter squash) and fresh red (bell) peppers, enlivened with a flurry of pungent Parmesan. It is a delicate and memorable dish, best served as a rich first course rather than a main plateful.

1 onion, chopped
1 clove garlic, chopped
40g/1½ oz butter
450g/1 lb pumpkin, peeled and diced
½ red pepper, diced
½ vegetable stock cube
250ml/8 fl oz water
300ml/10 fl oz single cream
Large pinch of dried thyme
Black and cayenne pepper to taste
325g/12 oz dried fettuccine or 450g/1 lb fresh fettuccine
Freshly grated Parmesan cheese to serve

1 onion, chopped
1 clove garlic, chopped
3 tablespoons butter
1 lb winter squash such as Hubbard or acorn, or pumpkin, peeled and diced
½ red bell pepper, diced
½ vegetable bouillion cube
1 cup water
1¼ cups whipping cream
Large pinch of dried thyme
Black and cayenne pepper to taste
12 oz dried fettuccine or 1 lb fresh fettuccine
Freshly grated Parmesan cheese to serve

1. Lightly sauté the onion and garlic in two-thirds of the butter until softened, then add the pumpkin (or winter squash) and sauté until lightly browned and almost tender. Add the red (bell) pepper and continue cooking for a few minutes.
2. Add stock cube (bouillion cube) and water, raise the heat, and cook until the liquid is reduced by about three-quarters. The pumpkin should be cooked through.
3. Add the cream, heat through, and season with the thyme, black pepper, and cayenne pepper. Keep this mixture warm while you cook the pasta. (The sauce may be made in advance, then reheated with a little water when ready to serve.)
4. When the pasta is *al dente*, drain and toss with the sauce, then serve immediately, each portion topped with a good dusting of Parmesan cheese.

Farfalle with Pumpkin and Mild Red Chilli

SERVES 4–6

The spicy flavours of America's Southwest: garlic, pumpkin, tomatoes and mild red chilli season this pasta. It is informal, dryish rather than saucy, and very easily put together. For health reasons the dish may be made with olive oil, and it is good, but I must confess that I often use butter: the taste of butter-sautéed garlic, pumpkin and red chilli is utterly seductive.

Any sort of chunky or flat pasta may be used instead of the farfalle.

125g/8 oz pumpkin, peeled and diced
40g/1½ oz butter
5–8 cloves garlic, coarsely chopped
5–8 ripe fresh or well-drained tinned tomatoes, diced
2 teaspoons mild red chilli powder
1 teaspoon paprika
¼ teaspoon cumin, or to taste
450g/1 lb pasta of choice
Salt to taste
50g/2 oz Parmesan cheese, freshly grated

½ lb winter squash such as Hubbard or acorn, or pumpkin, peeled and diced
3 tablespoons butter
5–8 cloves garlic, coarsely chopped
5–8 ripe fresh or well-drained canned tomatoes, diced
2 teaspoons red chilli powder or pure ground mild chillies such as ancho .
1 teaspoon paprika
¼ teaspoon cumin, or to taste
1 lb pasta of choice
Salt to taste
½ cup freshly grated Parmesan cheese

1. Lightly sauté the pumpkin in half the butter for several minutes until just becoming tender, then add the garlic and cook for another moment or two.
2. Add the tomatoes, stir around and cook through, then sprinkle in the chilli powder, paprika and cumin. Cook a minute or two longer, then remove from the heat.
3. Meanwhile, boil the pasta until *al dente*.
4. Drain and toss with the remaining butter and the sauce. Season with salt to taste and toss with Parmesan cheese. Serve immediately.

Pasta with Courgettes (Zucchini), Red (Bell) Peppers and Tomatoes

SERVES 4–6

In this dish spaghetti is tossed with a ratatouille-like vegetable mixture. Sautéing the onions and (bell) peppers separately from the other vegetables is very important: you end up with the taste of each vegetable distinct from the others, rather than the flavours simply merging together. The vegetable mixture is even better the day after preparation; make a double batch for an appetizer the first day and a pasta dish the day after.

2 red peppers, cut into strips or diced
1 onion, coarsely chopped
3 tablespoons olive oil, or as needed
3 courgettes, cut into bite-sized pieces
3 cloves garlic, chopped
Salt to taste
225g/8 oz diced fresh or tinned
    tomatoes, drained (reserve the juice)
Several sprigs of fresh rosemary
100ml/4 fl oz tomato juice
2 tablespoons tomato paste
325–450g/12–16 oz spaghetti
Freshly grated Parmesan cheese to
    serve

2 red bell peppers, cut into strips or
    diced
1 onion, coarsely chopped
3 tablespoons olive oil, or as needed
3 zucchini, cut into bite-sized pieces
3 cloves garlic, chopped
Salt to taste
8 ripe fresh tomatoes, diced, or 1 cup
    canned diced tomatoes, drained
    (reserve the juice)
Several sprigs of fresh rosemary
½ cup tomato juice
2 tablespoons tomato paste
12–16 oz spaghetti
Freshly grated Parmesan cheese to
    serve

1. Sauté the (bell) peppers and the onion in a small amount of the oil until softened, then place in an ovenproof earthenware casserole.
2. In the same pan you used for the peppers and onions, sauté the courgettes (zucchini) in several batches, using just a little olive oil. Do not brown, just let some turn a light golden. Add the garlic and salt to taste, then place in the casserole. Add the diced tomatoes and rosemary sprigs.
3. Put the tomato juice and any juices from the drained tomatoes in the sauté pan. Cook down until reduced in volume by about half, then pour over the vegetables.
4. Bake the vegetable mixture in the oven at 190°C/375°F/gas mark 5 for 30 minutes or so, then remove. If the mixture is very liquidy, pour the juices into a pan, reduce over a high heat, then pour back over the vegetables. Season well with salt and stir in the tomato paste to thicken the mixture.
5. Cook the pasta until *al dente*, then drain. Toss with the vegetables and serve immediately, each portion sprinkled with Parmesan cheese.

Garlic-Parsley Macaroni with Cauliflower, Courgettes (Zucchini), and Red (Bell) Peppers

SERVES 4

5 cloves garlic, coarsely chopped
4 tablespoons olive oil
2 red peppers, cut into strips or diced
½ green pepper, cut into strips or diced
2 courgettes, sliced
½ head cauliflower, divided into small florets
3 tablespoons tomato paste
100–175ml/4–6 fl oz water
Salt and freshly ground black or cayenne pepper, to taste
Handful of fresh parsley, coarsely chopped
325g/12 oz small macaroni

5 cloves garlic, coarsely chopped
¼ cup olive oil
2 red bell peppers, cut into strips or diced
½ green bell pepper, cut into strips or diced
2 zucchini, sliced
½ small cauliflower, divided up into small florets
3 heaping tablespoons tomato paste
½–⅔ cup water
Salt and freshly ground black or cayenne pepper, to taste
2 tablespoons fresh parsley, coarsely chopped
12 oz small macaroni

1. Sauté half the garlic in half the olive oil, then add the red and green (bell) peppers and cook together for a few minutes until softened. Remove from the pan.
2. Brown the courgettes (zucchini) briefly in the pan, then remove. Sauté the cauliflower for a few minutes. Return the (bell) peppers and courgettes (zucchini) to the pan with the cauliflower, then add the tomato paste and water. Season with salt and black or cayenne pepper and simmer for 10–15 minutes, or until the vegetables are tender.
Add half the parsley and set aside.
3. Cook the pasta until _al dente_. Drain.
4. Heat the remaining garlic in the remaining olive oil until lightly golden, then add the drained pasta. Season with salt and black or cayenne pepper.
5. Serve the pasta topped with the vegetable mixture. This is good without cheese, but I sometimes serve it with a fresh vegetable relish, such as beetroot (beets), fennel, diced carrot and tomatoes, tossed in vinaigrette.

Macaroni with Roasted Green (Bell) Peppers, Tomatoes and Goat Cheese

SERVES 4

Strongly flavoured with the taste of Italy's sun-drenched South, this dish is fresh tasting and vibrant. That fresh quality, however, depends upon ripe, sweet and tangy tomatoes: when not available, another recipe is probably your best bet.

2 green peppers
4 cloves garlic, chopped
3–4 tablespoons olive oil
8–10 small, very ripe fresh tomatoes, cut into eighths
325g/12 oz shortcut macaroni
1 tablespoon tomato paste
150g/5 oz fresh goat cheese, preferably garlic- and herb-flavoured
Dried oregano, crumbled, to taste
Salt and freshly ground black pepper, to taste
Freshly grated cheese such as Parmesan or other hard grating cheese to serve

2 green bell peppers
4 cloves garlic, chopped
3–4 tablespoons olive oil
8–10 small, very ripe fresh tomatoes, cut into eighths
12 oz macaroni, preferably a small chubby shape
1 tablespoon tomato paste
5 oz fresh goat cheese, preferably garlic- and herb-flavoured one
Dried oregano, crumbled, to taste
Salt and freshly ground black pepper, to taste
Freshly grated cheese such as Parmesan or other hard grating cheese to serve

1. Roast the green (bell) peppers as described on page 262, then cut into large dice.
2. Heat half the garlic in about 2 tablespoons of the olive oil, then add the tomatoes and brown lightly, then add the diced (bell) peppers and simmer while the pasta cooks.
3. Meanwhile, cook the pasta until *al dente*. Drain.
4. Add the tomato paste to the vegetables, then toss in the drained pasta, the remaining chopped garlic, and the remaining olive oil.
5. Toss in half the goat cheese, season with oregano, salt and black pepper and top with the remaining goat cheese. Serve immediately, accompanied by the grated cheese.

Fettuccine with Yellow and Red (Bell) Peppers in Garlicky Cream Sauce

SERVES 4–6

Strips of roasted yellow and red (bell) pepper awash with garlic-scented cream, served over supple chewy fettuccine. Blanket it with lots of freshly grated Parmesan cheese, and serve as a first course, in bowls, followed by a sauté of asparagus and strong-flavoured mushrooms.

2 red peppers
2 yellow peppers
40g/1½ oz butter
4–6 cloves garlic, chopped
100ml/4 fl oz dry white wine
350ml/12 fl oz single cream
325–450g/12–16 oz fettuccine
Handful of fresh basil leaves, coarsely shredded
A generous amount of freshly grated Parmesan cheese, to serve
Freshly ground black pepper to taste

2 red bell peppers
2 yellow bell peppers
3 tablespoons butter
4–6 cloves garlic, chopped
½ cup dry white wine
1½ cups whipping cream
12–16 oz fettuccine
2–3 tablespoons coarsely shredded fresh basil leaves
A generous amount of freshly grated Parmesan cheese, to serve
Freshly ground black pepper to taste

1. Roast the (bell) peppers as described on page 262, then slice into thin strips. Set aside.
2. Heat the butter gently and warm the garlic in it. Add the (bell) peppers, then pour in the wine. Raise the heat and cook over high heat until the wine is reduced to a thickened, almost syrupy essence, then add the cream. Reduce heat and cook until warmed through and thickened, then remove from heat, cover, and keep warm.

3. Meanwhile, cook the pasta until *al dente*. Drain.
4. Toss the drained pasta with the sauce and the basil. Serve in shallow bowls, each portion blanketed with fresh Parmesan cheese. Pass the peppermill and a chunk of Parmesan cheese along with a grater for those who would like more cheese.

Rotelle, Penne or Rigatoni with Tomato Sauce, Broccoli and Ricotta Cheese

SERVES 4–6

Toothsome chewy pasta, served up with fennel-scented tomato sauce, punctuated with nuggets of broccoli and dollops of snowy ricotta cheese.

4–6 cloves garlic, chopped
1 small onion, chopped
1 small carrot, diced
1 small celery stalk, chopped
2 tablespoons olive oil
1½ teaspoons fennel seeds
1 teaspoon fresh thyme or ½ teaspoon dried thyme, crushed
Pinch of dried marjoram, crushed (optional)
675g/1½ lb ripe fresh tomatoes, chopped, or 1½ 400g/14 oz tins chopped tomatoes
1 small tin tomato puree
Pinch of sugar
2 tablespoons coarsely chopped fresh rosemary or 3 tablespoons thinly sliced fresh basil leaves
450g/1 lb rotelle, penne, or rigatoni
2 heads broccoli, cut into bite-sized florets
225g/8 oz fresh ricotta cheese
Freshly grated Parmesan, Pecorino, aged Asiago, or other grating cheese
Salt and freshly ground black pepper

4–6 cloves garlic, chopped
1 small onion, chopped
1 small carrot, chopped
1 small celery stalk, chopped
2 tablespoons olive oil
1½ teaspoons fennel seeds
1 teaspoon fresh thyme or ½ teaspoon dried thyme, crushed
Pinch of dried marjoram, crushed (optional)
1½ lb ripe fresh tomatoes, chopped or 2 cups chopped canned tomatoes
3 heaping tablespoons tomato paste
Pinch of sugar
2 tablespoons coarsely chopped fresh rosemary or 3 tablespoons thinly sliced fresh basil leaves
1 lb rotelle, penne, or rigatoni
2 heads broccoli, cut into bite-sized florets
8 oz fresh ricotta cheese
Freshly grated Parmesan, Pecorino, aged Asiago, or similar cheese, to serve
Salt and freshly ground black pepper

1. Sauté the garlic, onion, carrot and celery in the olive oil until softened, then add the fennel seeds, thyme, marjoram, if using, tomatoes, tomato paste, and sugar.
2. Bring to the boil, then reduce the heat, and simmer uncovered until thick and flavourful, about 10 minutes. Remove from the heat and add the rosemary or basil.
3. Cook the pasta until half done, then add the broccoli and continue cooking until both are *al dente*. Drain.
4. Toss the broccoli and pasta with the sauce, then serve immediately, each portion topped with a generous dollop of ricotta cheese and a sprinkling of grated cheese. Season with salt and black pepper, if needed.

Fettuccine with Broccoli and Spinach and Carrot-Butter

SERVES 4–6

450g/1 lb spinach leaves	1 lb spinach leaves
300–325g/10–12 oz broccoli, cut into florets, the stems peeled and sliced	10–12 oz broccoli, cut into florets, the stems peeled and sliced
4 young carrots	4 young carrots
125ml/4 fl oz dry white wine	½ cup dry white wine
125ml/4 fl oz vegetable stock	½ cup vegetable stock
4–5 shallots, chopped	4–5 shallots, chopped
2 cloves garlic, chopped	2 cloves garlic, chopped
Pinch of tarragon	Pinch of tarragon
4 tablespoons butter, cut into 6–8 pieces	4 tablespoons butter, cut into 6–8 pieces
325g/12 oz fettuccine, preferably fresh	12 oz fettuccine, preferably fresh

1. Steam the spinach until just bright green. Remove from the heat and leave to cool. Squeeze out the excess liquid and chop into bite-sized pieces.
2. Steam the broccoli until bright green and still crunchy, then remove from the steamer and set aside with the spinach.
3. Diced two of the carrots and place in a small pan with the wine, stock, shallots, garlic and tarragon. Bring to the boil, cover, and cook until the carrots are tender. Uncover and boil until the liquid is reduced to about 2 tablespoons. Remove from heat.
4. Mash the cooked carrots with their liquid, using a fork or food processor. When the mixture cools to just warm, whisk in the small chunks of butter, one or two at a time, letting it combine into a creamy sauce before adding more. Set aside.
5. Grate the remaining carrots.
6. Cook the pasta until _al dente_. Drain and toss with the spinach and broccoli, then spoon on the carrot-butter and serve immediately, sprinkled with the grated carrots.

Fettuccine or Tagliatelle with Creamy Onion Sauce

SERVES 6

This sauce of sautéed onions and garlic awash with nutmeg-scented cream is as delicious as it is unusual. A generous sprinkling of crunchy toasted breadcrumbs gives the dish character and makes it outstanding.

Since it is fairly rich, serve as a first course or side dish.

50g/2 oz stale peasant-style bread such as ciabatta
2 tablespoons vegetable oil or 25g/1 oz butter, for frying breadcrumbs
Salt and freshly ground black pepper, to taste
6 onions, coarsely chopped
3 cloves garlic, coarsely chopped
40g/1½ oz butter
600ml/1 pint single cream
Pinch of freshly grated nutmeg
450g/1 lb fettuccine or tagliatelle
Freshly grated Parmesan cheese to serve

2 oz (2 large slices) stale peasant-style style bread such as ciabatta
2 tablespoons vegetable oil or butter, for toasting breadcrumbs
Salt and freshly ground black pepper, to taste
6 onions, coarsely chopped
3 cloves garlic, coarsely chopped
3 tablespoons butter
2–2¼ cups whipping cream
Pinch of freshly grated nutmeg
1 lb fettuccine or tagliatelle
Freshly grated Parmesan cheese to serve

1. Grate the bread on the large holes of a grater to make crumbs. Toast the crumbs in the vegetable oil or butter in a heavy frying pan (skillet) over medium heat until golden brown. Remove from the heat, season with salt and black pepper, and set aside.
2. Sauté the onion and garlic in the remaining butter until lightly browned. Stir in the cream, cook through a minute or two, then season with the nutmeg and salt and black pepper. Set aside.
3. Meanwhile, cook the pasta until *al dente*.
4. Drain and toss the pasta in the sauce, then serve sprinkled generously with the toasted breadcrumbs and Parmesan cheese.

Three Spaghettini Dishes Made with Braised Onions

SERVES 4–6

Onions, braised until golden and caramelized as if you were making onion soup or pissaladière, make a delicious basis for simple, gutsy pasta dishes. Since the onions are so tender and sweet, they are best combined with tangy, acidic or pungent ingredients, such as capers, tomatoes, red wine, etc.

Below is the method for braising the onions. That is followed by three variations, all as different from each other as they are good. Since the braised onions make a savoury, forceful sauce I especially like them on thin strands of spaghettini, though the thicker spaghetti could be used instead.

900g/2 lbs onions, thinly sliced
2–3 tablespoons olive oil

1. Toss the onions with the olive oil in a heavy pan. Cover, and cook over very low heat, stirring occasionally, for about 30 minutes or until the onions have softened and turned lightly golden.
2. Remove the lid and stir, then return the lid and continue to cook for another 30–40 minutes over low to medium heat, adding a little more olive oil if needed to keep the onions from sticking. In the end the onions should be meltingly tender, slightly browned and sticky in parts. Use as the basis for any of the following three recipes.

Braised Onions with Red Wine and Tomato

SERVES 4–6

The shreds of onion take on a glazed, translucent quality and the red wine evaporates almost completely, leaving behind its tell-tale deep red colour and equally deep flavour.

Braised onions from above recipe
350ml/12 fl oz dry red wine – it doesn't have to be a brilliant wine, but should be good enough for pleasant drinking
2–3 tablespoons tomato paste
1–2 tablespoons chopped fresh parsley
Pinch of dried thyme, herbes de Provence or mixed herbs
Salt and freshly ground black pepper, to taste
450g/1 lb spaghettini
Squeeze of lemon juice
Freshly grated Parmesan or other hard grating cheese to serve

Braised onions from above recipe
1½ cups dry red wine
2–3 heaping tablespoons tomato paste
1–2 tablespoons chopped fresh parsley
Pinch of dried thyme, herbes de Provence or mixed herbs
Salt and freshly ground black pepper, to taste
1 lb spaghettini
Squeeze of lemon juice
Freshly grated Parmesan cheese or other hard grating cheese to serve

1. Put the braised onions in a heavy pan and add the red wine. Cook over high heat until the wine has evaporated.
2. Remove from the heat and add the tomato paste, parsley, dried thyme or other herbs and salt and black pepper. Set aside and keep warm.

3. Meanwhile, cook the spaghettini until *al dente*. Drain and toss with the onions, then serve immediately, with a squeeze of lemon juice and some freshly grated cheese.

Spaghettini with Provençal Onion Sauce, Seasoned with Capers and Tomatoes

SERVES 4–6

3 cloves garlic, chopped
2 tablespoons olive oil
12 ripe fresh tomatoes, peeled, seeded
    and diced or 1½ 400g/14 oz tins
    chopped tomatoes
Braised onions from first recipe
Large pinch of dried thyme
Pinch of sugar
Salt and freshly ground black pepper,
    to taste
2 tablespoons capers
450g/1 lb spaghettini
Freshly grated Parmesan or other hard
    grating cheese to serve

3 cloves garlic, chopped
2 tablespoons olive oil
12 ripe fresh tomatoes, peeled, seeded
    and diced or 2 cups canned
    chopped tomatoes
Braised onions from first recipe
Large pinch of dried thyme
Pinch of sugar
Salt and freshly ground black pepper,
    to taste
2 tablespoons capers
1 lb spaghettini
Freshly grated Parmesan or other hard
    grating cheese to serve

1. Heat the garlic in the olive oil and when fragrant but not browned, add the tomatoes. Stir through to perfume and heat the tomatoes, then remove from the heat and toss with braised onions. Season with the thyme, sugar, salt and black pepper and capers. Set aside and keep warm.

2. Meanwhile, cook the spaghettini until *al dente*. Drain and toss with the sauce. Serve immediately, sprinkled generously with cheese.

Pasta with Pissaladière-Style Sauce of Onions and Olives

SERVES 4–6

Braised onions and salty black olives makes an intriguing plateful: the combination is traditional for the Niçoise flat bread pissaladière, and while it may be a surprise served on pasta, it is hearty and delicious.

450g/1 lb spaghettini
Braised onions from first recipe
20–30 black Italian, French or Greek
   olives, pitted and cut into quarters
Marjoram, thyme or other herbs,
   either fresh or dried, to taste
Salt and freshly ground black pepper,
   to taste
Freshly grated Parmesan cheese to
   serve

1 lb spaghettini
Braised onions from first recipe
20–30 black Italian, French or Greek
   olives, pitted and cut into quarters
Marjoram, thyme or other herbs,
   either fresh or dried, to taste
Salt and freshly ground black pepper
Freshly grated Parmesan cheese to
   serve

1. Cook the spaghettini until *al dente*.
2. Meanwhile, heat the braised onions over medium high heat, then remove from the stove. Add the olives, herbs, salt if needed (the olives are salty) and the black pepper.
3. Drain the pasta and toss with the onion sauce, then serve immediately, sprinkled generously with cheese.

Pasta with Aubergine (Eggplant) and Tomato Sauce

SERVES 6

A savoury sauce of tomatoes simmered with red wine and chunks of sautéed aubergine (eggplant), then tossed with pasta and mozzarella cheese until the cheese is just warm and softened.

1 large or 2 small aubergines, cut into large dice
Several tablespoons of olive oil
1 onion, diced
3 cloves garlic, chopped
350ml/12 fl oz tomato passata
100–175ml/4–6 fl oz dry red wine
Pinch of sugar (optional)
Salt and freshly ground black pepper, to taste
Large pinch of dried oregano, crushed between the fingers
325–450g/12–16 oz spaghetti, fusilli, rigatoni, or other hearty pasta shape
225g/8 oz mozzarella cheese (a firm one, for slicing) or other mild white cheese, cut into bite-sized pieces

1 large or 2 small eggplants, cut into large dice
Several tablespoons of olive oil
1 onion, diced
3 cloves garlic, chopped
1½ cups tomato passata or tomato sauce
½–¾ cups dry red wine
Pinch of sugar (optional)
Salt and freshly ground black pepper, to taste
Large pinch of dried oregano, crushed between the fingers
12–16 oz spaghetti, fusilli, rigatoni, or other hearty pasta shape
8 oz/1 cup diced mild white cheese such as mozzarella, Monterey Jack, etc.

1. Sauté the aubergine (eggplant) in olive oil until lightly browned. Remove from the pan and set aside. (The aubergine [eggplant] may be salted, rinsed and drained before browning if preferred. This will remove any bitterness and prevent it from absorbing excess oil.)
2. Lightly sauté the onion and garlic in about 1 tablespoon of olive oil until softened, then add the tomato passata and red wine. Bring to the boil, then reduce the heat and simmer for 15–20 minutes or until richly flavoured. Season with sugar, if needed, salt and black pepper, and the oregano.
3. Return the browned aubergine (eggplant) to the sauce and continue to simmer while the pasta cooks.
4. Cook the pasta until *al dente*. Drain.
5. Toss the pasta with the sauce to mix well, then add the cheese and serve immediately.

Fusilli Siracusani

SICILIAN AUBERGINE [EGGPLANT] PASTA

SERVES 4–6

Diced aubergine (eggplant), roasted (bell) peppers, tomatoes and lots of black olives and capers season this garlicky, basil-scented tomato sauce that clings to the fat curly strands of pasta known as fusilli lunghi. Spaghetti is also delicious in this Sicilian dish, and may be used instead.

1 red pepper
1 yellow pepper
1 aubergine, cut into bite-sized pieces
Olive oil for sautéeing
5 cloves garlic, chopped
1 onion, thinly sliced
900g/2 lb ripe fresh tomatoes, diced, or 2 400g/14 oz tins chopped tomatoes
Pinch of sugar (optional)
4 tablespoons tomato paste
15 black olives such as Gaeta or Kalamata, pitted and diced
2 tablespoons capers
Dash of balsamic vinegar (optional)
450g/1 lb fusilli lunghi or spaghetti
Handful of fresh basil leaves, torn or coarsely chopped
Salt and freshly ground black pepper, to taste
Freshly grated Parmesan cheese to serve

1 red bell pepper
1 yellow bell pepper
1 eggplant, cut into bite-sized pieces
Olive oil for sautéeing
5 cloves garlic, chopped
1 onion, thinly sliced
2 lb ripe fresh tomatoes, diced or 3 cups canned chopped tomatoes
Pinch of sugar (optional)
4 tablespoons tomato paste
15 black olives such as Gaeta or Kalamata, pitted and diced
2 tablespoons capers
Dash of balsamic vinegar (optional)
1 lb fusilli lunghi or spaghetti
¼ cup fresh basil leaves, torn or coarsely chopped
Salt and freshly ground black pepper, to taste
Freshly grated Parmesan cheese to serve

1. Roast the (bell) peppers as described on page 262, then cut into strips. Set aside.
2. Brown the aubergine (eggplant) in as little olive oil as possible to avoid greasiness (it may be salted, rinsed and drained, then dried before browning, if preferred). Add the garlic and set aside.
3. Lightly brown the onions in a small amount of the olive oil, then add the tomatoes and cook over medium heat for about 15 minutes or until the consistency is saucelike.
4. Add the reserved (bell) peppers, aubergine (eggplant), and the tomato paste. Cook for another 15 minutes, or until the aubergine (eggplant) is tender, then add the olives and capers, plus the balsamic vinegar, if using. Taste for seasoning.
5. Cook the pasta until *al dente*, then drain. Toss with the sauce and lots of fresh basil. Serve with Parmesan cheese.

Penne or gnocchetti alla Boscaiola

PASTA WITH A PESTO OF MUSHROOMS AND BLACK OLIVES

SERVES 4–6

Mushrooms and olives cooked into a paste are used to cloak al dente pasta. It tastes outstanding with the woodsy scent and flavour of the forest.

Penne, gnocchetti and chunky pastas are a good choice: not only are they sturdy but the little hollows and folds trap bits of the savoury mushroom and olive paste. However, a flat, narrow pasta such as vermicelli or tagliarini is also quite good.

325g/12 oz mushrooms, coarsely shredded
2–3 cloves garlic, chopped
3–4 tablespoons olive oil, plus extra for tossing the pasta
100g/4 oz black olive paste or Kalamata olives, pitted and finely chopped
325–450g/12–16 oz penne, gnocchetti, or other chunky pasta
1½ teaspoons chopped fresh rosemary, or to taste
Large pinch of dried mixed herbs
Freshly ground black pepper to taste

¾ lb mushrooms, coarsely shredded
2–3 cloves garlic, chopped
3–4 tablespoons olive oil plus extra for tossing the pasta
½ cup black olive paste, or pitted and finely chopped Kalamata olives
12–16 oz penne, gnocchetti, or other chunky pasta
1½ teaspoons chopped fresh rosemary, or to taste
Large pinch of dried mixed herbs
Freshly ground black pepper to taste

1. Sauté the mushrooms and garlic in the olive oil until the mushrooms are cooked through and the mixture is quite pastelike. Add the olive paste and set aside.
2. Cook the pasta until *al dente*; drain.
3. Toss the pasta with a little olive oil and the rosemary, mixed herbs, black pepper, and reserved mushroom and olive mixture. Serve immediately.

Spaghetti alla Norma

SERVES 4–6

This comes from Sicily, where pasta and aubergine (eggplant) dishes, usually bearing the name Norma, abound. The name refers to the composer Bellini, who was born in Sicily. His opera Norma *was such a resounding success that it became a term of excellence, and eventually was used to describe Sicily's aubergine (eggplant) and pasta dishes.*

While it can refer to nearly any combination of the two, this simple one is my favourite: a mound of pasta topped with tomato sauce and fresh herbs, and surrounded by a border of browned aubergine (eggplant) slices.

In Sicily this can be nearly instant fare: ready-fried aubergines (eggplants) are sold in the markets, so all you really have to do at home is boil the spaghetti and make the simple sauce. Ricotta salata, salted ricotta cheese that is aged and firm enough for grating, is the authentic cheese for this dish; if you have access to it, by all means use it in place of the more easily available Parmesan.

2 large aubergines, sliced 3–6mm/⅛–¼ inch thick
Salt
Olive oil
1 onion, chopped
3 cloves garlic, chopped
Pinch of sugar
600ml/1 pint tomato passata, or 450g/ 2 lb ripe fresh tomatoes, diced, or 2 400g/14 oz tins chopped tomatoes
Freshly ground black pepper to taste
450g/1 lb spaghetti
Freshly grated Parmesan, Pecorino or ricotta salata cheese to serve
Handful of fresh herbs: basil, parsley, oregano, thyme, marjoram, etc.

2 large eggplants, sliced ⅛–¼ inch thick
Salt
Olive oil
1 onion, chopped
3 cloves garlic, chopped
Pinch of sugar
2½–3 cups tomato passata or tomato sauce, or 2 lb ripe fresh tomatoes, diced, or 3 cups canned chopped tomatoes
Freshly ground black pepper to taste
1 lb spaghetti
Freshly grated Parmesan, Pecorino or ricotta salata cheese to serve
¼ cup combination of coarsely chopped fresh herbs such as basil, parsley, oregano, thyme, marjoram, etc.

1. Sprinkle the aubergine (eggplant) liberally with salt, and leave for at least an hour.
2. Rinse and pat dry with a clean towel or absorbent paper.
3. Brown the aubergine (eggplant) in heavy frying pan (skillet) in olive oil, taking care not to crowd the pan and cooking only one layer at a time. (The aubergine [eggplant] can be lightly dredged in flour to prevent it from absorbing too much oil; I like the flavour of the aubergine [eggplant] rather than a floury crust, but the choice is yours.)

Place the browned aubergine (eggplant) slices on a flat baking sheet and set aside.

4. Prepare the sauce by sautéeing the onions and garlic in about 2 tablespoons olive oil until softened, then add the sugar and tomatoes or passata and simmer for 15 minutes or until full-flavoured. Keep warm.

5. Cook the spaghetti until *al dente*; at the same time, reheat the aubergine (eggplant) slices in a medium hot oven.

6. Drain the spaghetti, arrange on a platter ringed by a border of aubergine (eggplant) slices, then ladle the tomato sauce over the pasta. Serve immediately, sprinkled generously with cheese and fresh herbs.

Tagliatelle with Mushrooms and Tomatoes

SERVES 4–6

The simplest sauce of sautéed mushrooms and tomatoes, finished with a sprinkling of parsley and served with tagliatelle or any ribbon-shaped pasta. This recipe uses only ordinary white-brown mushrooms, since with all of the tomatoey flavour there is no need to use anything more subtly flavoured or expensive.

3 cloves garlic, chopped
450g/1 lb mushrooms, thinly sliced
2-3 tablespoons olive oil
1 lb ripe fresh tomatoes, diced or 1 400g/14 oz tin chopped tomatoes, drained
Salt and freshly ground black pepper, to taste
325–450g/12–16 oz tagliatelle
2 tablespoons chopped fresh parsley
Freshly grated Parmesan cheese to serve

3 cloves garlic, chopped
1 lb mushrooms, thinly sliced
2-3 tablespoons olive oil
1 lb ripe fresh tomatoes, diced or 1½ cups canned chopped tomatoes, drained
Salt and freshly ground black pepper, to taste
12-16 oz tagliatelle
2 tablespoons chopped fresh parsley
Freshly grated Parmesan cheese to serve

1. Sauté the garlic and mushrooms quickly in the olive oil. Do it in several batches to keep the mushrooms firm and lightly browned; crowding the pan encourages sogginess.

2. Combine the sautéed mushrooms with the tomato and bring to the boil. Reduce heat to medium and cook until it has a nice thick saucelike consistency, about 15 minutes (longer if you are using fresh tomatoes). Add some of the parsley and season with salt and black pepper.

3. Meanwhile, cook the pasta until *al dente*.

4. Drain, toss with the sauce and serve sprinkled with the remaining parsley and Parmesan cheese.

Fettuccine with Tarragon-Scented Mushroom Sauce Aurora

SERVES 4–6

Sautéed diced mushrooms, much like the French duxelles, are the basis for this complex pasta sauce. A French accent continues to romp through the recipe, with tarragon, shallots and a splash of white wine.

325g/12 oz mushrooms, diced	¾ lb mushrooms, diced
5 shallots, chopped	5 shallots, chopped
40–50g/1½–2 oz butter	3–4 tablespoons butter
100ml/4 fl oz dry white wine	½ cup dry white wine
2 tablespoons flour	2 tablespoons flour
100ml/4 fl oz hot milk	½ cup hot milk
100ml/4 fl oz vegetable stock	½ cup vegetable stock
¼ teaspoon dried tarragon, or chopped fresh tarragon, to taste	¼ teaspoon dried tarragon, or chopped fresh tarragon, to taste
175ml/6 fl oz tomato passata, or 6 ripe fresh or tinned chopped tomatoes	¾ cup tomato passata or tomato sauce, or 4–6 ripe fresh or canned tomatoes, chopped
1 tablespoon tomato paste	1 tablespoon tomato paste
Salt and freshly ground black pepper, to taste	Salt and freshly ground black pepper, to taste
450g/1 lb fettuccine	1 lb fettuccini
Freshly grated Parmesan cheese to serve	Freshly grated Parmesan cheese to serve

1. Sauté the mushrooms and shallots in about half the butter. When the mushrooms are lightly browned and the shallots softened, pour in the white wine. Raise the heat and cook until the wine is evaporated to about half its volume, then remove from the pan and set aside.

2. In the pan in which the mushrooms were cooked, heat the remaining butter and when melted, sprinkle in the flour. Cook for a moment or two until pale golden, then remove from the heat and whisk in the hot milk until it forms a thickish paste, then add the stock. Return to the heat and cook over medium to high heat until thickened.

3. Add the reserved mushroom mixture, the tarragon, tomato passata or tomatoes, and tomato paste. Simmer for about 10 minutes to combine the flavours. Taste for seasoning, adding salt, black pepper and more tarragon if needed.

4. Meanwhile, cook the pasta until *al dente*. Serve tossed with the hot sauce, and pass the Parmesan cheese.

Farfalle with Creamy Tarragon and Shredded Mushroom Sauce

SERVES 4

Shredding the mushrooms brings out their foresty flavour, producing an almost truffle-like effect. The shredded mushrooms are added to a tarragon-scented béchamel, along with lots of Parmesan cheese, then tossed with farfalle. It is an unusual pasta dish with a French flavour.

40g/1½ oz butter
1 tablespoon flour
225ml/8 fl oz milk, hot, but not boiling
325g/12 oz farfalle or similar pasta shape
325g/12 oz mushrooms, coarsely shredded on the large holes of a grater
Generous pinch of dried tarragon or 1–2 teaspoons fresh chopped tarragon
40g/1½ oz Parmesan cheese, freshly grated
Salt and freshly ground black pepper, to taste

3 tablespoons butter
1 tablespoon flour
1 cup milk, hot, but not boiling
12 oz farfalle or similar pasta shape
¾ lb mushrooms, coarsely shredded on the large holes of a grater
Generous pinch of dried tarragon or 1–2 teaspoons fresh chopped tarragon
⅓–½ cup freshly grated Parmesan or similar hard grating cheese
Salt and freshly ground black pepper, to taste

1. Heat one-third of the butter and sprinkle with the flour. Cook for a minute or so, then remove from the heat and whisk in the milk. Return to the heat, whisking or stirring, and cook until the mixture thickens. Set aside and keep warm.
2. Cook the pasta until *al dente*. Drain.
3. Meanwhile, quickly brown the mushrooms in the remaining butter. Add the sauce to the mushrooms, heat through, then season with the tarragon and stir in the Parmesan cheese.
4. Toss the pasta with the sauce, season with salt and black pepper, and serve.

Variation

Pasta Soufflé: For a soufflé-like baked variation, add 4 egg yolks to the sauce, then whip the whites up until stiff and fold into the sauce. Fold half the sauce into cooked pasta such as fettuccine, top with remaining sauce, then bake in the oven at 220°C/425°F/ gas mark 7 until it is well risen and golden brown.

Pasta in Creamy Porcini Sauce

SERVES 4–6

Foresty, fragrant porcini mushrooms are one of the great pleasures of Tuscany. If you are lucky enough to visit when these mushrooms are in season, sample them grilled over an open fire, simmered into soup, or tossed in pasta. If, however, you miss porcini season, comfort yourself with the fact that the dried mushrooms are very good – some might argue that they are even better than fresh, as the strong flavours become concentrated during the drying process.

25g/1 oz dried porcini
250ml/8 fl oz hot, but not boiling,
   vegetable stock
450g/1 lb mushrooms, thinly sliced
40g/1½ oz butter
5 shallots, chopped
2 cloves garlic, chopped
2 tablespoons brandy
350ml/12 fl oz single cream
¼ teaspoon fresh grated nutmeg
Salt and freshly ground black pepper,
   to taste
450g/1 lb fettuccine or pappardelle,
   preferably fresh
50g/2 oz Parmesan cheese, freshly grated

1 oz dried porcini
1 cup hot, but not boiling, vegetable
   stock
1 lb mushrooms, thinly sliced
3 tablespoons butter
5 shallots, chopped
2 cloves garlic, chopped
2 tablespoons brandy
1½ cups whipping cream
¼ teaspoon freshly grated nutmeg
Salt and freshly ground black pepper,
   to taste
1 lb fettuccine or pappardelle,
   preferably fresh
½ cup freshly grated Parmesan cheese

1. Rehydrate the porcini in the hot broth as described on page 262, reserving the soaking liquid. Coarsely chop the soaked mushrooms if they are large.
2. Sauté the fresh mushrooms in half the butter, then set aside.
3. When porcini are softened, heat the remaining butter and lightly sweat the shallots and garlic in it, then stir in the porcini and reserved sautéed mushrooms. Cook a moment, then pour in the reserved soaking liquid.
4. Cook down until reduced in volume by about half, then add the brandy and continue cooking for a few minutes until the alcohol has evaporated. Add the cream, nutmeg, salt and black pepper. Keep warm.
5. Meanwhile, cook the pasta until *al dente*. Drain and toss with the mushroom sauce, and sprinkle generously with the Parmesan cheese.

Variations

Spaghettini con Whisky, Porcini, e Panna: This recipe is said to have originated with British and American soldiers in Italy during World War II. It has a heady whisky scent, even though most of the alcohol does cook out.

Omit the brandy. Substitute 100ml/4 fl oz (½ cup) whisky for half of the stock. Heat together keeping well away in case it ignites. Pour over the porcini and soak, then proceed as above.

Orzo Pilaff with Porcini: Add 500ml/16 fl oz (2 cups) vegetable stock to the sautéed mushroom mixture, after you have added the brandy, then add 325g/12 oz orzo and cook until *al dente*. If the orzo gets too dry, add more water or stock. When the pasta is cooked there should be only a small amount of liquid to bind it. Proceed as above, warming through with cream and serving with grated cheese.

Fresh Fettuccine with Nutmeg-Scented Morel Cream: Dried morel mushrooms with their smoky scent make an elegant, rich pasta dish. Follow the basic recipe, using morels instead of the porcini, and the best-quality fettuccine you can find. Marsala may be used instead of the brandy.

Pasta with Sage Sauce

SERVES 4

Potent sage purée is mellowed with a little stock and enriched with a small amount of butter. Sometimes I omit the stock and serve the buttered, sage-dressed pasta sprinkled with Parmesan cheese or tossed with a little tangy, soft goat cheese. Wide pastas such as pappardelle or lasagne are good with this; stuffed pastas are better still.

I often serve the sage-dressed pasta tossed with diced ripe tomatoes, or with diced cooked beetroot (beet) and a drizzle of its scarlet juice.

2 cloves garlic, chopped
25ml/1 fl oz olive oil
Small handful of fresh sage leaves, finely chopped
325g/12 oz wide pasta of choice, or stuffed pasta
25g/1 oz unsalted butter
2 tablespoons vegetable stock
Coarsely chopped fresh parsley, preferably flat leaf, to serve

2 cloves garlic, chopped
2 tablespoons olive oil
¼ cup fresh sage leaves, finely chopped
12 oz wide pasta of choice, or stuffed pasta
2 tablespoons unsalted butter
2 tablespoons vegetable stock
2 tablespoons chopped fresh parsley, preferably flat leaf, to serve

1. Combine the garlic, olive oil and sage and process in liquidizer (blender) or food processor or pound in a mortar and pestle until it becomes a potent, pungent, bright green balm. It doesn't need to be smooth; small bits of sage add welcome texture.
2. Cook the pasta until *al dente*. Drain and toss with the butter, stock and sage sauce, then serve immediately, sprinkled with parsley.

Capellini with Peas, Porcini and Tomatoes

SERVES 4

Porcini mushrooms scent the zesty tomatoes and bright green peas in this flavoursome pasta dish.

The amount of porcini you use will, of course, affect the flavour of the sauce, but it is equally good if you add only a few. Finishing the dish with a little nugget of melting butter and a scattering of snipped basil gives it an even richer flavour.

25g/1 oz dried porcini	1 oz dried porcini
175ml/6 fl oz very hot, but not boiling, vegetable stock or water	¾ cup very hot, but not boiling, vegetable stock or water
1 small onion, coarsely chopped	1 small onion, coarsely chopped
2 cloves garlic, chopped	2 cloves garlic, chopped
40g/1½ oz butter	3 tablespoons butter
8 ripe fresh tomatoes, diced, or 1 400g/14 oz tin chopped tomatoes, drained and diced	8 ripe fresh tomatoes, diced, or 1½ cups chopped canned tomatoes, drained
1 tablespoon tomato paste	1 tablespoon tomato paste
Salt and freshly ground black pepper, to taste	Salt and freshly ground black pepper, to taste
Tiny pinch of sugar (optional)	Tiny pinch of sugar (optional)
325g/12 oz capellini	12 oz capellini
100g/4 oz fresh young peas or frozen petits pois	½ cup fresh young peas or frozen petits pois
5–8 fresh basil leaves, thinly sliced	5–8 fresh basil leaves, thinly sliced
Freshly grated Parmesan or similar hard grating cheese to serve	Freshly grated Parmesan or similar hard grating cheese to serve

1. Rehydrate the porcini in the stock or water as described on page 262, reserving the liquid.
2. Lightly sauté the onion and garlic in two-thirds of the butter until softened, then add the porcini and cook a moment. Add the reserved soaking liquid, bring to the boil and cook until reduced to less than half.
3. Add the tomatoes and cook for a minute or two longer, then add the tomato paste and season with salt, black pepper and the sugar, if needed.
4. Meanwhile, cook the pasta and peas together in boiling water, then drain. Toss with the sauce, then with the remaining butter. Serve immediately, sprinkled with the basil. Offer Parmesan cheese separately.

Pasta with Creamy Sauce of Puréed Mushrooms and Porcini

SERVES 4–6

This sauce is based on a combination of cultivated mushrooms and the more flavourful porcini, simmered with cream, then puréed into a rich mushroom essence.

15g/½ oz dried porcini
250ml/8 fl oz hot, but not boiling, vegetable stock or water
1 onion, chopped
2 tablespoons olive oil
225g/8 oz mushrooms, coarsely chopped
3 cloves garlic, chopped
Several gratings of fresh nutmeg
100ml/4 fl oz single cream
Salt and freshly ground black pepper, to taste
450g/1 lb fresh pasta such as fettuccine
15g/½ oz butter
Freshly grated Parmesan cheese to serve

½ oz dried porcini
1 cup hot, but not boiling, vegetable stock or water
1 onion, chopped
2 tablespoons olive oil
½ lb mushrooms, coarsely chopped
3 cloves garlic, chopped
Several gratings of fresh nutmeg
½ cup whipping cream
Salt and freshly ground black pepper, to taste
1 lb fresh pasta such as fettuccine
1 tablespoon butter
Freshly grated Parmesan cheese to serve

1. Rehydrate the porcini in the stock or water as described on page 262, reserving the liquid.
2. Sauté the onion in the olive oil until softened and lightly browned in places, then add the fresh mushrooms and the garlic, and continue to cook until the mushrooms are browned and reduced in size.
3. Add the porcini to the mushrooms, then add several tablespoons of the soaking liquid and cook down until the liquid has evaporated.

Remove from the heat and add the nutmeg.
3. In a liquidizer (blender) or food processor purée the mushroom mixture with the cream and 100 ml/4 fl oz (½ cup) of the soaking liquid. Blend until smooth and season with salt and black pepper. Keep warm.
4. Cook the pasta until *al dente*, then drain and toss in the butter. Toss with the sauce and serve immediately, with Parmesan cheese.

Capellini or Fettuccine with Asparagus and a Creamy Purée of Hazelnuts, Porcini and Mascarpone Cheese

SERVES 4

The subtle flavours of hazelnuts, porcini mushrooms and mascarpone cheese make a luscious sauce, especially when served with very delicate pasta and asparagus. If asparagus is out of season, however, don't worry: the dish is delicious without it.

Notice there is no Parmesan here; I like the strong flavours of this sauce to shine through rather than be blanketed by the cheese.

25g/1 oz dried porcini
175–225ml/6–8 fl oz hot, but not
  boiling, vegetable stock
50g/2 oz hazelnuts
2 cloves garlic, chopped
175–225g/6–8 oz mascarpone cheese
50ml/2 fl oz Marsala or brandy (optional)
Salt and freshly ground black pepper,
  to taste
325g/12 oz capellini or fettuccine,
  preferably fresh
225–325g/8–12 oz asparagus, tough ends
  trimmed, cut into bite-sized pieces
15–25g/½–1 oz butter (optional)

1 oz dried porcini
¾–1 cup hot, but not boiling,
  vegetable stock
½ cup hazelnuts
2 cloves garlic, chopped
6–8 oz/⅓–½ lb mascarpone cheese
¼ cup Marsala or brandy (optional)
Salt and freshly ground black pepper,
  to taste
12 oz capellini or fettuccine, preferably
  fresh
8–12 oz asparagus, tough ends
  trimmed, cut into bite-sized pieces
1–2 tablespoons butter (optional)

1. Rehydrate the porcini in the stock as described on page 262, reserving the liquid.
2. Lightly toast the hazelnuts in an ungreased heavy frying pan (skillet) until lightly browned in parts. Remove from the pan, place in a clean towel and rub the nuts against each other to remove the skins. Leave to cool.
3. In a blender or food processor finely chop the garlic, then add the toasted hazelnuts and process until some are finely ground, others quite chunky. Add the rehydrated porcini, the soaking liquid and the mascarpone cheese, then process together and set aside. (This may be done up to a day in advance and stored in the refrigerator.)
4. Add the marsala or brandy, if using, to the sauce and cook over medium to high heat until the liquid is reduced by about half and intensified in colour and flavour. Season to taste with salt and black pepper.
5. Meanwhile, cook the pasta and asparagus in boiling water. If using fresh pasta add the asparagus at the same time; if using dried pasta, cook it first for about 4 minutes, then add the asparagus. Drain.

6. Serve the hot pasta and asparagus, first tossed in the butter, then with the rich sauce.

Couscous Pilaff with Shiitake

SERVES 4–6

Shiitake mushrooms, also known as Chinese black mushrooms, give this wonderful woodsy couscous a European flavour. You could use fresh shiitake, or any of the more unusual mushrooms, but dried ones have a more concentrated flavour, along with the bonus of their soaking liquid.

This makes a cosy supper served with a salad of Continental leaves such as frisée, rocket (arugula), chives, etc., and perhaps a nice chunk of cheese and plate of ripe nectarines or pears to end the meal.

10–15 dried shiitake
900ml/1½ pints hot, but not boiling, vegetable stock
325g/12oz instant couscous
1 onion, coarsely chopped
3 cloves garlic, coarsely chopped
40g/1½ oz butter
Several large pinches of thyme or dried mixed herbs such as herbes de Provence
Light grating of fresh nutmeg
Salt and freshly ground black pepper, to taste

10–15 dried shiitake
3½ cups hot, but not boiling, vegetable stock
12 oz instant couscous
1 onion, coarsely chopped
3 cloves garlic, coarsely chopped
3 tablespoons butter
Several large pinches of thyme or dried mixed herbs such as herbes de Provence
Light grating of fresh nutmeg
Salt and freshly ground black pepper, to taste

1. Rehydrate the shiitakes in the stock as described on page 262, reserving the soaking liquid. Cut the stems off the mushrooms and discard. Slice the caps and set aside.
2. Moisten the couscous with 75–100ml/3–4 fl oz (⅓–½ cup) cold water, mix well, and set aside.
3. Sauté the onion and garlic in two-thirds of the butter until softened, then add the shiitake and cook until the mixture is golden and lightly browned in places, about 5–7 minutes. Season with the thyme or mixed herbs, nutmeg, salt and black pepper.
4. Pour the reserved soaking liquid into the pan and bring to the boil. Continue to boil for a minute or two, then pour into the couscous and mix well. Cover and leave for 5 minutes, or long enough for the couscous to plump up.
5. Serve immediately, dotted with the remaining butter to melt in.

Autumn-Day Capellini with Roasted Garlic, Mushrooms and Tomatoes

SERVES 4–6

2 heads garlic, separated into cloves but left unpeeled, plus 4 cloves garlic, peeled and chopped
4 tablespoons olive oil
225g/8 oz mushrooms, thinly sliced
Salt and freshly ground black pepper, to taste
About 15 ripe sweet fresh tomatoes, seeded and diced and drained of excess liquid (save for soup or sauce)
450g/1 lb capellini
Freshly grated Pecorino or similar hard grating cheese, to serve (optional)
Fresh herbs such as parsley, oregano, thyme, marjoram, etc., or pinch of dried thyme or herbes de Provence, to serve

2 heads garlic, separated into cloves but left unpeeled, plus 4 cloves garlic, peeled and chopped
¼ cup olive oil
½ lb mushrooms, thinly sliced
Salt and freshly ground black pepper, to taste
10–15 ripe fresh tomatoes, seeded and diced, and drained of excess juice (save for soup or sauce)
1 lb capellini
Freshly grated Pecorino or similar hard grating cheese to serve (optional)
¼ cup fresh herbs such as parsley, oregano, thyme, marjoram, etc., or pinch of dried thyme or herbes de Provence, to serve

1. Place the whole garlic cloves in a baking dish and toss with a small amount of the olive oil. Bake in the oven at 180°C/350°F/gas mark 4 for about 30 minutes or until the garlic is tender. Leave to cool, then peel, keeping it from falling apart into a purée as much as you can. Set aside.

2. Over a high heat, sauté the sliced mushrooms with half the chopped raw garlic in a tablespoon or so of the olive oil, then add the tomatoes and sauté together for a minute or two. Season with salt and black pepper and set aside.

3. Cook the capellini until *al dente*, then drain and toss with the remaining olive oil and chopped raw garlic.

4. Toss this garlicky pasta with the reserved roasted garlic and the mushroom and tomato mixture. Serve immediately, sprinkled with cheese, if using, and fresh or dried herbs.

Greek-Flavour Lemon Orzo with Yogurt-Vegetable Topping

SERVES 4

Delicious as a side dish, especially alongside a Mediterranean-style tomato and aubergine (eggplant) stew. The orzo may be prepared up to an hour in advance. Add a few spoonfuls of water when you reheat over a medium flame, and you might need to add more lemon juice just before serving.

325g/12 oz orzo
40g/1½ oz butter
1 egg, lightly beaten
Finely grated rind and juice of
    1 lemon, more if needed
Salt and freshly ground black pepper,
    to taste
Pinch of dried mint (optional)
2 tablespoons coarsely chopped fresh
    parsley, preferably flat leaf
2 cloves garlic, chopped
250ml/8 fl oz Greek yogurt, preferably
    sheep's milk
1 small green pepper, diced
1 small onion, coarsely chopped
1 teaspoon paprika

12 oz orzo
3 tablespoons butter
1 egg, lightly beaten
Zest and juice of 1 lemon, more if
    needed
Salt and freshly ground black pepper,
    to taste
Pinch of dried mint (optional)
2 tablespoons coarsely chopped fresh
    parsley, preferably flat leaf
2 cloves garlic, chopped
1 cup yogurt, preferably whole milk
    yogurt
1 small green bell pepper, diced
1 small onion, coarsely chopped
1 teaspoon paprika

1. Cook the orzo in boiling salted water until *al dente*. Drain and toss with the butter.
2. Mix the egg and the lemon rind (zest) and juice together, then toss with the hot buttered orzo, taking care that it mixes into a creamy pasta rather than turning into scrambled eggs.
3. Season with salt and black pepper, the mint, parsley and half the garlic.
4. Combine the yogurt, green (bell) pepper, onion, and remaining garlic in a serving bowl and sprinkle with the paprika.
5. Serve each portion of creamy, tangy orzo topped with a spoonful of the yogurt mixture.

Melissa's Spaghetti

SERVES 4–6

My young niece, Melissa, is mad about celery. Because of her passion, I have become reacquainted with this often-overlooked vegetable, and very fond of this Tuscan pasta dish. The fiery heat makes a splendid contrast to the fresh, light celery. It is an unusual dish, and very simple to prepare.

1 head celery, stalks cut into short
   batons
6–8 cloves garlic, coarsely chopped
3–4 tablespoons olive oil
1 dried hot red chilli pepper, or more,
   to taste
Salt
450g/1 lb spaghetti

1 head celery, stalks cut into short
   batons
6–8 cloves garlic, coarsely chopped
3–4 tablespoons olive oil
1 dried hot red chilli pepper, or more,
   to taste
Salt
1 lb spaghetti

1. Blanch the celery in a large pan of boiling water, then remove with a slotted spoon, leaving the celery-scented water to cook the pasta in.
2. Sauté the garlic and blanched celery in the olive oil with the hot pepper until lightly golden brown. Remove the hot pepper and season with salt to taste.
3. Cook the spaghetti in the celery water until *al dente*, then drain and toss with the garlic and celery mixture, adding more salt if needed.

Variation

Breadcrumbs, either fresh or toasted, add crispy texture to the dish for a delicious variation. Sprinkle over a tablespoon or two per person.

Lumache or Penne with Creamy Spinach and Ricotta Sauce

SERVES 4–6

Spring (green) onions add fresh flavour to this creamy spinach sauce. If the sauce becomes too rich and thick, thin it with a little water or milk.

225g/8 oz fresh spinach or 175g/6 oz frozen spinach
2 spring onions, chopped
1 clove garlic, chopped
25g/1 oz butter
1 tablespoon flour
250 ml/8 fl oz hot, but not boiling, milk
225g/8 oz ricotta cheese or fromage frais
40g/1½ oz Parmesan cheese, freshly grated
Large pinch of dried mixed herbs or 1 tablespoon chopped fresh basil
Small pinch of freshly grated nutmeg
Salt and freshly ground black pepper, to taste
325g/12 oz lumache (shells) or penne (quills)

8 oz fresh spinach or 6 oz frozen spinach
2 green onions, chopped
1 clove garlic, chopped
2 tablespoons butter
1 tablespoon flour
1 cup hot, but not boiling, milk
8 oz/1 cup ricotta cheese or fromage frais
½ cup freshly grated Parmesan cheese
Large pinch of dried mixed herbs or 1 tablespoon chopped fresh basil
Small pinch of freshly grated nutmeg
Salt and freshly ground black pepper, to taste
12 oz lumache (shells) or penne (quills)

1. Cook the spinach until bright green and tender. Rinse in cold water and squeeze dry. Chop coarsely and set aside.
2. Lightly sauté the spring (green) onions and garlic in the butter, then when soft sprinkle with the flour and stir until the flour is cooked through. Off the heat, stir in the milk, then return to the heat and continue stirring until the mixture thickens. Add the spinach and heat for a minute or two, then stir in the ricotta cheese or fromage frais, Parmesan cheese, mixed herbs, nutmeg, and salt and black pepper. Set aside and keep warm while you cook the pasta.
3. Cook the pasta until *al dente*. Drain and toss with the hot sauce. Serve immediately, sprinkled with more Parmesan cheese.

Variation

Add about 10 diced or sliced sun-dried tomatoes to the spinach sauce. If using dried ones, cook with the pasta; if using oil-marinated ones, add to the sauce with the spinach.

Orzo with Greek Island Flavours

SERVES 4–6

This is a variation of a dish I enjoyed time and again during a winter on a Greek Island. It has all the hallmark Greek flavours: tomatoes, cinnamon and allspice, onions and garlic, along with the tangy nip of feta cheese. I was surprised, therefore, when a friend from the Sudan exclaimed that she ate this all the time at home. Her version was much simplified, however, and used spaghetti rather than orzo.

1 onion, coarsely chopped
4 cloves garlic, chopped
3 tablespoons olive oil
250ml/8 fl oz tomato passata
225g/8 oz diced tomatoes (either ripe and fresh, or tinned)
Pinch each of cinnamon and allspice or cloves
Pinch of sugar (optional)
1 bunch fresh spinach, cooked and coarsely chopped or 12 oz frozen spinach, defrosted
¼ teaspoon dried oregano
325g/12 oz orzo
100g/4 oz feta cheese, coarsely crumbled
Salt and freshly ground black pepper, to taste
Chopped fresh parsley (optional)

1 onion, coarsely chopped
4 cloves garlic, chopped
3 tablespoons olive oil
1 cup tomato passata or tomato sauce
8 ripe fresh or canned tomatoes, diced
Pinch each of cinnamon and allspice or cloves
Pinch of sugar (optional)
1 bunch fresh spinach, cooked and coarsely chopped or 12 oz frozen spinach, defrosted
¼ teaspoon dried oregano
12 oz orzo
¼ lb feta cheese, coarsely crumbled
Salt and freshly ground black pepper, to taste
Chopped fresh parsley (optional)

1. Lightly sauté the onion and garlic in the olive oil until softened, then add the tomato passata and tomatoes. Bring to the boil, season with the cinnamon, allspice or cloves, and sugar, if needed, then add spinach and simmer over medium heat until reduced in volume and flavourful. Season with the oregano and set aside.
2. Meanwhile, cook the orzo until half tender. Drain and add to the tomato and spinach mixture. Simmer together until the orzo is tender.
3. Toss the sauced pasta with three-quarters of the feta cheese and sprinkle with the rest, then with the parsley (if using). Check the seasoning, adding more cinnamon, oregano, salt and pepper if needed. Serve immediately.

Pasta with Pungent Greens and Cherry Tomatoes

SERVES 4–6

675g/1½ lb greens – turnip tops,
   cabbage greens, dandelion greens,
   beet greens, broccoli tops, broccoli,
   spinach, or a combination
Salt
450g/1 lb orecchiette
4 tablespoons olive oil
3 cloves garlic, chopped
15–20 cherry tomatoes, halved
Salt and freshly ground black pepper
   or cayenne pepper, to taste
Freshly grated or shaved Parmesan
   cheese to serve

1½ lb greens – turnip tops, beet
   greens, green outer cabbage leaves,
   dandelion greens, broccoli tops,
   broccoli, spinach, or a combination
1 lb orecchiette
¼ cup olive oil
3 cloves garlic, chopped
15–20 cherry tomatoes, halved
Salt and freshly ground black pepper
   or cayenne pepper, to taste
Freshly grated or shaved Parmesan or
   other grating cheese to serve

1. Cook the greens in boiling salted water for about 5 minutes, then add the pasta and cook until _al dente_. Drain and toss with 1 tablespoon of the olive oil.
2. Meanwhile, heat the remaining olive oil and the garlic, then quickly sauté the tomatoes over medium to high heat for about 3–5 minutes.
3. Combine the pasta and greens with the sautéed tomatoes and serve immediately, seasoned well with salt and either black pepper or cayenne pepper, and tossed with Parmesan cheese.

Variations

Instead of fresh tomatoes, tomato passata (or tomato sauce) may be used. Sprinkle with parsley along with the cheese.

Orecchiette with Cherry Tomatoes, Celery and Garlic Croûtons: Omit the greens and sauté 1 chopped onion and 1 chopped celery stalk with the garlic, then add the cherry tomatoes. To make garlic croûtons, brown 1 thick slice of country-style or French bread, diced, in a tablespoon or so of olive oil. Toss the orecchiette in the celery and tomato sauce, then serve topped with garlic croûtons.

Pasta with a Sauce of Spinach, Peas, and Rosemary Cream

SERVES 4–6

Hearty and thick, filled with a garden full of vegetables and a splash of cream. While I never throw away the liquid from cooking vegetables, sometimes I am at a loss as to what to do with it. Here the decision is made for the cook, with a sauce conveniently based on the vegetable cooking water mixed with a stock cube.

450g/1 lb fresh spinach or 325g/12 oz
    frozen spinach
½ vegetable stock cube
1 onion, chopped
5 cloves garlic, chopped
40g/1½ oz butter
1 tablespoon olive oil
1 tablespoon chopped fresh rosemary,
    or to taste
100–175g/4–6 oz fresh or frozen peas
450g/1 lb penne, or other short
    chubby shapes such as lumache
    (shells), etc.
3 courgettes, cut into large dice
250ml/8 fl oz single cream
2 teaspoons lemon juice, or to taste
Salt and freshly ground black pepper
Fresh herbs such as basil, rosemary or
    parsley, to serve (optional)
Freshly grated Parmesan to serve

1 lb fresh spinach or 12 oz frozen
    spinach
½ vegetable bouillion cube
1 onion, chopped
5 cloves garlic, chopped
3 tablespoons butter
1 tablespoon olive oil
1 tablespoon chopped fresh rosemary,
    or to taste
½–¾ cup fresh or frozen peas
450g/1 lb penne, or other short
    chubby shapes such as lumache
    (shells), etc.
3 zucchini, cut into large dice
1 cup whipping cream
2 teaspoons lemon juice, or to taste
Salt and freshly ground black pepper
Fresh herbs such as rosemary, basil or
    parsley, to serve (optional)
Freshly grated Parmesan to serve

1. Cook the spinach in 125ml/4 fl oz (½ cup) water until spinach is bright green. Remove from cooking liquid (reserving liquid), rinse with cold water and drain. When cool enough to handle, squeeze the spinach until nearly dry, reserving the green liquid that results. Add this and the ½ vegetable stock (vegetable bouillion) cube to the cooking liquid and set aside for the sauce.

2. Lightly sauté the onion and garlic in the butter and olive oil until softened; stir in 250ml/8 fl oz (1 cup) of the spinach cooking liquid and cook down until reduced to about a quarter of its original volume.

3. Add the reserved spinach, the rosemary and peas, and cook for a few more minutes, adding a little more of the spinach cooking water if the mixture is in danger of burning. The mixture should not be soupy, but nearly dry. Set aside and keep warm.

4. Cook the pasta and courgettes (zucchini) in rapidly boiling water until *al dente*.
5. Drain, then add to the spinach and pea mixture with the cream and lemon juice. Taste for seasoning, adding salt and black pepper, and herbs to taste, then serve immediately, each portion topped with a sprinkling of Parmesan cheese.

Variation

This hearty vegetable and pasta dish makes a good casserole: pour into an earthenware casserole, top with a layer of fontina or Asiago cheese and a sprinkling of Parmesan, then bake in the oven at 190°C/375°F/gas mark 5 until the top is lightly browned in parts. Serve immediately.

Orecchiette with Turnip Tops

SERVES 4

Orecchiette is a smallish, flat round pasta, whimsically named little ears because of its shape. Classically it is paired with strong, simple flavours such as leafy greens, as in this speciality from Italy's deep South. Any greens may be used instead of turnip tops, such as beet greens, spinach, or leafy broccoli tops. However if using particularly bitter-tasting greens be sure to blanch them first, then discard the cooking water.

If you cannot find orecchiette, use seashells or dried gnocchi, or even spaghetti.

675g/1½ lb turnip tops or other leafy greens
325g/12 oz orecchiette
3 tablespoons olive oil
3–6 cloves garlic, finely chopped
Salt and freshly ground black pepper, to taste

1½ lb turnip tops or other leafy greens
12 oz orecchiette
3 tablespoons olive oil
3–6 cloves garlic, finely chopped
Salt and freshly ground black pepper, to taste

1. Remove the tough stems from the greens and wash well. Boil in salted water until almost tender, then add the pasta and cook until the pasta is *al dente* and the greens completely tender. Drain.
2. Meanwhile, heat the oil and garlic together until the garlic is golden, then add the drained pasta and greens. Toss together and season well with salt and black pepper. Serve immediately.

Variations

Add a pinch of hot red pepper flakes to the olive oil and garlic as it heats.

Add a spoonful or two of black olive paste at the end.

Fusilli with Diced Autumn Vegetables

SERVES 4–6

A selection of coarsely chopped vegetables, combined with the strong flavour of porcini mushrooms, makes an unusual sauce. Toss with supple chewy fusilli – the kind that curls around rather than twists. If it is unavailable, capellini would be nice.

The sautéed vegetable mixture makes the basis for a delightful frittata – if you have leftovers or feel like making a double batch.

15g/½ oz dried porcini
100g/4 oz mushrooms, coarsely chopped
3 tablespoons olive oil
2 onions, coarsely chopped
3 cloves garlic, coarsely chopped
Salt and freshly ground black pepper, to taste
½ carrot, coarsely chopped
½ courgette, coarsely chopped
4 fresh or tinned artichoke hearts, cut into coarse dice (to prepare fresh artichoke hearts, see page 263)
2 ripe fresh tomatoes or 3 tinned ones, diced
325–450g/12–16 oz fusilli or capellini
15g/½ oz butter
Freshly grated Parmesan cheese to serve

½ oz dried porcini
¼ lb mushrooms, coarsely chopped
3 tablespoons olive oil
2 onions, coarsely chopped
3 cloves garlic, coarsely chopped
Salt and freshly ground black pepper, to taste
½ carrot, coarsely chopped
½ zucchini, coarsely chopped
4 artichoke hearts, fresh or canned, cut into coarse dice (to prepare fresh artichokes, see page 263)
2 ripe fresh tomatoes, diced or 3 canned tomatoes, diced
12–16 oz fusilli or capellini
1 tablespoon butter
Freshly grated Parmesan cheese to serve

1. Rehydrate the porcini as described on page 262 (reserve the soaking liquid for another use). Coarsely chop the porcini and set aside.
2. Sauté the fresh mushrooms in half the oil with half the onions and cook until lightly browned in places and richly flavoured. Add the rehydrated porcini and half the garlic, then season with salt and black pepper. Remove the mixture from the pan and set aside.
3. In the same pan, sauté the remaining onion and garlic, plus the carrot and courgette (zucchini) in the remaining olive oil; when softened, add the artichoke hearts and sauté for a moment or two, then add the tomatoes and cook over medium to high heat until it becomes slightly saucelike.
3. Cook the pasta until *al dente*, then drain and toss in the butter. Toss with the vegetable mixture and serve sprinkled with Parmesan cheese.

Variation

Autumn Vegetable Ragu: Purée the vegetable mixture with 250ml/8 fl oz (1 cup) of the mushroom soaking liquid and 2 small tins (6–8 tablespoons) tomato paste. Season with a drop or two of lemon juice, salt and black pepper, and several large pinches of mixed herbs. This mixture also makes a delicious pizza topping: smear a tablespoon or so of tomato paste atop a pizza (dough) base, then top with several spoonfuls of the vegetable sauce. Sprinkle with olive oil, raw garlic and finely grated cheese, then bake until lightly browned. Serve topped with several spoonfuls of chopped raw tomatoes and a generous sprinkling of mixed herbs such as herbes de Provence.

Pasta alla Giardino
PASTA FROM THE GARDEN
SERVES 4–6

1 onion, chopped
2 cloves garlic, chopped
1 spring onion, including the green part, finely sliced
1 tablespoon chopped fresh parsley
25g/1 oz butter
1–2 courgettes, diced
4 artichoke hearts (see page 263 for preparation directions), cut into eighths (frozen or tinned are fine)
225g/8 oz fresh or frozen peas
8–10 ripe fresh or tinned tomatoes, diced
1–2 tablespoons tomato paste
Salt and freshly ground black pepper, to taste
Pinch of sugar (optional)
450g/1 lb spaghetti
Freshly grated Parmesan, Pecorino or similar cheese, to serve
Fresh herbs such as marjoram, basil or oregano, to serve

1 onion, chopped
2 cloves garlic, chopped
1 green onion, including the green part, finely sliced
1 tablespoon chopped fresh parsley
2–3 tablespoons butter
1–2 zucchini, diced
4 artichoke hearts (see page 263 for preparation directions), cut into eighths (frozen or canned is fine)
1 cup fresh or frozen peas
8–10 ripe fresh or canned tomatoes, diced
1–2 tablespoons tomato paste
Salt and freshly ground black pepper, to taste
Pinch of sugar (optional)
1 lb spaghetti
Freshly grated Parmesan, Pecorino, or similar cheese, to serve
1–2 tablespoons chopped fresh herbs such as marjoram, basil or oregano, to serve

1. Gently sauté the onion, garlic, spring (green) onion and parsley in half of the butter until softened. Add the courgettes (zucchini) and artichoke hearts and cook gently for about 5 minutes.
2. Add the peas, tomatoes and tomato paste, plus 50–75ml/2–3 fl oz (¼–⅓ cup) water and cook over medium to high heat until saucelike; another few minutes.
3. Season with salt and freshly ground black pepper and with sugar, if needed.
4. Cook the spaghetti until *al dente*. Drain and toss with the remaining butter, then toss with the sauce.
5. Serve immediately, sprinkled with finely grated cheese and a handful of chopped fresh herbs.

Conchiglie with Yellow (Bell) Peppers and Aubergine (Eggplant) Sauce

SERVES 4–6

This dish is inspired by the the myriad sun-drenched pasta and vegetable dishes I've eaten in Italy. You can, of course, vary the vegetables: add courgettes (zucchini) and you will have a ratatouille-like sauce, red (bell) pepper instead of yellow,. or diced fennel, will give yet another effect.

1 onion, coarsely chopped
4 cloves garlic, coarsely chopped
1 yellow pepper, diced
6 tablespoons olive oil
1 aubergine, cut into bite-sized cubes
6 small to medium fresh ripe tomatoes, diced, or 275g/10 oz tin chopped tomatoes
Salt and freshly ground black pepper, to taste
Pinch of sugar (optional)
1 teaspoon fresh or ½ teaspoon dried oregano or marjoram
325g/12 oz conchiglie (pasta shells)
100g/4 oz green beans, cut into bite-sized lengths
4 tablespoons freshly grated Parmesan cheese

1 onion, coarsely chopped
4 cloves garlic, coarsely chopped
1 yellow bell pepper, diced
⅓ cup olive oil
1 eggplant, cut into bite-sized cubes
6 small to medium ripe fresh tomatoes, diced, or 1 cup chopped canned tomatoes
Salt and freshly ground black pepper, to taste
Pinch of sugar (optional)
1 teaspoon fresh or ½ teaspoon dried oregano or marjoram
12 oz conchiglie (pasta shells)
¼ lb green beans (or, if available, a combination of green and yellow beans), cut into bite-sized lengths
¼ cup freshly grated Parmesan or similar grating cheese

1. Sauté the onion, garlic and (bell) pepper in about half the olive oil until soft. Remove from the pan and brown the aubergine (eggplant) in the remaining olive oil. Remove from the pan and set aside.
2. Cook the tomatoes in the pan, adding a little more oil if necessary. When saucelike, return the vegetables to the pan. Season with salt and black pepper, the sugar, if needed, and the oregano or marjoram. Set aside.
3. Cook the pasta until about half done, then add the beans and continue cooking until both are *al dente*.
4. Drain and mix with the sauce. Toss with the cheese and serve immediately.

Roasted Tomato and Green Bean Couscous with Ginger

SERVES 4–6

This couscous has Italian flavours, reminiscent of Sicilian couscous rather than the highly spiced affairs of Morocco and Tunisia. It makes a particularly good side dish for grilled vegetable kebabs, together with a salad of slightly bitter frisée leaves.

3 cloves garlic, chopped
2 tablespoons olive oil
6–8 tomatoes, roasted, peeled and diced (see page 261)
225g/8 oz green beans, fresh and blanched or frozen, cut into bite-sized lengths
600ml/1 pint vegetable stock, more if needed
325g/12 oz instant couscous
½ teaspoon powdered ginger, or to taste
Dash of Tabasco sauce or pinch of cayenne pepper
Salt to taste

3 cloves garlic, chopped
2 tablespoons olive oil
6–8 tomatoes, roasted, peeled and diced (see page 261)
½ lb green beans, fresh and blanched or frozen, cut into bite-sized lengths
2–3 cups vegetable stock, more if needed
12 oz instant couscous
½ teaspoon powdered ginger, or to taste
Dash of Tabasco sauce or pinch of cayenne pepper
Salt to taste

1. Sauté the garlic in the olive oil then add the roasted tomatoes and cook for a few moments.
2. Add the stock and bring to the boil, then add the couscous. Remove from the heat, cover and leave for 10 minutes. Halfway through check to see if it is moist enough, if not add more stock.
3. Add the ginger, reheat to warm up the couscous, and season with Tabasco or cayenne pepper and salt. Serve immediately.

Spaghetti Sauced with a Purée of Roasted Vegetables

SERVES 4–6

A culinary experiment described in mouthwatering detail over a transatlantic telephone line by my US editor and friend, Janice Gallagher, then recreated in my London kitchen. The sauce is made of roasted vegetables, enlivened with Southwestern spices. Despite the fact that the vegetables are puréed together, they need to be roasted separately to maintain their individual flavours.

The sauce is rather like a spicy roasted-vegetable gazpacho, and could probably be used as the basis of one: simply thin with a little vegetable stock and chill.

Leftover sauce tastes good with a spinach omelette and makes a zesty pizza topping.

2 green peppers	2 green bell peppers
20 small ripe fresh tomatoes	20 small ripe fresh tomatoes
2 onions, cut into quarters	2 onions, cut into quarters
2 heads of garlic, separated into cloves but left unpeeled	2 heads of garlic, separated into cloves but left unpeeled
125–250ml/4–8 fl oz tomato juice	½–1 cup tomato juice
3–4 tablespoons olive oil	3–4 tablespoons olive oil
1 tablespoon wine vinegar	1 tablespoon wine vinegar
¼ teaspoon cumin seeds, or to taste	¼ teaspoon cumin seeds, or to taste
¼ teaspoon mild chilli powder	¼ teaspoon mild chilli powder
Salt	Salt
450g/1 lb spaghetti	1 lb spaghetti
25g/1 oz butter or 2 tablespoons olive oil for tossing with pasta	2 tablespoons butter or olive oil for tossing with the pasta
Freshly grated Parmesan or similar grating cheese, to serve	Freshly grated Parmesan or similar grating cheese, to serve

1. Roast the green (bell) peppers as described on page 262 then dice and set aside.
2. Roast the tomatoes as described on page 261. Leave to cool, then chop roughly (don't worry about peeling – the skin adds flavour).
3. Place the onions and garlic in an ungreased heavy frying pan (skillet) over medium to high heat and let char slightly. Reduce the

heat and cover, then cook over low heat until tender, about 15–25 minutes. Remove and leave to cool, then dice the onions and peel the garlic.

4. Place all the vegetables in a liquidizer (blender) or food processor, then add the tomato juice, olive oil and vinegar. Blend to a fairly smooth but still slightly chunky mixture, adding more tomato juice if

necessary to obtain the correct consistency, then season with the chilli powder and cumin. Taste for salt.

5. Meanwhile, cook the spaghetti until _al dente_. Drain. If eating hot, toss in the butter; if eating cool, toss in the 2 tablespoons of olive oil.

6. Toss the pasta with the cool sauce. If eating hot, serve with a little finely grated cheese.

Variation

Add 175g/6 oz (¾ cup) fresh or frozen peas to the pasta as it cooks. Drain and sauce.

Spaghettini with Diced Roasted Tomatoes and Pungent Raw Garlic

SERVES 4–6

Once you have the tomatoes roasted, the rest of this dish is a cinch. I find that roasting the tomatoes the day before is not only easier, but the tomatoes taste better and their juices have thickened nicely.

20 smallish ripe, red fresh tomatoes
5 cloves garlic, coarsely chopped
3 tablespoons olive oil
Salt and freshly ground black pepper,
  to taste
450g/1 lb spaghettini
15–25g/½–1 oz butter (optional)

20 smallish ripe, red fresh tomatoes
5 cloves garlic, coarsely chopped
3 tablespoons olive oil
Salt and freshly ground black pepper,
  to taste
1 lb spaghettini
1–2 tablespoons butter (optional)

1. Roast the tomatoes as described on page 261.
2. Combine the chopped roasted tomatoes with their juices, the garlic and the olive oil. Season with salt and black pepper.

3. Cook the pasta until _al dente_, then drain and toss in the butter, if using.
4. Toss the pasta with the tomato mixture, then serve immediately.

Pasta with Grilled Summer Vegetables, Northern California Style

SERVES 6

Vegetables on the grill are as much a part of Californian eating and cooking as garlic, olive oil and local wines. One of the delightful things about grilled vegetables is the way their smoky flavour enhances other dishes such as soups, pizza, sandwiches, or the following pasta dish.

2-3 courgettes, and/or other summer squash, sliced lengthwise about 6mm/¼ inch thick

1 red, 1 yellow and 1 green pepper

1 Japanese-style aubergine, sliced lengthwise

Bunch of spring onions, trimmed but left whole

1 bulb fresh fennel, sliced lengthwise about 6mm/¼ inch thick

100ml/4 fl oz olive oil

Juice of ½–1 lemon

6 cloves garlic, finely chopped

Dried thyme or herbes de Provence, to taste

6 ripe fresh tomatoes

450g/1 lb fresh or 325g/12 oz dried pasta of choice

8 oil-marinated sun-dried tomatoes, sliced into thin strips

Salt and freshly ground black pepper, to taste

Handful of mixed fresh herbs: basil, oregano, parsley, thyme, etc.

2-3 zucchini, and/or other summer squash, sliced lengthwise about ¼ inch thick

1 red, 1 yellow and 1 green bell pepper

1 Japanese-style eggplant, sliced lengthwise

Bunch of green onions, trimmed but left whole

1 bulb fresh fennel, sliced lengthwise about ¼ inch thick

½ cup olive oil

Juice of ½–1 lemon

6 cloves garlic, finely chopped

Dried thyme or herbes de Provence, to taste

6 ripe fresh tomatoes

1 lb fresh or 12 oz dried pasta of choice

8 oil-marinated sun-dried tomatoes, sliced into thin strips

Salt and freshly ground black pepper, to taste

¼ cup fresh mixed fresh herbs: basil, oregano, parsley, thyme, etc.

1. Place the courgettes (zucchini), (bell) peppers, aubergine (eggplant), and spring (green) onions and fennel in a baking dish and pour over the olive oil and lemon juice. Sprinkle over half the garlic and the dried herbs and leave for at least an hour.

2. Remove the vegetables from the dish and reserve the marinade. Grill the marinated vegetables and the whole tomatoes over an open fire or under a hot grill (broiler –

though this will not have the lovely smoky aroma) until tender but still quite firm. Remove from the grill. Peel and dice the tomatoes; slice the other vegetables into matchsticks. Keep warm.

3. Cook the pasta until *al dente*.

4. Drain and toss with the reserved marinade, the remaining garlic, the sun-dried tomatoes and the grilled vegetables. Season with salt and black pepper and serve strewn with lots of fresh herbs.

Linguine with Roasted Tomatoes, Basil, Garlic and Pine Nuts

SERVES 4–6

3 tablespoons pine nuts
4 cloves garlic, coarsely chopped
4 tablespoons olive oil
Large handful of fresh basil leaves, coarsely torn or cut up
About 15 small to medium tomatoes, roasted, peeled and diced (see page 261)
4 tablespoons dry white wine
4 tablespoons vegetable stock
Pinch of sugar, optional
Salt and freshly ground black pepper, and cayenne pepper, to taste
450g/1 lb linguine
Freshly grated Parmesan cheese to serve

3 tablespoons pine nuts
4 cloves garlic, coarsely chopped
¼ cup olive oil
¼ cup fresh basil leaves, coarsely torn or cut up
About 15 small to medium tomatoes, roasted, peeled and diced (see page 261)
¼ cup dry white wine
¼ cup vegetable stock
Pinch of sugar, optional
Salt and freshly ground black pepper and cayenne pepper, to taste
1 lb linguine
Freshly grated Parmesan cheese to serve

1. Toast the pine nuts in an ungreased heavy frying pan (skillet) over medium heat, tossing and stirring occasionally, until golden brown in spots. Do not let them get too brown as they can burn very suddenly. Remove from the heat.

2. Sauté the garlic in the olive oil, then add the basil and the roasted tomatoes and cook over a medium to high heat for a minute or so. Add the wine and stock and cook over high heat until reduced in volume by about half. Season with the sugar, salt, black pepper and cayenne pepper.

3. Meanwhile, cook the pasta until *al dente*. Drain.

4. Toss the pasta with the sauce and pine nuts, then serve immediately, sprinkled with the Parmesan cheese.

Spaghetti with Hazelnut Pesto

SERVES 4

This rich yet savoury hazelnut paste is very similar to pesto, but with a strong taste of pounded nuts rather than the herbal flavour of basil. The similarity between the two sauces should be no surprise, since both hail from Liguria, and hazelnuts are enjoyed in nearly as many dishes there as is basil. In season the nuts are sold from impromptu street stalls, threaded on to strings like chunky necklaces. While their destination is usually sweets and baked goods, here they star in a deliciously unusual pasta, a satisfying dish for autumn or winter.

75–100g/3–4 oz shelled hazelnuts
4–5 cloves garlic, chopped
About 50ml/2 fl oz olive oil
325g/12 oz spaghetti
1 tablespoon fresh thyme leaves or
   ¼–½ teaspoon dried thyme
Freshly ground black pepper to taste
25g/1oz Parmesan cheese, freshly
   grated, or to taste
25g/1 oz fresh parsley, chopped, or to
   taste

1 cup shelled hazelnuts
4–5 cloves garlic, chopped
About ¼ cup olive oil
12 oz spaghetti
1 tablespoon fresh thyme or
   ¼–½ teaspoon dried thyme
Freshly ground black pepper to taste
¼ cup freshly grated Parmesan cheese,
   or to taste
½ cup chopped fresh parsley, or to
   taste

1. Toast the hazelnuts in an ungreased heavy frying pan (skillet) over medium to high heat, tossing them frequently to prevent burning. They should become flecked with dark brown. When they are nearly ready their skins will split and begin to fall off. (Hazelnuts may also be roasted in the oven at 200°C/400°F/gas mark 6 for about 10 minutes.) Place the hazelnuts in a clean towel and rub them against each other briskly to remove their skins.

2. In a food processor or liquidizer (blender) finely chop the garlic then add the hazelnuts and process to a coarse mealy texture. Add enough olive oil to make a thinnish paste, then set aside.

3. Cook the pasta until *al dente*. Drain and toss with the hazelnut paste and the thyme, adding a little more olive oil if the paste is too thick.

4. Serve immediately, sprinkled with the Parmesan cheese and parsley.

Pasta with Basil-Scented Walnut Pesto

SERVES 4

This is a Tuscan pesto-like sauce of pounded nuts and basil. You can vary the amounts of basil and walnuts to taste and the garlic is optional but not traditional. Another version of the sauce, Ravioli con Salsa di Noci (see page 97), includes mascarpone, which makes it richer and smoother, a classic to slather over Genoese spinach- and ricotta-stuffed ravioli (pansotti).

Several large handfuls of fresh basil, about 50 leaves, coarsely chopped
200g/7 oz shelled walnuts, coarsely chopped
Salt and freshly ground black pepper or cayenne pepper, to taste
50 g/2 oz Parmesan cheese, freshly grated, plus extra to serve
175ml/6 fl oz olive oil
325g/12 oz pasta of choice

1 cup coarsely chopped fresh basil
1½ cups coarsely chopped shelled walnuts
Salt and freshly ground black pepper or cayenne pepper, to taste
½ cup freshly grated Parmesan cheese, plus extra to serve
¾ cup olive oil
12 oz pasta of choice

1. Chop the basil and grind the walnuts. This can be done together in a liquidizer (blender) or food processor.
2. Season with salt and black pepper or cayenne pepper, combine with the Parmesan cheese and olive oil, and mix to a creamy consistency.
3. Cook the pasta until *al dente*, then drain and toss with the sauce. Serve with extra Parmesan cheese to taste.

Tiny Seashells or Orzo with Radicchio

SERVES 4

Radicchio, with its slightly bitter and invigorating flavour, pairs pleasingly with the wine, tomato and cream sauce. If radicchio is unavailable, use a different bitter salad leaf such as chicory (Belgian endive) or Treviso.

1 onion, chopped
3 cloves garlic, coarsely chopped
3 tablespoons olive oil
2–3 heads radicchio, trimmed and coarsely chopped
250ml/8 fl oz dry red wine
4 ripe fresh or tinned tomatoes, peeled and diced
250ml/8 fl oz single cream
450g/1 lb small seashell-shaped pasta or orzo
Freshly grated Parmesan cheese or crumbled Gorgonzola cheese to serve
Handful of fresh basil, chopped or thinly sliced, or parsley if basil is unavailable

1 onion, chopped
3 cloves garlic, chopped
3 tablespoons olive oil
2–3 heads radicchio, trimmed and coarsely chopped
1 cup dry red wine
4 ripe fresh or canned tomatoes, peeled and diced
1 cup whipping cream
1 lb small seashell-shaped pasta or orzo
Freshly grated Parmesan cheese or crumbled Gorgonzola cheese to serve
2–3 tablespoons chopped fresh basil or parsley if basil is unavailable

1. Lightly sauté the onion and garlic in the olive oil until softened, then add the radicchio and stir through the flavourful oil.
2. Pour in the wine and cook over medium to high heat until reduced by about half. Add the tomatoes and cream and simmer until the liquid becomes a thinnish sauce.
3. Meanwhile, cook the pasta until *al dente*. Drain and toss with the radicchio sauce, then sprinkle with the Parmesan or Gorgonzola cheese and the basil or parsley.

PASTA WITH CHEESE

Pasta with Sautéed Onions and Vignottes Cheese

SERVES 4–6

Sautéed onions combine with pungent Vignottes cheese for pasta with a French accent.
Vignottes has a delicate heart, with a rind that gets rather stinky as it grows older.

100g/4 oz stale, crusty peasant-style
    bread, coarsely grated into crumbs
40g/1½ oz butter
3 onions, chopped
2 cloves garlic, chopped
100ml/4 fl oz single cream (optional)
300g/11 oz Vignottes cheese
Salt and freshly ground black pepper,
    to taste
450g/1 lb spaghetti or fettuccine

4 oz stale, crusty peasant-style bread,
    coarsely grated into crumbs
3 tablespoons butter
3 onions, chopped
2 cloves garlic, chopped
½ cup whipping cream (optional)
11oz Vignottes cheese
Salt and freshly ground black pepper,
    to taste
1 lb spaghetti or fettuccine

1. Toast the bread crumbs in about half the butter until golden and crisp. Remove from the pan and set aside.
2. In the remaining butter lightly sauté the onions and garlic until softened and lightly browned, then add the cream, if using, and cook for a minute or two until thickened.
3. Cut the cheese into small pieces. If the rind is very pungent, remove some or all of it. Toss the cheese into the hot pan, swirl through, then remove from the heat.
4. Meanwhile, cook the pasta until *al dente*. Drain and toss with the onion and cheese mixture; season with salt and pepper to taste. Serve immediately, sprinkled with the toasted breadcrumbs.

Linguine alla Pizzaiola
WITH TOMATOES, MOZZARELLA, AND BASIL

SERVES 4–6

Classic flavours of Italian summertime.

3 cloves garlic, coarsely chopped
2 tablespoons olive oil
8 ripe sweet fresh tomatoes, peeled, seeded and diced (tinned diced tomatoes are okay), drained of excess juice (reserve the juice)
2 tablespoons tomato paste
Salt and freshly ground black pepper, to taste
325–450g/12–16 oz linguine
175–250g/6–9 oz fresh milky mozzarella cheese, cut into large dice
Several large handfuls of fresh basil leaves, coarsely torn or left whole

3 cloves garlic, coarsely chopped
2 tablespoons olive oil
8 ripe sweet fresh tomatoes, peeled, seeded and diced (canned diced tomatoes are okay) drained of their excess juice (reserve the juice)
2 tablespoons tomato paste
Salt and freshly ground black pepper, to taste
12–16 oz linguine
½ lb fresh milky mozzarella cheese, cut into large dice
¼ cup fresh basil leaves, coarsely torn or left whole

1. Warm the garlic in the olive oil just long enough to bring out its fragrance. Add the diced tomatoes and tomato paste and cook for a minute or two, adding some of the tomato juice if needed. Season with salt and black pepper, then set aside and keep warm.
2. Cook the linguine until *al dente*, then drain.
3. Toss the pasta with the hot sauce and the mozzarella cheese. Scatter basil over the top and serve immediately.

Variation

Breadcrumbs, either toasted or fresh, are very good with tomato- and basil-dressed pasta. Omit the mozzarella if you prefer.

Pasta and Green Beans (or Asparagus) with Mascarpone and Breadcrumb Sauce

SERVES 6

I often make a few changes to this outstanding traditional Italian Alpine dish: asparagus is the vegetable most often used, but as the season here is short and the vegetable delicate, I often substitute green beans. As for cheeses, fontina or Gruyère are the usual choice, but I often opt for Parmesan instead.

100g/4 oz stale country-style bread
1 tablespoon oil or 15g/½ oz butter
450g/1 lb pasta of choice
225g/8 oz green beans, cut into bite-sized lengths, or asparagus, tough stems broken off and the stalks cut into bite-sized lengths
350ml/12 fl oz vegetable stock
150–225g/5–8 oz mascarpone cheese, at room temperature
175g/6 oz fontina or Gruyère cheese, grated, or several heaped tablespoons freshly grated Parmesan cheese
Salt and freshly ground black pepper, to taste

4 oz/about 4 slices stale country-style bread
1 tablespoon oil or butter
1 lb pasta of choice
½ lb green beans cut into bite-sized lengths, or asparagus, tough stems broken off and stalks cut into bite-sized lengths
1½ cups vegetable stock
⅔–1 cup mascarpone cheese, at room temperature
6 oz fontina or Gruyère cheese, grated or several heaping tablespoons freshly grated Parmesan cheese
Salt and freshly ground black pepper, to taste

1. Make breadcrumbs by grating the bread then toasting in a heavy frying pan (skillet) over low to medium heat in the oil or butter. When crisp and golden brown, remove from the heat.
2. Boil the pasta until half cooked, then add the green beans or asparagus and continue to cook until both are *al dente*. Drain.
3. Meanwhile, heat the stock until it bubbles around the edges, then add the breadcrumbs and mascarpone cheese. Stir until the cheese melts creamily into the sauce, then toss the sauce with the pasta and vegetables. Add the cheese of choice, season with salt and black pepper and serve immediately.

Variation

Cauliflower and Farfalle Gratin: Instead of green beans or asparagus use 1 cauliflower, cut into florets. Blanch the cauliflower, then sauté, after sautéeing the breadcrumbs. For the pasta choose farfalle or another short, chubby shape.

Add the cooked cauliflower to the pasta and creamy breadcrumb sauce, then top with additional grated cheese and grill or bake in a hot oven until the cheese has melted.

Farfalle or Penne with Sun-Dried Tomato and Goat Cheese Purée

SERVES 4

Since this tangy sauce needs no cooking it is almost like a pesto in simplicity of preparation and freshness of flavour. Try it on pasta stuffed with mushrooms, spinach, or other vegetables that are strong enough in flavour to stand up to the sun-dried tomatoes and goat cheese.

3 cloves garlic, chopped
About 15 oil-marinated sun-dried
   tomatoes, coarsely chopped
150g/5 oz goat cheese, crumbled
Large pinch of fresh or dried thyme
2 tablespoons olive oil
325g/12 oz farfalle or penne
15 fresh basil leaves, thinly sliced or
   coarsely chopped

3 cloves garlic, chopped
About 15 oil-marinated sun-dried
   tomatoes, coarsely chopped
5 oz/⅔ cup goat cheese, crumbled
Large pinch of fresh or dried thyme
2 tablespoons olive oil
12 oz farfalle or penne
15 fresh basil leaves, thinly sliced or
   coarsely chopped

1. In the liquidizer (blender) or food processor combine the garlic, sun-dried tomatoes, goat cheese, thyme and olive oil. Process until it is a creamy pinkish paste, then set aside.

2. Cook the pasta until *al dente*.
3. Drain and toss with the purée, then serve immediately, sprinkled with the basil.

Spaghetti with Browned Onions, Spinach and Blue Cheese

SERVES 4

A delightfully different pasta dish with the sweet-savoury flavour of browned onions, the freshness of lightly cooked spinach, and the salty tang of blue cheese.

6–8 onions, sliced 3–6mm/⅛–¼ inch thick
50–75ml/2–3 fl oz olive oil, or as needed
325g/12 oz spaghetti
1 bunch spinach leaves, well washed then torn into pieces
100–150g/4–5 oz blue cheese, crumbled
Freshly ground black pepper to taste

6–8 onions, sliced ⅛–¼ inch thick
¼ cup olive oil, or as needed
12 oz spaghetti
1 bunch spinach leaves, well washed then torn into pieces
4–5 oz/¼ lb blue cheese, crumbled
Freshly ground black pepper to taste

1. Brown the onion slices in a heavy frying pan (skillet) with as little of the olive oil as possible, cooking them quickly until slightly softened and browned in spots; they should not be limp and darkly browned. Set aside.
2. Boil the spaghetti until half cooked, then add the spinach and continue cooking until the pasta is *al dente* and the spinach is tender and bright green. Drain and toss in the remaining olive oil.
3. Top the pasta and spinach with the onions, then crumble the blue cheese over. Season with black pepper and serve immediately.

Rigatoni and Green Beans with Chorreadas Sauce

SERVES 4–6

Chorreadas is a spicy Bolivian tomato and cheese sauce, seasoned with ginger and turmeric. It is especially good served with thick, robust pasta such as rigatoni and tossed with crisp green beans.

4 onions, diced
2 tablespoons olive oil
225g/8 oz diced, ripe fresh tomatoes,
    or 1 400g/14 oz tin chopped tomatoes
325g/12 oz rigatoni
225g/8 oz fresh or frozen green beans,
    cut into bite-sized pieces
½–1 fresh chilli, chopped
½–¾ teaspoon turmeric
¼ teaspoon cumin
Pinch of sugar (optional)
100ml/4 fl oz Greek yogurt or sour cream
325–400g/12–14 oz white cheese such as
    Cheddar, fontina, Jarlsberg, etc., cubed
Salt and freshly ground black pepper
    or cayenne pepper, to taste
15–25g/½–1 oz butter, at room
    temperature
Pinch of dried ginger
1 clove garlic, chopped
1 tablespoon chopped fresh coriander
    leaves

4 onions, diced
2 tablespoons olive oil
1 cup diced, ripe fresh or canned
    tomatoes
12 oz rigatoni
½ lb fresh or frozen green beans
½–1 fresh chilli, chopped
½–¾ teaspoon turmeric
¼ teaspoon cumin
Pinch of sugar (optional)
4 oz/½ cup sour cream
¾ lb white cheese such as Monterey
    Jack, fontina, Jarlsberg, white
    Cheddar, etc., cubed
Salt and freshly ground black pepper
    or cayenne pepper, to taste
1–2 tablespoons butter, at room
    temperature
Pinch of dried ginger
1 clove garlic, chopped
1 tablespoon chopped fresh cilantro
    leaves

1. Sweat the onions in the olive oil until softened. Add the tomatoes then sauté together for a few minutes. Do not stir into a sauce but let it remain at an almost relish-like consistency.
2. Meanwhile, boil the rigatoni until half cooked, then add the green beans and continue cooking until both pasta and beans are *al dente*; drain.
3. Add the chilli pepper, turmeric, cumin, sugar if using, Greek yogurt or sour cream, and cheese to the onion and tomato mixture. Cook over medium heat, stirring all the time, until the cheese melts, then season with salt and black pepper or cayenne pepper.
4. Toss the pasta and green beans with the sauce, then toss in the butter, ginger, and garlic. Serve immediately, garnished with the chopped coriander leaves (cilantro).

Sardinian-Inspired Pasta with Tomato Sauce and Mint-Seasoned Ricotta Cheese

SERVES 4–6

Sardinians often use ricotta seasoned with fresh mint for stuffing ravioli. Here, I've taken the mixture and used it as a topping for a zesty tomato-sauced pasta. Fresh mint adds a fragrant freshness to the bland ricotta cheese, and a sprinkling of Parmesan or Pecorino cheese gives it all a salty tang.

2 small to medium onions, coarsely chopped
4 cloves garlic, coarsely chopped
1 celery stalk, diced
2 tablespoons chopped fresh parsley
2–3 tablespoons olive oil
600–900ml/1–1½ pints tomato passata
Pinch of sugar (optional)
Salt and freshly ground black pepper, to taste
Large pinch of oregano leaves, crumbled
225g/8 oz ricotta cheese
2 teaspoons chopped fresh mint leaves, preferably small peppermint or Corsican mint
325–450g/12–16 oz pasta: choose a chewy, dense shape such as gemelli, fusilli, orecchiette, small elbows, etc.

2 small to medium onions, coarsely chopped
4 cloves garlic, coarsely chopped
1 celery stalk, diced
2 tablespoons chopped fresh parsley
2–3 tablespoons olive oil
2½–3 cups tomato passata or tomato sauce
Pinch of sugar (optional)
Salt and freshly ground black pepper, to taste
Large pinch of oregano leaves, crumbled
1 cup ricotta cheese
2 teaspoons finely chopped fresh mint leaves, preferably small peppermint or Corsican mint
12–16 oz pasta: choose a chewy, dense shape such as genelli, fusilli, orecchiette, small elbows, etc.

1. Lightly sauté the onions, garlic, celery and parsley in the olive oil until the onions have softened, then add the tomato passata, sugar, salt and black pepper and oregano.
2. Bring to the boil, then reduce the heat and simmer for 5–10 minutes.
3. Meanwhile, combine the ricotta cheese with the mint and set aside.
4. Cook the pasta until *al dente*; drain.
5. Serve the pasta tossed with the tomato sauce and topped with dollops of the mint-seasoned ricotta cheese.

Pasta with Cabbage, Leeks and Tomatoes Topped with Cheese

SERVES 4–6

Consummately comforting.

½ head green or white cabbage, thinly sliced
1 leek, coarsely chopped
3–4 cloves garlic, coarsely chopped
25g/1 oz butter, plus extra for tossing with the pasta
2 tablespoons flour
250ml/8 fl oz hot, but not boiling, milk
450g/1 lb ripe fresh tomatoes, diced, or 1½ 400g/14 oz tins chopped tomatoes
Dried mixed herbs such as herbes de Provence or Italian herbs, to taste
Salt and freshly ground black pepper, to taste
450g/1 lb spaghetti or other pasta of choice
275g/10 oz mature Cheddar cheese, coarsely grated

½ green or white cabbage, thinly sliced
1 leek, coarsely chopped
3–4 cloves garlic, coarsely chopped
2 tablespoons butter, plus extra for tossing with the pasta
2 tablespoons flour
1 cup hot, but not boiling, milk
1 lb ripe fresh tomatoes, diced, or 1½ cups canned chopped tomatoes
Dried mixed herbs such as herbes de Provence or Italian herbs, to taste
Salt and freshly ground black pepper, to taste
1 lb spaghetti or other pasta of choice
⅔ lb/1½ cups coarsely grated cheese such as young Asiago, Monterey Jack, white Cheddar, fontina, etc.

1. Sauté the cabbage, leek and garlic in the butter. Sprinkle with the flour and cook for a few minutes, then stir in the milk and cook over medium heat until the sauce thickens and the vegetables are tender. Add the tomatoes and continue cooking until it becomes a thick chunky vegetable sauce. Season with dried mixed herbs and salt and black pepper.

2. Meanwhile, cook the pasta until *al dente*. Drain, then toss in a little butter.

3. Serve with the sauce, topped with a generous portion of the grated cheese. Serve immediately.

Buckwheat or Wholewheat Noodles with Cabbage and Blue Cheese

SERVES 4

A simplified version of a traditional dish from the hilly Valtellina region of northern Lombardy in Italy, in which flat, wide buckwheat pasta is prepared with rustic vegetables such as cabbage or chard and seasoned with sage and sharp cheese such as aged Asiago. Since the traditional buckwheat pasta, pizzoccheri, is not easily available elsewhere, I substitute the more accessible Asian buckwheat noodles or wholewheat spaghetti imported from Italy. This dish makes a marvellous winter supper.

15g/½ oz butter
1 tablespoon flour
250ml/8 fl oz milk, hot but not boiling
2 cloves garlic, chopped
2 tablespoons olive oil
1 green or white cabbage, thinly sliced
75–150ml/3–5 fl oz vegetable stock
325g/12 oz buckwheat or wholewheat noodles or fettuccine, spaghetti, etc.
½ teaspoon crumbled dry sage leaves, or 1 teaspoon thinly sliced fresh leaves, or to taste
100g/4 oz blue cheese, crumbled or diced
Salt and freshly ground black pepper, to taste

1 tablespoon butter
1 tablespoon flour
1 cup milk, hot but not boiling
2 cloves garlic, chopped
2 tablespoons olive oil
1 medium sized white or green cabbage, thinly sliced
⅓–⅔ cup vegetable stock
12 oz buckwheat or wholewheat pasta
½ teaspoon crumbled dried sage leaves, or 1 teaspoon finely sliced fresh leaves, or to taste
4 oz/¼ lb blue cheese, crumbled or diced
Salt and freshly ground black pepper, to taste

1. Heat the butter in a pan and sprinkle in the flour. Cook for a minute or two, then remove from the heat and gradually whisk or stir in the hot milk. Return to the heat and cook, stirring or whisking, until thickened. Set aside.
2. Sauté the garlic in the olive oil for a few moments, then add the cabbage and stir-fry quickly until softened. Add the béchamel sauce and enough stock to make a sauce the consistency of thin cream. Simmer for a few minutes, then remove from the heat and keep warm.
3. Cook the pasta until *al dente*, then drain.
4. Toss the pasta with the sauce, sage, and blue cheese, then season with salt, if needed, and black pepper.

Spaghetti with Toasted Cumin and Simmered Garlic in Tangy Cheese Sauce

SERVES 4

Greek yogurt adds a tangy quality to this cumin-scented cheese sauce. As untraditional and surprising as the recipe may sound, it makes a delicious bowlful.

10 cloves garlic, peeled but left whole
250ml/8 fl oz vegetable stock
325g/12 oz spaghetti
½ teaspoon cumin seeds, or to taste
3–4 tablespoons Greek yogurt or sour cream
175g/6 oz white cheese such as fontina, Cheddar, Jarlsberg, etc., diced or grated
Freshly ground black pepper to taste

10 cloves garlic, peeled but left whole
1 cup vegetable stock
12 oz spaghetti
½ teaspoon cumin seeds, or to taste
¼ cup sour cream
6oz/⅓ lb white cheese such as fontina, Monterey Jack, white Cheddar, Jarlsberg, etc., diced or grated
Freshly ground black pepper to taste

1. Simmer the garlic cloves in the stock until tender, about 15–20 minutes. Set aside.
2. Cook the pasta until *al dente*; drain.
3. Meanwhile, prepare the sauce: lightly toast the cumin seeds in an ungreased heavy frying pan (skillet) over medium heat for a minute or two until fragrant. Do not let them burn.
4. Add the garlic cloves and half of the vegetable stock, heat through, then add the Greek yogurt or sour cream and cheese. (Do not worry about the lumpy appearance of the sauce: it is the soft garlic cloves, and they make a nice surprise when bitten into.) Thin with remaining stock if needed, or reserve this for another purpose.
5. Toss the pasta with the sauce and serve immediately, seasoned with black pepper to taste.

Lumache or Penne with Ricotta Cheese and Black Olives

SERVES 4–6

1 onion, chopped
4 cloves garlic, chopped
25–50ml/1–2 fl oz olive oil
1 tablespoon chopped fresh rosemary
Freshly ground black pepper to taste
325–400g/12–14 oz ricotta cheese
About 25–35 black Mediterranean-style
  olives, pitted and diced
450g/1 lb lumache (seashells), penne,
  or other chubby-shaped pasta
Freshly grated Parmesan cheese to
  serve

1 onion, chopped
4 cloves garlic, chopped
2–4 tablespoons olive oil
1 tablespoon chopped fresh rosemary
Freshly ground black pepper to taste
¾ lb/1½ cups ricotta cheese
About 25–35 black Mediterranean-style
  olives, pitted and diced
1 lb lumache (seashells), penne, or
  other chubby-shaped pasta
Freshly grated Parmesan cheese to
  serve

1. Lightly sauté the onions and garlic in the olive oil until just softened.
2. Remove from the heat and add the rosemary, black pepper, ricotta cheese and olives. Set aside.
3. Cook the pasta until *al dente*. Drain and toss with the sauce, then with Parmesan cheese. Serve immediately.

Ditalini and Broccoli with Creamy Blue Cheese Sauce

SERVES 4

While combining blue cheese such as Gorgonzola with pasta is a delicious Italian tradition, adding richness and smoothness to the sauce, the pungency of the blue-veined cheese does mellow and lose its characteristic bite as it heats. Here, half the blue cheese is added at the beginning for its richness, and half at the end for its tangy jolt.

15g/½ oz butter
1 tablespoon flour
250ml/8 fl oz milk
250g/9 oz blue cheese, crumbled
Salt and freshly ground black pepper,
  to taste
Tiny pinch of cayenne pepper
325g/12 oz ditalini or similar pasta
1–2 bunches broccoli, cut into bite-
  sized florets

1 tablespoon butter
1 tablespoon flour
1 cup hot milk
9 oz blue cheese, crumbled
Salt and freshly ground black pepper,
  to taste
Tiny pinch of cayenne pepper
12 oz ditalini or similar pasta
1–2 bunches broccoli, cut into bite-
  sized florets

1. Melt the butter in a pan, then sprinkle with the flour. Cook for a few minutes until golden, then remove from the heat and stir in a little of the milk to make a smooth paste, then gradually add the rest. Return to the heat and cook, stirring, until thickened. Remove from the heat again and stir in half the blue cheese.

2. Cook the pasta until half done, then add the broccoli and continue cooking until both broccoli and pasta are *al dente*.

3. Drain and toss the broccoli and pasta with the sauce, then crumble the remaining blue cheese over, toss well, and serve immediately.

PASTAS WITH BEANS

Hearty, high-protein beans combined with chewy, supple pasta make satisfying main courses or supper dishes. The range is wide: tender cannellini (white kidney) beans or the even more tender pale green flageolets, sprightly black-eyed peas, mealy butter beans or lima beans, slightly sweet red kidney beans and nutty chickpeas (garbanzos), plus lentils of all colours.

Tinned (canned) beans may replace dried beans for speed and convenience in most recipes. Take care to adjust the salt, however, as most tinned beans are overly saline.

Soy products such as soya mince fill out pasta sauces, too, adding body and protein. For recipes using tofu, refer to the chapter on Far Eastern pasta, and do consult the chapter on Soups and Stews for other pasta dishes featuring beans.

Pappardelle with Broccoli and Red Beans

SERVES 6

Wide strips of noodles tossed with a brash and satisfying mixture of broccoli, tomatoes and red beans is a typical dish from the Mezzogiorno in the south of Italy.

Any fairly large pasta shape is good with this hearty bean and broccoli mixture: the hollow tubes called bucatini, rotelle (wagon wheels) or penne (quills).

3-4 cloves garlic, finely chopped
3 tablespoons olive oil
550g/1¼ lb broccoli, cut into bite-sized florets, the stems peeled and sliced
5 ripe fresh or tinned tomatoes, chopped
350ml/12 fl oz tomato passata
Pinch of sugar (optional)
400g/14 oz cooked or drained tinned kidney beans
450g/1 lb pappardelle, or other pasta shape of choice
Freshly grated Parmesan cheese to serve

3-4 cloves garlic, finely chopped
3 tablespoons olive oil
2 bunches broccoli, cut into bite-sized florets, the stems peeled and sliced
5 ripe fresh or canned tomatoes, diced
1½ cups tomato passata or tomato sauce
Pinch of sugar (optional)
1½ cups cooked or drained canned kidney beans
1 lb pappardelle, or other pasta shape of choice
Freshly grated Parmesan cheese to serve

1. Lightly sauté the garlic in the olive oil and add the broccoli. Cook over medium heat for a minute or two, then add the tomatoes and tomato passata or sauce and continue cooking for a few minutes longer or until it becomes saucelike. Raise the heat if it is too liquidy. Add the sugar if the sauce is too acidic.
2. Add the kidney beans and simmer while you cook the pasta.
3. Boil the pasta until *al dente*. Drain and serve with the sauce and Parmesan cheese.

Pasta with Chickpeas (Garbanzos) and Garlic-Rosemary-Lemon Sauce

SERVES 4–6

Browning garlic then simmering it with rosemary, stock, and lemon juice makes a tangy sauce for stubby-shaped macaroni and nutty chickpeas (garbanzos). Season with hot pepper for a spicy accent.

8 cloves garlic, coarsely chopped
2 tablespoons olive oil
15g/½ oz butter
2 tablespoons coarsely chopped fresh
  rosemary
100ml/4 fl oz vegetable stock
Several leaves chopped fresh spinach
  or 1 tablespoon cooked spinach,
  chopped (optional)
2 tablespoons lemon juice
400g/14 oz cooked or drained tinned
  chickpeas
325g/12 oz short pasta
Cayenne pepper or hot pepper flakes,
  to taste
Salt and freshly ground black pepper,
  to taste

8 cloves garlic, coarsely chopped·
2 tablespoons olive oil
1 tablespoon butter
2 tablespoons coarsely chopped fresh
  rosemary
½ cup vegetable stock
Several leaves chopped fresh spinach
  or 1 tablespoon chopped cooked
  spinach (optional)
2 tablespoons lemon juice
1½ cups cooked or drained canned
  garbanzos
12 oz short pasta
Cayenne pepper or hot pepper flakes,
  to taste
Salt and freshly ground black pepper,
  to taste

1. Cook the garlic in the olive oil and butter over medium heat until golden; add the rosemary, stir through, then add the stock and cook until reduced by about half.
2. Add the spinach, if using, and the lemon juice and cook over medium heat until strongly flavoured and almost syrupy. Add the chickpeas (garbanzos) and set aside.

3. Meanwhile, cook the pasta until *al dente*, then drain.
4. Toss the pasta with the sauce. Season with cayenne pepper or hot pepper flakes, and salt and black pepper if liked, then serve immediately, adding a squeeze of lemon juice at the last minute if needed.

Spaghetti with Curried Broccoli and Chickpeas (Garbanzos)

SERVES 4

1 onion, coarsely chopped
5 cloves garlic, chopped
1 tablespoon chopped fresh ginger root
½–1 fresh hot green chilli, chopped
25g/1 oz butter
1 teaspoon curry powder
½ teaspoon cumin
Seeds of 6 cardamom pods
200g/7 oz cooked or drained tinned
   chickpeas
2 teaspoons chickpea (besan) flour
   (optional)
175ml/6 fl oz vegetable stock
550g/1¼ lb broccoli, cut into bite-sized
   florets, stems peeled and sliced
175–200ml/6–8 fl oz yogurt
Salt and cayenne pepper, to taste
325g/12 oz spaghetti
Juice of ½ lemon
2 tablespoons chopped fresh coriander
   leaves

1 onion, chopped
5 cloves garlic, chopped
1 tablespoon chopped fresh ginger root
½–1 fresh hot green chilli such as
   jalapeno, chopped
2 tablespoons butter
1 teaspoon curry powder
½ teaspoon cumin
Seeds of 6 cardamon pods
1 cup cooked or drained canned
   garbanzos
2 teaspoons garbanzo flour (optional)
¾ cup vegetable stock
2 bunches broccoli, cut into bite-sized
   florets, stems peeled and sliced
¾–1 cup yogurt
Salt and cayenne pepper, to taste
12 oz spaghetti
Juice of ½ lemon
2 tablespoons chopped fresh cilantro

1. Lightly sauté the onion, garlic, ginger root and chilli in the butter until softened, then sprinkle in the spices and cook for a moment or two.
2. Add the chickpeas (garbanzos) and chickpea flour, if using, and cook for a few minutes, then stir in the stock and bring to the boil. Add the broccoli and cook until crisp-tender.
3. Remove the broccoli from the sauce with a slotted spoon, then raise the heat and cook the sauce until reduced in volume and very thick. Remove from the heat, stir in the yogurt, and return the broccoli to the pan. Add the salt and cayenne pepper, then cover and keep warm.
4. Cook the spaghetti until *al dente*.
5. Drain the pasta and serve with the broccoli sauce, sprinkled with the lemon juice and fresh coriander leaves (cilantro).

Curly Pasta with Curried Soya Mince (Textured Soy Protein), Browned Garlic Oil, and Minted Yogurt

SERVES 4–6

This unlikely and absolutely delicious dish is vaguely Middle Eastern in origin. The contrast of flavours and textures is marvellous. Though the recipe looks time-consuming, it is very easy to prepare.

10 cloves garlic, sliced or coarsely chopped
75ml/3 fl oz olive oil
250ml/8 fl oz yogurt
1 teaspoon dried mint, crumbled, or to taste
325–450g/12–16 oz thick twisting pasta such as fusilli lunghi, or thick straight pasta such as bucatini broken into shorter lengths

Curried Soya Mince
1 onion, chopped
2 cloves garlic, chopped
1 hot chilli, chopped
1.25cm/½ inch piece fresh ginger root, chopped
1 carrot, diced
½ red pepper, coarsely chopped
2 tablespoons vegetable or olive oil
Enough soya mince to make 450g/1 lb when rehydrated
3–4 chard or outer cabbage leaves, blanched and thinly sliced
½ teaspoon curry powder
¼ teaspoon turmeric
¼ teaspoon cumin
Pinch of lavender (optional)
1 vegetable stock cube
25g/1 oz fresh coriander, coarsely chopped
Dash of lemon juice
Salt and freshly ground black pepper, to taste

10 cloves garlic, sliced or coarsely chopped
⅓ cup olive oil
1 cup yogurt
1 teaspoon dried mint, crumbled, or to taste
12–16 oz thick curly pasta such as fusilli lunghi, or thick straight pasta such as bucatini broken into shorter lengths

Curried Soy Protein
1 onion, chopped
2 cloves garlic, chopped
1 hot chilli pepper such as a jalapeno, chopped
½ inch piece fresh ginger root, chopped
1 carrot, diced
½ red bell pepper, coarsely chopped
2 tablespoons vegetable or olive oil
Enough dehydrated textured soy protein to make 1 lb when rehydrated
3–4 chard or outer cabbage leaves, blanched and thinly sliced
½ teaspoon curry powder
¼ teaspoon turmeric
¼ teaspoon cumin
Pinch of lavender (optional)
1 vegetable bouillion cube
¼ cup coarsely chopped cilantro
Dash of lemon juice
Salt and freshly ground black pepper, to taste

1. Heat the garlic in the oil in a heavy frying pan (skillet) over medium heat until golden. Remove from the heat and set aside.
2. Mix together the yogurt and mint and chill.
3. To make the curried soya mince, sauté the onion, garlic, chilli, ginger root, carrot, and red (bell) pepper in the oil until softened, then add the soya mince (textured vegetable protein) and cook for a few more minutes over medium heat until lightly browned.
4. Add the chard or cabbage, curry powder, turmeric, cumin, lavender, if using, stock cube (bouillon cube), and enough water to rehydrate the soya mince or textured soy protein (follow the instructions on the packet). Cook for about 15–20 minutes, or until the mince is rehydrated and the mixture saucelike.
5. Add the coriander leaves (cilantro), lemon juice, and salt and black pepper.
6. Cook the pasta until *al dente*; drain.
7. Serve the pasta tossed with the browned garlic oil then topped with the curried soya mince (textured soy protein) and a dollop of minted yogurt.

Pasta al Ceci

PASTA WITH CHICKPEA [GARBANZO] AND TOMATO SAUCE

SERVES 6

Robust and lusty, this dish is filled with the flavours of Italy's sun-drenched South.

2 small to medium onions, chopped	2 small to medium onions, chopped
6 cloves garlic, chopped	6 cloves garlic, chopped
2 tablespoons olive oil	2 tablespoons olive oil
400g/14 oz cooked or drained tinned chickpeas	1½ cups cooked or drained canned garbanzos
1 litre/1¾ pints tomato passata	4 cups tomato passata or sauce
¼–½ teaspoon dried thyme, or to taste	¼–½ teaspoon dried thyme, or to taste
1 bay leaf	1 bay leaf
Pinch of sugar (optional)	Pinch of sugar (optional)
Salt and freshly ground black pepper, to taste	Salt and freshly ground black pepper, to taste
450g/1 lb spaghetti	1 lb spaghetti
Freshly grated Parmesan cheese to serve	Freshly grated Parmesan cheese to serve

1. Sauté the onions and garlic in the olive oil until softened.
2. Add the chickpeas (garbanzos), tomato passata, thyme and bay leaf then bring to the boil. Reduce the heat and simmer for 5–10 minutes, then season with the sugar, salt and black pepper.
3. Cook the spaghetti until *al dente*, then drain.
4. Toss with the sauce and serve with Parmesan cheese.

Rigatoni with White Beans, Tomato-Parsley Sauce and Red Pesto

SERVES 4–6

4–5 cloves garlic, chopped
2 tablespoons olive oil
15g/½ oz parsley, coarsely chopped
14 oz cooked or drained tinned white haricot beans or cannellini
450g/1 lb fresh ripe tomatoes, diced, or 1 400g/14 oz tin chopped tomatoes
Pinch of sugar (optional)
Salt and freshly ground black pepper, to taste
450g/1 lb rigatoni or other short thick pasta shape
200g/6 oz red pesto (see page 256)
2–3 tablespoons coarsely chopped fresh basil to serve (optional)
Freshly grated Parmesan cheese to serve

4–5 cloves garlic, chopped
2 tablespoons olive oil
¼ cup coarsely chopped parsley
1½ cups cooked or drained canned cannellini, Great Northern, or other white beans
1½ cups chopped fresh or canned tomatoes
Pinch of sugar (optional)
Salt and freshly ground black pepper, to taste
1 lb rigatoni or other short thick pasta shape
⅓ cup red pesto (see page 256)
2–3 tablespoons chopped fresh basil to serve (optional)
Freshly grated Parmesan cheese to serve

1. Heat the garlic in the olive oil until fragrant but not browned, then stir in the parsley and beans and cook for a few moments.
2. Add tomatoes and cook over medium to high heat for a minute or two until most of the liquid evaporates. Season with sugar, if using, and salt and black pepper. Set aside and keep warm.
3. Cook the pasta until *al dente*, then drain.
4. Toss the pasta with the sauce and red pesto.

Serve sprinkled with fresh basil and Parmesan cheese.

Variation

Instead of haricot beans or cannellini (white kidney beans), use cooked or drained tinned butter beans (large dried white lima beans). To the sautéeing garlic add 1 diced red (bell) pepper, then proceed as above.

FAR EASTERN PASTA

While the old belief that pasta was brought to Italy from China by Marco Polo has been pretty much debunked, there is no doubt that noodles have been eaten in the Far East for a very long time. Traditional Chinese, Japanese, Burmese, Vietnamese, Thai and other Southeast Asian pasta dishes abound. And well they should: their bland quality pairs so well with strong and pungent Far Eastern flavours: soy, sesame, chilli, lime and so on.

Far Eastern pasta is not always made from wheat: rice, buckwheat, mung beans, and potato flour are among the various ingredients used to make Asian noodles. They have slightly different qualities from Italian and other Western pasta, and use different seasoning ingredients: sharp and savoury, pungent sauces and soups rather than the more Mediterranean-flavoured or creamy sauces of the West. I have therefore grouped these Asian or Far Eastern dishes together in this chapter. There are a number scattered throughout other chapters of this book as well.

Black Mushroom Broth with Tofu, Tree Cloud Fungus, Broccoli and Cellophane Noodles

SERVES 4

Cellophane noodles are made from potato and pea starch. They are slithery and translucent, and light rather than starchy like most other noodles.

50g/2 oz dried Chinese black mushrooms (shiitake)

15g/½ oz tree cloud fungus

500ml/16 fl oz hot, but not boiling, water

50g/2 oz dried cellophane noodles

1 litre/1¾ pints vegetable stock

2 celery stalks, cut on the slant into bite-sized pieces

1.25cm/½ inch piece fresh ginger root, chopped

2 cloves garlic, chopped

1 tablespoon vegetable oil

1 bunch broccoli, cut into bite-sized pieces florets, the stems peeled and sliced

300g/11 oz firm tofu, cut into bite-sized squares

Soy sauce to taste

2 oz dried Chinese black mushrooms (shiitake)

½ oz tree cloud fungus

2 cups hot, but not boiling, water

2 oz dried cellophane noodles

1 quart vegetable stock

2 celery stalks, cut on the slant into bite-sized pieces

½ inch piece fresh ginger root, chopped

2 cloves garlic, chopped

1 tablespoon vegetable oil

1 bunch broccoli, cut into bite-sized florets, the stems peeled and sliced

11 oz firm tofu, cut into bite-sized squares

Soy sauce to taste

1. Rehydrate the black mushrooms and tree cloud fungus in separate bowls in the hot water, as described on page 262, reserving the soaking liquid. Cut off and discard the stalks, then cut the tree cloud fungus into small pieces.
2. Soak the cellophane noodles in cold water to cover for about 10 minutes. Drain and cut into 2.5–5 cm/1–2 inch lengths. Set aside.
3. Put the mushrooms, tree cloud fungus, and their soaking liquid in a pan with the vegetable stock and bring to the boil, then reduce the heat and simmer for 10–15 minutes.
4. Meanwhile, stir-fry the celery, ginger root and garlic in the oil, then add this mixture to the simmering soup, together with the noodles.
5. Simmer for another 5 minutes, then add the broccoli and tofu. Simmer until the broccoli is tender. Season with soy sauce to taste.

Variation

Hot and Sour Soup: Prepare the soup, adding thin shreds of Chinese leaves (Chinese or Napa cabbage) with the broccoli. Beat 2 eggs and thin with a little soy sauce, then drizzle into the soup, letting it form threads. Season generously with cayenne pepper and white vinegar, wine vinegar or sherry vinegar to taste – you should be aiming for a tart, hot flavour. Season with soy sauce if needed, then serve each bowful sprinkled with sesame oil, chopped spring onions (green onions) and fresh coriander leaves (cilantro).

Southeast Asian Rice Noodle Broth with Lime, Chillies, Salad and Peanuts

SERVES 4

This outstanding soup performs a balancing act of aromas, flavours, and textures; its chilli-heat and lightness make it particularly good summer fare, and it has the bonus of being quick and easy to prepare.

325g/12 oz dried wide rice noodles, preferably Vietnamese	12 oz dried wide rice noodles, preferably Vietnamese
1 litre/1¾ pints vegetable stock	1 quart vegetable stock
2 cloves garlic, coarsely chopped	2 cloves garlic, coarsely chopped
3–4 spring onions, thinly sliced	3–4 green onions, thinly sliced
1 cucumber, roughly chopped	1 cucumber, roughly chopped
2 tablespoons chopped fresh coriander leaves	2 heaping tablespoons chopped fresh cilantro
2 tablespoons chopped fresh mint leaves	2 heaping tablespoons chopped fresh mint leaves
3–4 tablespoons coarsely chopped dry-roasted peanuts	3–4 heaping tablespoons coarsely chopped dry-roasted peanuts
2 fresh green medium-hot chillies, thinly sliced	2 fresh green chillies such as jalapeno, thinly sliced
1 lime, cut into wedges	1 lime, cut into wedges

1. Soak the noodles in cold water for 10 minutes. Drain, then plunge into boiling water for 3–5 minutes. Drain.
2. Heat the stock with the garlic, then add the drained noodles and cook until heated through.
3. Serve immediately, garnished with the remaining ingredients.

South Pacific-East Asian Coconut Soup with Chinese Egg Noodles, Green Beans and Water Chestnuts

SERVES 4–6

*This broth is very rich yet clean-tasting, with a complexity that belies its simplicity.
I like to sip the mild creamy soup first, then when I reach the noodles, add a squeeze
of lemon or lime juice and a shake of hot pepper or Tabasco.*

325g/12 oz Chinese egg noodles, either fresh or dried
Soy sauce and sesame oil to season the noodles
3 spring onions, thinly sliced
10–15 water chestnuts, diced
2 heaped tablespoons coarsely chopped fresh coriander leaves
1 egg, lightly beaten
600ml/1 pint vegetable stock
50g/2 oz creamed coconut in block form (or reduce the stock by 250ml/8 fl oz and use 250ml/8 fl oz unsweetened coconut milk or cream)
Handful of green beans, cut into bite-sized lengths
Cayenne pepper to taste
1 lime or lemon, cut into wedges

12 oz Chinese egg noodles, either fresh or dried
Soy sauce and sesame oil to season the noodles
3 green onions, thinly sliced
10–15 water chestnuts, diced
2 heaping tablespoons coarsely chopped fresh cilantro
1 egg, lightly beaten
3 cups vegetable stock
1 cup unsweetened coconut milk or coconut cream
¼ lb green beans, cut into bite-sized lengths
Cayenne pepper to taste
1 lime or lemon, cut into wedges

1. Cook the noodles until *al dente*, then drain and rinse with cold water. Season with a few splashes of soy sauce and sesame oil, then mix with the spring onions (green onions), water chestnuts, coriander leaves (cilantro) and egg. Set aside. (This may be done up to a day in advance and kept covered in the refrigerator.)
2. Combine the vegetable stock, coconut milk or cream (if using a block, let it melt in as the stock heats) and green beans. Bring to the boil. Beans should be bright green and the broth should be creamy.
3. Add the noodle mixture to the soup and stir to combine, heating for a minute or two to cook the egg.
4. Serve immediately, each portion sprinkled with cayenne pepper and accompanied by a wedge of lime or lemon to squeeze in.

Vietnamese-Style Tomato Broth with Cellophane Noodles and Bean Sprouts

SERVES 4

Very light yet brightly flavoured, this soup makes a refreshing summer supper or winter first course.

50g/2 oz cellophane noodles
5 spring onions, thinly sliced
1–2 tablespoons vegetable oil
6–8 ripe fresh or tinned tomatoes, chopped
1 litre/1¾ pints vegetable stock
Cayenne pepper to taste
2 handfuls bean sprouts
Wedges of lime
3 tablespoons coarsely chopped peanuts

2 oz cellophane noodles
5 green onions, thinly sliced
1–2 tablespoons vegetable oil
6–8 ripe fresh or canned tomatoes, chopped
1 quart vegetable stock
Cayenne pepper to taste
¼–½ lb bean sprouts
Wedges of lime
¼ cup coarsely chopped peanuts

1. Put the noodles in a bowl and pour over hot, but not boiling, water to cover. Leave for 10 minutes or until softened. Drain and rinse in cold water, then cut into bite-sized strands. Set aside.

2. Lightly sauté the spring onions (green onions) in the oil until softened, then add the tomatoes and cook about 5 minutes. Add the stock, bring to the boil, then add the noodles and simmer for 5–10 minutes or until richly flavoured.

3. Season with cayenne pepper. Just before serving, add the bean sprouts and heat through. Serve each portion sprinkled with the peanuts and accompanied by wedges of lime.

Japanese-Style Noodles in Broth Topped with Savoury Custard

SERVES 1–2

The fat, thick noodles – called udon – are delicious in this Japanese noodle snack, but as they are usually available only in Japanese, Chinese or other Far Eastern groceries. I often substitute dried Chinese-style egg noodles, which are available in every supermarket.

75-100g/3-4 oz dried egg noodles, or
   fresh udon
250-300ml/8-10 fl oz vegetable stock
1 egg, lightly beaten
½ teaspoon soy sauce
1 spring onion, thinly sliced

3-4 oz dried egg noodles or fresh udon
1-1¼ cups vegetable stock
1 egg, lightly beaten
½ teaspoon soy sauce
1 green onion, thinly sliced

1. Cook the noodles until just tender. Drain.
2. Heat the stock to boiling; remove from the heat and keep hot. Combine the egg with the soy sauce and spring onion (green onion).
3. Add the noodles to the hot stock, then pour the egg mixture over the top. Do not stir together, but let it more or less float on top of the soup. Cover and cook over low to medium heat until the egg mixture is steamed to firmness.
4. Serve immediately, with extra soy sauce to taste.

Coconut Curry with Rice Noodles, Chinese Black Mushrooms (Shiitake) and Water Chestnuts

SERVES 4–6

This easily prepared, somewhat soupy noodle dish has a whiff of curry and the richness of coconut, paired with the earthy flavour of shiitake mushrooms. You can vary the dish by adding a little broccoli or asparagus.

15 dried Chinese black mushrooms or shiitake

1 litre/1¾ pints hot, but not boiling, water

375g/13 oz thin rice noodles (also called rice sticks or rice vermicelli)

2 vegetable stock cubes

100g/4 oz coconut cream in block form (or substitute unsweetened coconut milk for half the water)

10–15 fresh, blanched or drained tinned water chestnuts, diced

½ teaspoon curry powder, or to taste, plus a little extra for sprinkling

15 dried Chinese black mushrooms or shiitake

3 cups hot, but not boiling, water

13 oz rice noodles (also called rice sticks or rice vermicelli)

2 vegetable bouillion cubes

2 cups unsweetened coconut milk or coconut cream

10–15 canned and drained or fresh, blanched water chestnuts, diced

½ teaspoon curry powder, or to taste, plus a little extra for sprinkling

1. Rehydrate the mushrooms in the hot water as described on page 262, reserving the soaking liquid. Remove and discard the mushroom stems, then thinly slice the mushroom caps and set aside.
2. Soak the rice noodles in cold water for about 15 minutes. Drain then cook in boiling water for a few minutes only, until just tender. Drain and rinse with cold water. Set aside.
3. Heat the mushroom soaking liquid with the stock cubes, coconut cream, water chestnuts, curry powder and shiitake. Cook for a few minutes, until the liquid thickens slightly.
4. Add the noodles and serve immediately, sprinkled lightly with curry powder.

Variation

Rice Noodles with Shiitake and Tomatoes: Follow the recipe above, but heat the sauce in a frying pan instead of a saucepan. Add 2 diced ripe tomatoes to the sauce and cook over medium heat until the liquid is reduced and very thick. This will be a dryish noodle dish now, not a soup.

Add the noodles to the sauce and toss together for a moment on the heat. Serve immediately, each portion sprinkled with a generous amount of thinly sliced spring onions (green onions).

Rice Noodles with Shiitake, Tree Cloud Fungus, Greens, and the Scent of Sesame

SERVES 4

8-10 dried shiitake or Chinese black
  mushrooms
2-3 large tree cloud fungus
350ml/12 fl oz hot, but not boiling,
  vegetable stock
275g/10 oz thin rice noodles (also
  called rice sticks or rice vermicelli)
2 tablespoons vegetable oil
2 eggs, lightly beaten
2 onions, thinly sliced
3 cloves garlic, chopped
2 teaspoons chopped fresh ginger root
½ lb spinach or 1 head bok choy or
  ½ head Chinese leaves, cut into
  bite-sized pieces
1 teaspoon cornflour
Soy sauce and sesame oil for drizzling
Hot pepper sauce or chilli oil, to taste

8-10 dried shiitake or Chinese black
  mushrooms
2-3 large tree cloud fungus
1½ cups hot, but not boiling,
  vegetable stock
10 oz thin rice noodles (also called rice
  sticks or rice vermicelli)
2 tablespoons vegetable oil
2 eggs, lightly beaten
2 onions, thinly sliced
3 cloves garlic, chopped
2 teaspoons chopped fresh ginger root
½ bunch bok choy, 1 bunch spinach
  or chard, or ½ head Napa or Chinese
  cabbage, cut into bite-sized pieces
1 teaspoon cornstarch
Soy sauce and sesame oil for drizzling
Hot pepper sauce or chilli oil, to taste

1. Rehydrate the shiitake or Chinese black mushrooms and tree cloud fungus in separate bowls in the hot stock as described on page 262, reserving the soaking liquid. Cut the stems and tough parts from the mushrooms and discard. Slice the mushrooms and tree cloud fungus into small pieces and set aside.

2. Soak the rice noodles in cold water until they soften, about 15 minutes. Drain and cook in boiling water for just a few minutes until tender, then drain and set aside.

3. In about 1 tablespoon of the vegetable oil make a thin flat omelette with the beaten eggs. Cook on both sides, remove to a plate and roll up. Slice thinly and set aside.

4. Stir-fry the onions, garlic and ginger root in the remaining vegetable oil, add the mushrooms and tree cloud fungus and stir-fry for a moment or two. Remove from the pan, then stir-fry the spinach, bok-choy or Chinese leaves (Napa or Chinese cabbage) for a moment or two until crisp-tender. Remove and set aside.

5. Stir the cornflour (cornstarch) into the mushroom soaking liquid, then pour into the pan or wok and cook until slightly thickened. Add the reserved noodles and vegetables (including any juices) and heat through.

6. Serve immediately, drizzled with soy sauce and sesame oil, and topped with the thinly sliced omelette. Pass hot sauce or chilli oil for each person to add to taste.

Chinese Breakfast Noodles

SERVES 4

Tender noodles, freshly cooked and glistening with a splash of soy sauce and sesame oil, are a traditional Chinese breakfast food, dispensed by street stalls that park themselves enticingly outside the apartment blocks of residential neighbourhoods. Rice noodles are often used, but I find fresh wonton noodles or other fresh pasta make an excellent substitute.

Toppings might include crunchy toasted sesame seeds or a drizzle of fiery hot chilli oil. This recipe gives my favourite combination: sesame oil, soy sauce, and spring onions (green onions), with a sprinkling of crushed peanuts as a last-minute consideration; it is delicious either with or without.

325g/12 oz wonton noodles
1–2 tablespoons soy sauce, to taste
2–3 tablespoons sesame oil, to taste
Dash of hot sauce such as Tabasco or
 chilli oil (optional)
4–6 spring onions, thinly sliced
1–2 tablespoons coarsely crushed or
 chopped roasted peanuts (optional)

12 oz wonton noodles
1–2 tablespoons soy sauce, to taste
2–3 tablespoons sesame oil, to taste
Dash of hot sauce such as Tabasco or
 chilli oil (optional)
4–6 green onions, thinly sliced
1–2 tablespoons coarsely crushed or
 chopped roasted peanuts (optional)

1. Cook the wonton noodles in boiling water until just tender. Take care when you drop them into the water that they do not stick together in one large chunk of noodle.

2. Drain and season with the soy sauce, sesame oil, and hot pepper sauce if using. Top with the spring onions (green onions) and peanuts, if using, and serve immediately.

Crisp-Fried Rice Noodle Cloud Over Spicy-Sweet Mixed Vegetable Stir-Fry

SERVES 4

Thin rice noodles fry up into a crispy, light, cloud-like mass, making a delightful counterpoint to savoury stir-fries or tangy fresh vegetable salads.

125g/4½ oz thin rice noodles (also called rice stick or rice vermicelli)
Vegetable oil for deep frying, plus a very small amount for stir-frying
1–2 onions, thinly sliced
3 cloves garlic, chopped
1 tablespoon chopped fresh ginger root
1 green pepper, diced
1 red pepper, diced
Handful of green beans, mangetout, sugar snap peas or asparagus, cut into 5cm/2 inch lengths
10–15 mushrooms, quartered
1 courgette, sliced on the diagonal
125g/4½ oz water chestnuts, quartered or sliced
Handful of bean sprouts
100ml/4 fl oz hoisin sauce
100ml/4 fl oz vegetable stock
1 tablespoon cornflour
1 tablespoon soy sauce, or to taste
1 tablespoon sugar
Hot pepper seasoning to taste
1–2 tablespoons chopped fresh coriander leaves

4–5 oz thin rice noodles (also called rice sticks or rice vermicelli)
Vegetable oil for deep frying, plus a very small amount for stir-frying
1–2 onions, thinly sliced
3 cloves garlic, chopped
1 tablespoon chopped fresh ginger root
1 green bell pepper, diced
1 red bell pepper, diced
2 cups green beans, snow peas, sugar snap peas or asparagus, cut into 2 inch lengths
10–15 mushrooms, quartered
1 zucchini, sliced on the diagonal
¾ cup quartered or sliced water chestnuts
¼ lb bean sprouts
½ cup hoisin sauce
½ cup vegetable stock
1 tablespoon cornstarch
1 tablespoon soy sauce, or to taste
1 tablespoon sugar
Hot pepper seasoning to taste
1–2 tablespoons chopped fresh cilantro

1. Deep fry the dry rice noodles in very small batches in medium hot oil. It will take only a few minutes for them to sizzle and expand dramatically, becoming light and crisp. Do not let the noodles become golden; when they are crispy light and still white, but no longer tough or crunchy and hard, remove with a slotted spoon and leave on absorbent paper to drain. Set aside.

2. In a wok or heavy frying pan (skillet), stir-fry the onions, garlic, ginger root, green and red (bell) peppers in a very little oil. When tender-crunchy remove from the pan and set aside, then stir-fry in separate batches the

green beans (or mangetout [snow peas], sugar snap peas or asparagus) with the mushrooms, the courgette (zucchini), and the water chestnuts with the bean sprouts. Set all the vegetables aside.

3. Mix the hoisin sauce with the stock, cornflour (cornstarch), soy sauce, sugar and hot pepper seasoning. Pour into the hot wok and stir until thickened, then return the vegetables to the pan and toss with the sauce.

4. Serve immediately, arranging the vegetables on a platter, topping them with a halo of crisp rice noodles and finishing with a sprinkling of coriander leaves (cilantro).

Spicy Rice Noodle Snack from the Streets of Hong Kong

SERVES 2–4

Just one of the endless noodle dishes ladled up by the street vendors of Hong Kong. The seller reaches into the steamy cauldron, lifts out a portion of hot noodles, splashes on a little sauce and sprinkles on a garnish, and you immediately have a spicy treat.

225g/8 oz dried flat rice noodles, about 3mm/⅛ inch wide or 325g/12 oz fresh rice noodles
2 tablespoons hoisin sauce
2 teaspoons chilli bean sauce
Pinch of sugar, optional
1 tablespoon sesame oil
1–1 ½ tablespoons soy sauce
1–2 tablespoons fresh coriander leaves (optional)
2 tablespoons toasted sesame seeds (optional)

8 oz dried flat rice noodles, about ⅛ inch wide, or 12 oz fresh rice noodles
2 tablespoons hoisin sauce
2 teaspoons hot bean sauce or chilli bean sauce
Pinch of sugar, optional
1 tablespoon sesame oil
1–1½ tablespoons soy sauce
1–2 tablespoons fresh cilantro leaves (optional)
2 tablespoons toasted sesame seeds (optional)

1. If using dried rice noodles, soak first for 15 minutes to soften. Cook the soaked or fresh rice noodles until just tender. Drain.

2. Stir together the hoisin sauce, hot bean (or chilli bean) sauce, sugar if using, sesame oil and soy sauce.

3. Serve the hot noodles topped with the sauce and sprinkled with the fresh coriander leaves (cilantro) and sesame seeds, if using.

Southeast Asian Rice Noodles with Ginger-Garlic Green Beans and Peanut Sauce

SERVES 4–6

This was inspired by a dish I enjoyed at the table of London cookery writer and illustrator, Leslie Forbes. She served the noodles as a side dish, but I have served them since as a central dish accompanied by a selection of crunchy salad vegetables, such as diced cucumbers sprinkled with cayenne pepper, diced red (bell) pepper, crisp-tender carrot slices in sesame oil and rice vinegar, and, perhaps, coarsely chopped peanuts.

325g/12 oz 6mm/¼ inch wide dried rice noodles (also called rice sticks or rice vermicelli)

225g/8 oz peanut butter (either smooth or crunchy)

100ml/4 fl oz coconut milk or 25–50g/1–2 oz coconut cream dissolved in 100ml/4 fl oz water

Cayenne pepper and salt, to taste

1 tablespoon sugar or honey, or to taste

Juice of 1 lime, or to taste

5 cloves garlic, coarsely chopped

1.25cm/½ inch piece fresh ginger root, chopped

1 tablespoon vegetable oil

225g/8 oz green beans, cut into 5cm/2 inch lengths (if other than young and tender, blanch first)

2 tablespoons coarsely chopped fresh coriander leaves

12 oz ⅛–¼ inch wide dried rice noodles (also called rice sticks or rice vermicelli)

¾ cup peanut butter, either smooth or crunchy

½ cup unsweetened coconut milk

Cayenne pepper and salt, to taste

1 tablespoon sugar or honey, or to taste

Juice of 1 lime, or to taste

5 cloves garlic, coarsely chopped

½ inch piece fresh ginger root, chopped

1 tablespoon vegetable oil

½ lb green beans, cut into 2 inch lengths (if other than young and tender, blanch first)

2 tablespoons coarsely chopped fresh cilantro

1. Soak the rice noodles in cold water and cook according to the instructions on the packet. Drain and set aside.
2. Combine the peanut butter and coconut milk in a pan and heat gently until melted; stir to mix well then remove from the heat. Season with cayenne pepper, salt, sugar or honey, and lime juice. Set aside.
3. Stir-fry the garlic and ginger root in the vegetable oil until softened and fragrant, then add the green beans and stir-fry together for a minute or two until crisp-tender. Season with salt.
4. Add the noodles to the green beans, toss through once or twice, then serve on a platter, topped with the peanut sauce and sprinkled with fresh coriander leaves (cilantro).

Don Don Mein

SICHUAN NOODLES WITH SPICY SAUCE

SERVES 4

In China, noodle dishes such as these are served for birthday celebrations, as the long strands of pasta signify longevity.

325g/12 oz dried or fresh Chinese egg noodles, either thin or thick
3 cloves garlic, chopped
1–2 dried hot red chillies
2 tablespoons vegetable oil
1 tablespoon tomato ketchup
1 tablespoon Chinese bean sauce
300g/11oz firm tofu, drained and diced
2–3 spring onions, thinly sliced
1 tablespoon finely minced Sichuan turnip (a hot chillied pickle available from Chinese groceries)
1 teaspoon chopped fresh ginger root
1 tablespoon sesame oil
50ml/2 fl oz vegetable stock
1 tablespoon sherry

12 oz dried or fresh Chinese egg noodles, either thin or thick
3 cloves garlic, chopped
1–2 dried hot red chillies
2 tablespoons vegetable oil
1 tablespoon tomato ketchup
1 tablespoon Chinese bean sauce
11 oz firm tofu, drained and diced
2–3 green onions, thinly sliced
1 tablespoon finely minced Sichuan hot chillied pickled turnip
1 teaspoon chopped fresh ginger root
1 tablespoon sesame oil
¼ cup vegetable stock
1 tablespoon sherry

1. Cook the noodles until just tender, then rinse with cold water and drain. Set aside.
2. Heat the garlic and chillies in the oil until the garlic is golden; take care to keep your face away from the wok or frying pan as the fumes from the chillies can irritate your eyes and nose. Remove the chillies and add the ketchup and bean sauce, then stir-fry the tofu in this mixture.
3. Add the spring onions (green onions), Sichuan (Szechuan) turnip, ginger root, sesame oil, vegetable stock and sherry. Heat through, then add the noodles and cook until they are hot. Serve immediately.

Cold Buckwheat Soba with Mangetout (Snow Peas) and Water Chestnuts

SERVES 4

325g/12 oz buckwheat soba, about the same width as fettuccine

100g/4 oz mangetout

2 tablespoons sesame oil

1 tablespoon vegetable oil

3 spring onions, thinly sliced

2-3 tablespoons soy sauce, preferably dark

Dash of hot pepper seasoning such as Tabasco or hot chilli oil

1 tablespoon lemon juice, balsamic vinegar or Chinese black vinegar

2 teaspoons sugar, or to taste

Salt to taste

About 10 water chestnuts, tinned or fresh and blanched, sliced

2 tablespoons toasted sesame seeds or slivered almonds (optional)

12 oz buckwheat soba, about the same width as fettuccine

¼ lb snow peas or sugar snap peas

2 tablespoons sesame oil

1 tablespoon vegetable oil

3 green onions, thinly sliced

2-3 tablespoons soy sauce, preferably dark

Dash of hot pepper seasoning such as Tabasco or hot chilli oil

1 tablespoon lemon juice, balsamic vinegar or Chinese black vinegar

2 teaspoons sugar, or to taste

Salt to taste

About 10 water chestnuts, canned or fresh and blanched, sliced

2 tablespoons toasted sesame seeds or slivered almonds (optional)

1. Cook the buckwheat soba until almost tender then add the mangetout (snow peas) or sugar snap peas and cook for a minute or two longer until the noodles are *al dente* and the vegetables are bright green and crisp-tender. Drain and rinse with cold water.
2. Mix with the sesame oil, vegetable oil, spring onions (green onions), soy sauce, hot pepper seasoning, lemon juice (or vinegar), sugar, and salt to taste. Add the water chestnuts and chill for at least an hour. Taste for seasoning. Garnish with the sesame seeds or almonds if using.

Broccoli Chow Fun

SERVES 4

Chow fun are sold in Chinese groceries. They are fat soft rolled sheets of rice noodles and utterly delicious, even if just served with a drizzle of sesame oil, soy sauce and spring onions (green onions). They are also good stir-fried with any number of vegetables and sauces. This is a variation on a dish I used to eat in San Francisco's Chinatown, late at night when the rest of the city was asleep but my favourite Chinese restaurant was wide awake and very busy.

3 tablespoons sesame seeds
450g/1 lb chow fun
3 cloves garlic, chopped
1–2 teaspoons chopped fresh ginger root
2–3 tablespoons vegetable oil
1–2 bunches broccoli, cut into bite-sized florets, stems peeled and sliced
4 oz bean sprouts (optional)
2 tablespoons sherry
2 teaspoons cornflour
2 tablespoons soy sauce, preferably dark
2 tablespoons vegetable stock
2 tablespoons sesame oil
2 spring onions, chopped

3 tablespoons sesame seeds
1 lb chow fun
3 cloves garlic, chopped
1–2 teaspoons chopped fresh ginger root
2–3 tablespoons vegetable oil
1–2 bunches broccoli, cut into bite-sized florets, stems peeled and sliced
¼ lb bean sprouts (optional)
2 tablespoons sherry
2 teaspoons cornstarch
2 tablespoons soy sauce, preferably dark
2 tablespoons vegetable stock
2 tablespoons sesame oil
2 green onions, chopped

1. Toast the sesame seeds in an ungreased heavy frying pan (skillet) over low to medium heat, turning every so often until fragrant and golden brown. Set aside.
2. Cut the chow fun into noodle shapes. Since it will be shaped like a large, fat, rolled pancake, cut it into strips about 4cm/1½ inch wide, then unroll. Set aside.
3. Heat the garlic and ginger root in half the oil in a wok or heavy frying pan (skillet), then stir-fry the broccoli until crisp-tender and bright green. Remove from the wok and reserve. If using bean sprouts, stir-fry quickly then remove from the wok and set aside.

4. Mix together the sherry, cornflower (cornstarch), soy sauce and vegetable stock. Set aside.
5. Heat the remaining oil until hot but not smoking. Add the chow fun and stir-fry for 2–3 minutes. Remove from the wok, add the sauce and stir until thickened, then return the chow fun and reserved vegetables to the wok and heat through.
6. Serve immediately, drizzled with the sesame oil, and sprinkled with the spring onions (green onions) and toasted sesame seeds.

East-West Pasta Primavera

SERVES 4–6

Any vegetables in season would be delicious in this East-West potful: try carrots sliced on the diagonal, Chinese leaves (Chinese or Napa cabbage) cut into strips, blanched sliced spring greens, sliced courgettes (zucchini), and so on.

325g/12 oz lasagne, or 1 packet fresh wonton noodles
1 tablespoon sesame oil, plus extra for seasoning
2–3 spring onions, thinly sliced
3–4 cloves garlic, chopped
1.25 cm/½ inch piece fresh ginger root, chopped
2 tablespoons vegetable oil
275–325g/10–12 oz broccoli, cut into bite-sized pieces
100g/4 oz asparagus, cut into bite-sized lengths
1 red pepper, cut into strips
100ml/4 fl oz vegetable stock
1 tablespoon cornflour, mixed into a paste with a little water
Soy sauce to taste
2 tablespoons chopped fresh coriander leaves

12 oz lasagne noodles or 1 package fresh wonton noodles
1 tablespoon sesame oil, plus extra for seasoning
2–3 green onions, thinly sliced
3–4 cloves garlic, chopped
½ inch piece fresh ginger root, chopped
2 tablespoons vegetable oil
1 bunch broccoli, cut into bite-sized pieces
¼ lb asparagus, cut into bite-sized lengths
1 red bell pepper, cut into strips
½ cup vegetable stock
1 tablespoon cornstarch, mixed into a paste with a little water
Soy sauce to taste
2 tablespoons chopped fresh cilantro

1. Cook the lasagne or wonton until just tender. Drain, rinse in cold water, then toss in the sesame oil and set aside.
2. In a large frying pan (skillet) or wok, stir-fry half the spring onions (green onions), garlic and ginger root in 1 tablespoon of the oil, then add the broccoli and cook until crisp-tender. Remove and set aside.
3. In the remaining oil stir-fry the remaining spring onions (green onions), garlic and ginger root, then add the asparagus and red (bell) pepper and cook until just tender. Remove and set aside.
4. Mix the stock and cornflour (cornstarch) until smooth, then pour it into the hot pan or wok and stir together until it thickens. Add the lasagne or wonton noodles and the vegetables, then toss to heat through. Remove from the heat, season with soy sauce and sesame oil, then serve immediately sprinkled with the coriander leaves (cilantro).

Cal-Asian Salad

SERVES 3–4

Fresh and invigorating for a summer lunch.

225g/8 oz thin rice noodles (also called rice sticks or rice vermicelli)
½ Cos lettuce, leaves rolled and cut into thin shreds
½ cucumber, diced
3–5 spring onions, thinly sliced
Pinch of dried mint leaves, crumbled
2 tablespoons olive oil
1 tablespoon lemon juice, or to taste
Salt to taste
1 red pepper, diced
2 tablespoons lightly crushed peanuts
2 teaspoons sesame oil
5–10 fresh mint leaves, cut into thin strips
½ teaspoon mild chilli powder, or to taste

½ lb thin rice noodles (also called rice sticks or rice vermicelli)
½ head Romaine lettuce, leaves rolled and cut into thin shreds
½ cucumber, diced
3–5 green onions, thinly sliced
Pinch of dried mint leaves, crumbled
2 tablespoons olive oil
1 tablespoon lemon juice, or to taste
Salt to taste
1 red bell pepper, diced
2 tablespoons lightly crushed peanuts
2 teaspoons sesame oil
5–10 fresh mint leaves, cut into thin strips
½ teaspoon chilli powder, or to taste

1. Soak the rice noodles for 10 minutes, then cook until tender. Drain and rinse in cold water, then set aside.
2. Combine the lettuce with the cucumber, spring onions (green onions) and dried mint, then dress with olive oil, lemon juice and salt. (Both steps 1 and 2 may be done up to a day in advance and kept, well covered, in the refrigerator.)
3. Place the green salad in a mound on a serving dish and surround with the noodles. Top the salad with the diced red (bell) pepper and the crushed peanuts and sprinkle with the sesame oil, fresh mint leaves and chilli powder.

Mee Goreng

SERVES 3–4

Mee Goreng is a spicy noodle dish from the street stalls and coffee shops of Singapore. These are run by Indians, and although Mee Goreng has none of the curry spices one usually associates with foods from the Indian subcontinent and is completely unknown in any part of India, in Singapore and Malaysia it is known as Indian-style noodles.

175–225g/6–8 oz Chinese-style dried noodles
2 teaspoons soy sauce
5–6 cloves garlic, chopped
3 tablespoons vinegar
1 teaspoon Tabasco sauce or other hot pepper sauce
1 tablespoon sugar
3 tablespoons tomato ketchup
2 tablespoons vegetable oil, more if needed
¼ green or white cabbage, cut into small dice
6 spring onions, thinly sliced
1 tomato, diced
Several 2.5 cm/1 inch squares deep-fried tofu, cut into 6mm/¼ inch slices (optional)
10–15 tinned or fresh and blanched water chestnuts, diced
2 eggs, lightly beaten
100g/4 oz bean sprouts
3–4 tablespoons crunchy roasted peanuts or about 2 tablespoons crisp-fried shallot flakes
1 fresh green chilli, cut into thin strips
2 tablespoons fresh coriander leaves
¼ cucumber, halved lengthwise then thinly sliced
Lemon or lime wedges

6–8 oz Chinese-style dried noodles
2 teaspoons soy sauce
5–6 cloves garlic, chopped
3 tablespoons vinegar
1 teaspoon Tabasco sauce or other hot pepper sauce
1 tablespoon sugar
3 tablespoons catsup
2 tablespoons vegetable oil, more if needed
¼ green or white cabbage, cut into small dice
6 green onions, thinly sliced
1 tomato, diced
Several 1 inch squares deep-fried tofu, cut into ¼ inch slices (optional)
10–15 fresh and blanched or canned water chestnuts, diced
2 eggs, lightly beaten
¼ lb bean sprouts
¼ cup dry roasted peanuts, or about 2 tablespoons crisp-fried shallot flakes
1 fresh green chilli such as jalapeno, cut into thin strips
2 tablespoons fresh cilantro
¼ cucumber, halved lengthwise then thinly sliced
Lemon or lime wedges

1. Cook the noodles in rapidly boiling salted water with half the soy sauce. Drain and rinse with cold water then set aside.

2. Make a sauce by combining the remaining soy sauce with 1 clove of the chopped garlic, the vinegar, Tabasco or other hot sauce,

sugar and tomato ketchup (catsup). Set aside.

3. Heat about three-quarters of the oil in a wok or heavy frying pan (skillet), add the remaining garlic and sauté quickly until golden. Over high heat, add the cabbage, half the spring onions (green onions), the tomato, the tofu, if using, and the water chestnuts. Stir-fry for about 30 to 60 seconds or until tender but still crisp.

4. Add the noodles and the sauce, toss over the heat and, if using a large wok, push the mixture to one side; if there is not enough

room, transfer the mixture to a platter or casserole dish and keep warm.

5. Add the remaining oil to the pan and pour in the eggs, stirring them until scrambled, then add the bean sprouts and toss until wilted.

6. Combine the noodle mixture with the eggs and bean sprouts and serve immediately, topped with the peanuts or crisp shallots, the chilli strands, coriander leaves (cilantro), cucumber and remaining spring onions (green onions). Serve accompanied by lemon or lime wedges.

Pasta with East-West Pesto

SERVES 4–6

Fresh coriander (cilantro) and chillies are pounded with peanuts into a pesto-like seasoning paste, then tossed with rice noodles.

3 cloves garlic, chopped
2–3 fresh green chillies, chopped
3 tablespoons peanut butter or coarsely chopped roasted peanuts
25g/1 oz fresh coriander leaves, chopped
25g/1 oz fresh mint leaves, chopped, or additional coriander leaves
Pinch of sugar
Salt to taste
Juice of ½ lemon or lime
325g/12 oz rice noodles (also called rice sticks or rice vermicelli)
Soy sauce and sesame oil, to taste

3 cloves garlic, chopped
2–3 fresh green chillies, such as jalapenos, chopped
3 tablespoons peanut butter or coarsely chopped roasted peanuts
½ cup coarsely chopped fresh cilantro
¼ cup coarsely chopped fresh mint leaves or additional cilantro
Pinch of sugar
Salt to taste
Juice of ½ lemon or lime
12 oz rice noodles (also called rice sticks and rice vermicelli)
Soy sauce and sesame oil, to taste

1. In a liquidizer (blender) or food processor process the garlic, chillies, peanut butter or chopped peanuts, coriander (cilantro) and mint, if using, sugar, salt and lemon or lime juice. Add a little soy sauce if needed to get the right consistency.

2. Soak and cook the noodles according to directions on the packet, then drain, and toss with soy sauce and sesame oil to taste. Serve each portion topped with a few spoonfuls of the thick green paste, and toss together.

Spicy Black Bean Chow Mein with Stir-Fried Cabbage and Shiitake

SERVES 4

Chow mein is quite familiar to anyone with a penchant for Chinese food, but this Cantonese speciality is only one of a wide variety of Chinese noodle dishes. A chewy-crisp pillow of noodles combined with stir-fried vegetables and aromatics, chow mein can be made with anything from your garden, and seasoned with a vast array of flavours. Here the vegetables are a combination of the humble and the exotic: cabbage, carrots and bean sprouts with a scattering of dried shiitake mushrooms and tree cloud fungus. And it's all spiced up with fermented black beans, fresh chilli and coriander (cilantro).

325g/12 oz dried or fresh Chinese egg
  noodles
About 3 tablespoons vegetable oil
About 10 dried shiitake mushrooms
2–3 large tree cloud fungus
3 cloves garlic, chopped
6mm/¼ inch piece fresh ginger root,
  chopped
1 carrot, diced
½ green or white cabbage, diced
Pinch of sugar
225g/4 oz bean sprouts
2 tablespoons fermented black beans
1 tablespoon cornflour
175ml/6 fl oz vegetable stock
½–1 fresh chilli, thinly sliced, or
  cayenne pepper or other hot
  seasoning, to taste
Soy sauce to taste
2 teaspoons sesame oil, or to taste
3 spring onions, thinly sliced
2–3 tablespoons coarsely chopped fresh
  coriander leaves

12 oz fresh or dried Chinese egg
  noodles
About 3 tablespoons vegetable oil
About 10 dried shiitake mushrooms
2–3 large tree cloud fungus
3 cloves garlic, chopped
¼ inch thick slice of ginger root,
  chopped
1 carrot, diced
½ green or white cabbage, diced
Pinch of sugar
¼ lb bean sprouts
2 tablespoons fermented black beans
1 tablespoon cornstarch
¾ cup vegetable stock
½–1 fresh chilli such as jalapeno or
  serrano, thinly sliced, or cayenne
  pepper or other hot seasoning, to
  taste
Soy sauce to taste
2 teaspoons sesame oil, or to taste
3 green onions, thinly sliced
2–3 tablespoons coarsely chopped fresh
  cilantro

1. Boil the noodles until just tender; drain and rinse with cold water then drain well again.
2. Rub a baking sheet with 1 tablespoon of the oil and spread the cooked noodles evenly over it. Bake in the oven at 200°C/400°F/gas mark 6 for 20 minutes, then turn over and brown for 10 more minutes. The noodles will stick together in a crispy, golden, sheet-like pancake. (They may be prepared up to two days in advance, and kept at room temperature away from moisture. To reheat and recrisp, place in the oven at 130°C/250°F/gas mark ½ for about 20 minutes).
3. Rehydrate the shiitake and tree cloud fungus in hot, but not boiling, water to cover, as described on page 262, reserving the soaking liquid for another use (for this recipe, you may soak them together instead of separately). Cut the stems off the mushrooms and discard. Slice the shiitake into halves, or smaller pieces if they are very large, and slice the tree cloud fungus into thin strips. Set aside.
4. In a wok or frying pan (skillet) stir-fry the garlic, ginger root, carrot and soaked mushrooms in 1 tablespoon of the oil, then add the cabbage and sugar and stir-fry for about 30 seconds or until the cabbage wilts slightly. Remove from the pan.
5. Add the remaining oil to the pan, if needed, and quickly stir-fry the bean sprouts until just wilted. Remove from the pan and add to the cabbage mixture.
6. Lightly crush the fermented black beans with the back of a spoon or the handle of a Chinese cleaver. Mix with the cornflour (cornstarch), stock, and chilli or other hot seasoning, and add to the pan. Cook until thickened, then return the vegetables to the sauce and toss through. Add the noodles, broken up into several pieces, and heat through for a few seconds.
7. Serve on a platter, sprinkled with the soy sauce, sesame oil, spring onions (green onions), and fresh coriander leaves (cilantro).

Variation

Black Bean Chow Mein with Vegetables and Tofu: Replace the cabbage with green beans, cut into bite-sized lengths, courgettes (zucchini) cut into matchsticks, and diced firm or crisp-fried tofu.

Panthe Kaukswe

BURMESE NOODLES WITH CURRY SAUCE AND ASSORTED TOPPINGS

SERVES 4–6

Chickpea (garbanzo) flour, also known as besan or gram flour, has a nutty flavour and is almost as high in protein as soy flour. It is much used throughout India and parts of the Far East, especially Burma, where it forms the basis for this sauce, Burma's national dish.

Panthe Kaukswe can be made with any sort of Far Eastern noodles: rice, cellophane, mung bean threads, or egg noodles. The spicy sauce is splashed on, and condiments are sprinkled on at the table, to taste, so no two bites are ever the same.

The sauce, by the way, is not only easily prepared a day ahead but it tastes best that way too.

4 onions, chopped
6–8 cloves garlic, chopped
1½ tablespoons chopped fresh ginger
   root
1 teaspoon turmeric
1 teaspoon curry powder
1 stalk lemon grass, peeled, cut into
   5cm/2 inch lengths, and slightly
   crushed
Generous pinch of cayenne pepper or
   hot red pepper flakes
2 tablespoons vegetable oil
1 tablespoon sesame oil
2 tablespoons chickpea (besan) flour
500ml/16 fl oz coconut milk, or block
   of coconut cream dissolved in
   500ml/16 fl oz hot water
250ml/8 fl oz vegetable stock
Juice of 1 lime or lemon
325–450g/12–16 oz noodles of choice:
   cellophane, mung bean, rice, or egg
   noodles

4 onions, chopped
6–8 cloves garlic, chopped
1½ tablespoons chopped fresh ginger
   root
1 teaspoon turmeric
1 teaspoon curry powder
1 stalk lemon grass, peeled, cut into 2
   inch lengths, and slightly crushed
Generous pinch of cayenne pepper or
   hot red pepper flakes
2 tablespoons vegetable oil
1 tablespoon sesame oil
2 tablespoons garbanzo (besan) flour
2 cups unsweetened coconut milk
1 cup vegetable stock
Juice of 1 lime or lemon
12–16 oz Asian noodles of choice:
   cellophane, mung bean, rice, or egg
   noodles

For the garnishes:
10 cloves garlic, thinly sliced
2 tablespoons vegetable oil
Several squares fried tofu, cut into thin
strips, or fresh firm tofu, diced
3 hard-boiled eggs, diced
5–8 spring onions, thinly sliced
2–4 fresh green chillies, thinly sliced
1–2 lemons, cut into wedges
Small bowl of fresh coriander leaves
for sprinkling

For the garnishes:
10 cloves garlic, thinly sliced
2 tablespoons vegetable oil
Several squares fried tofu, cut into thin
strips, or fresh tofu, diced
3 hard-cooked eggs, diced
5–8 green onions, thinly sliced
2–4 fresh green chillies such as
jalapenos, thinly sliced
1–2 lemons, cut into wedges
Small bowl of fresh cilantro for
sprinkling

1. In a heavy frying pan (skillet) or wok sauté the onions, garlic, ginger root, turmeric, curry powder, lemon grass and cayenne pepper or red pepper flakes in the vegetable oil and sesame oil, cooking slowly until the onions are very soft and browned, about 15–20 minutes.
2. Sprinkle in the chickpea (garbanzo) flour, then pour in the coconut milk and the stock. Simmer until the sauce is thickened, about 20 minutes. If it becomes too thick or starts to separate, add a little water. Season with lemon juice and keep warm.
3. Meanwhile, soak and cook the noodles according to the directions on the packet. Drain.
4. Prepare the garnishes: sauté the sliced garlic in the vegetable oil until golden brown but not dark and bitter. Place on a small plate. Arrange the other garnishes on plates or in bowls.
5. Serve the noodles tossed with the sauce and accompanied by the garnishes, and let everyone help themselves.

Vietnamese Noodle-Lettuce Parcels

SERVES 4

Wrapping savoury and spicy ingredients into cool leafy greens, garnished with fresh and crispy toppings such as chillies, vegetables, nuts, herbs, etc. is a deliciously typical Southeast-Asian idea, and the contrasts of textures and flavours make for very exciting eating.

Don't try to eat this politely with your knife and fork: roll up your sleeves and pick it up with your fingers. It tastes even better.

225g/8 oz thin rice noodles (also called rice sticks or rice vermicelli)
3 cloves garlic, chopped
225g/8 oz soya mince
1 tablespoon vegetable oil
125g/4 oz fresh and blanched or tinned and drained water chestnuts, diced
175ml/6 fl oz hoisin sauce
100ml/4 fl oz vegetable stock
Soy sauce to taste
1 tablespoon tomato ketchup
2 tablespoons sugar
1–2 tablespoons red or white wine vinegar (optional)
Hot pepper sauce or cayenne pepper, to taste
150–175g/5–6 oz roasted peanuts, coarsely chopped
1 large head lettuce such as Cos or 2 smaller round lettuces, broken into whole leaves
Handful of bean sprouts, either raw or blanched
½ cucumber, diced
1–2 carrots, grated
2–3 spring onions, thinly sliced
Fresh coriander leaves
Fresh mint leaves

8 oz thin rice noodles (also called rice sticks or rice vermicelli)
3 cloves garlic, chopped
8 oz dry textured vegetable protein
1 tablespoon vegetable oil
½ cup diced fresh and blanched or canned and drained water chestnuts
¾ cup hoisin sauce
½ cup vegetable stock
Soy sauce to taste
1 tablespoon catsup
2 tablespoons sugar
1–2 tablespoons red or white wine vinegar (optional)
Hot pepper sauce or cayenne pepper, to taste
½ cup coarsely chopped dry-roasted peanuts
1 head leafy lettuce such as Romaine or Boston (butter), broken into whole leaves
¼ lb bean sprouts, either raw or blanched
½ cucumber, diced
1–2 carrots, grated
2–3 green onions, thinly sliced
¼ cup fresh cilantro
¼ cup fresh mint leaves

1. Soak and cook noodles according to directions on the packet, then drain and rinse in cold water. Set aside.
2. Stir-fry the garlic and soya mince (textured vegetable protein) in the vegetable oil until the soya mince is lightly browned, then stir in the water chestnuts.
3. Add the hoisin sauce, stock, soy sauce, tomato ketchup and sugar, then simmer for 5 minutes or until slightly thickened (different brands of soya mince [vegetable protein] take varying amounts of time to cook). When ready, the mixture should be soupy, since it will thicken when the peanuts are added. Season with vinegar to balance the sweetness, and add hot pepper sauce or cayenne pepper to taste.
4. Add the peanuts and set aside.
5. Serve the noodles on one platter, the soya-mince (textured vegetable protein) filling in a bowl, and the lettuce leaves, vegetables and herbs on another plate. Each person takes a lettuce leaf and places a spoonful of cool rice noodles inside, then tops it with some hot sauce, then sprinkles on vegetables and herbs, then rolls the whole thing up in the lettuce leaf.

Mu Shu Vegetables Lo Mein

SERVES 4

Long Chinese egg noodles, or mein, take the place of the traditional pancake-like wrappers with this vegetable mixture. A dab of hoisin sauce and a sprinkling of spring onions (green onions) completes the mu shu theme.

About 30 lily buds (available from
  Chinese grocers) (optional)
Handful of small tree cloud fungus or
  3 large ones, or 3 large wood ear fungus
5–8 large dried shiitake
325g/12 oz dried thin Chinese egg
  noodles
2 tablespoons oil
1 green or white cabbage, thinly sliced
1 carrot, coarsely grated
1 teaspoon chopped fresh gingerroot
Pinch of sugar
White pepper to taste
2 tablespoons rice wine or dry sherry
1 tablespoon soy sauce, plus extra for
  seasoning noodles
1 teaspoon sesame oil, plus extra for
  seasoning noodles
3–4 tablespoons coarsely chopped fresh
  coriander leaves
3 spring onions, thinly sliced
Hoisin sauce to taste

About 30 lily buds (available in
  Chinese grocery shops) (optional)
Handful of small tree cloud fungus or
  3 large ones, or 3 large wood ear
  fungus
5–8 large dried shiitake
12 oz dried Chinese egg noodles
2 tablespoons oil
1 green or white cabbage, thinly sliced
1 carrot, coarsely grated
1 teaspoon chopped fresh ginger root
Pinch of sugar
White pepper to taste
2 tablespoons rice wine or dry sherry
1 tablespoon soy sauce, plus extra for
  seasoning noodles
1 teaspoon sesame oil, plus extra for
  seasoning noodles
3–4 tablespoons coarsely chopped fresh
  cilantro
3 green onions, thinly sliced
Hoisin sauce to taste

1. In separate small bowls rehydrate the lily buds, tree cloud fungus and shiitake in hot, but not boiling, water to cover, as described on page 262, reserving the soaking liquid for another use. Discard the hard ends or stems of each; chop the lily buds, and thinly slice the tree cloud fungus and shiitake.

2. Cook the noodles until just tender, then drain and rinse with cold water. Dress with soy sauce and sesame oil then set aside and keep warm.

3. Heat the oil in a wok or large frying pan (skillet) and stir-fry the cabbage, carrot and ginger root until just crunchy, about 30 seconds, then add the lily buds, tree cloud fungus and shiitake. Season with the sugar, white pepper, and rice wine or sherry, and cook for a minute or two, add the soy sauce.

4. Serve the hot vegetables atop the noodles, drizzle it all with the sesame oil, sprinkle with the fresh coriander leaves (cilantro) and spring onions (green onions) and serve each portion with a generous dab of hoisin sauce.

Chinese Noodles with Spicy Peanut Butter Sauce and Salad

SERVES 6

This makes a lovely summer meal, first course, or even picnic fare.

1 teaspoon Sichuan peppercorns
6 cloves garlic, chopped
2 teaspoons chopped fresh ginger root
4 tablespoons peanut butter
2 tablespoons tahini
75ml/3 fl oz strong brewed tea
50ml/2 fl oz soy sauce or to taste
2 tablespoons tomato ketchup
2 tablespoons dry sherry
4 tablespoons sesame oil
1½ tablespoons wine vinegar
50g/2 oz sugar or to taste
1 teaspoon chilli oil or about
　½ teaspoon cayenne pepper
450g/1 lb thin Chinese egg noodles
½ cucumber, diced
1 carrot, grated
4 spring onions, thinly sliced
Handful of bean sprouts, blanched
　(optional)
3 tablespoons chopped fresh coriander
　leaves

1 teaspoon Sichuan peppercorns
6 cloves garlic, chopped
2 teaspoons chopped fresh ginger root
4 tablespoons peanut butter
2 tablespoons tahini
⅓ cup strong brewed tea
¼ cup soy sauce or to taste
2 tablespoons catsup
2 tablespoons dry sherry
¼ cup sesame oil
1½ tablespoons wine vinegar
3 tablespoons sugar or to taste
1 teaspoon chilli oil or about
　½ teaspoon cayenne pepper
1 lb thin Chinese egg noodles
½ cucumber, diced
1 carrot, grated
4 green onions, thinly sliced
¼ lb bean sprouts, blanched (optional)
3 tablespoons chopped fresh cilantro

1. Lightly toast the Sichuan peppercorns in an ungreased heavy frying pan (skillet), then crush coarsely either in a mortar and pestle or with a rolling pin.
2. In a food processor or liquidizer (blender) combine the peppercorns with the garlic, ginger root, peanut butter, tahini, tea, soy sauce (reserving a little to toss with the noodles), tomato ketchup (catsup), sherry, half the the sesame oil, wine vinegar, sugar and chilli oil or cayenne pepper. Blend to a smooth sauce.
3. Cook the noodles then drain and rinse in cold water. Toss with the reserved soy sauce and remaining sesame oil and set aside.
4. Serve the noodles at room temperature or chilled, with the peanut sauce and the cucumber, carrot, spring onions (green onions), bean sprouts, if using, and fresh coriander leaves (cilantro).

BAKED PASTA

Baked pasta is usually a hale and hearty affair, great sizzling casseroles filled with vivid flavours and a variety of ingredients. Their character is completely different from quickly tossed *al dente* pasta with a simple sauce, or the light and breezy pasta recipes of summertime. Baked pasta dishes make robust fare and emanate comfort and hospitality: there is always enough for an extra at the table.

Besides macaroni cheese, lasagne is probably the best known baked pasta dish in both Britain and America. Regardless of how many exotic, well-cooked pasta dishes I have eaten, a good lasagne and macaroni baked with cheese remain my favourites, and I frequently make them in endless guises and variations.

There are fewer fried pasta dishes, yet occasionally one finds specialities made from fresh noodle dough, fried to a golden crisp and utterly irresistible. Wontons and egg rolls, stuffed and fried, are such pasta. Unfilled wonton or egg roll noodles, fried until crispy and golden then sprinkled with icing (confectioners') sugar, make an excellent biscuit- (cookie-) like sweet, or if sprinkled with savoury spices instead of sugar, a cracker-like snack to accompany drinks. Fresh ravioli, too, can be quickly fried until golden and eaten as an appetizer-like nibble.

Macaroni and Cheddar Cheese Gratin with Tangy Beetroot Relish

SERVES 4–6

If you ate at my table for a month, inevitably you would be served this crusty-topped macaroni gratin, enlivened with a tangy relish of beetroot (beets) and onions. It is probably my favourite, most comforting dish, perfect for a rainy evening. The relish keeps the dish from being ordinary, and its tanginess lifts the heavier nature of the baked pasta.

450g/1 lb pasta such as farfalle, pennine (small quills), elbows, lumachine (seashells), etc.
25g/1 oz butter
2 tablespoons flour
500ml/16 fl oz hot milk
2 cloves garlic, chopped
Pinch of freshly grated nutmeg
Salt and freshly ground black pepper, to taste
225g/8 oz fresh and blanched or frozen peas
400g/14 oz mature Cheddar cheese, grated
1 onion, chopped
4 beetroot, cooked and diced
Pinch of sugar or a little honey (optional)
2 teaspoons red or white wine vinegar

1 lb pasta such as farfalle, pennine (small quills), elbows, lumachine (seashells) etc.
2 tablespoons butter
2 tablespoons flour
2 cups hot milk
2 cloves garlic, chopped
Pinch of freshly grated nutmeg
Salt and freshly ground black pepper, to taste
1½ cups fresh and blanched or frozen peas
¾–1 lb sharp Cheddar or combination of cheeses
1 onion, chopped
4 beets, cooked and diced
Pinch of sugar or a little honey (optional)
2 teaspoons vinegar

1. Cook the pasta until just *al dente*, then drain.
2. Melt the butter in a saucepan, sprinkle with the flour and cook for a few minutes, then remove from the heat and stir in the milk. Return to the heat, and cook, stirring, until the mixture thickens. Season with the garlic, nutmeg, salt and black pepper.
3. Combine the pasta with the sauce, peas, and three-quarters of the cheese. Spoon into a baking dish and top with the remaining cheese. Bake in the oven at 200°C/400°F/gas mark 6 until the cheese topping is crusty and golden, about 30 minutes.
4. Meanwhile, prepare the relish: combine the onion, beetroot (beets), sugar or honey, if using, and vinegar.
5. Serve the hot baked pasta with a spoonful of the cool, tangy relish alongside.

Casserole of Aubergine (Eggplant) and Small Pasta with Ricotta and Mozzarella Cheese

SERVES 6

Serve this hearty casserole with a light and tangy salad of rocket (arugula) and a milder young lettuce.

2 aubergines, sliced
Olive oil for frying
450g/1 lb small seashell pasta or other small pasta such as anellini (little rings)
4 cloves garlic, chopped
1/4–1/2 teaspoon fennel seeds
Large pinch of dried oregano
900ml/1½ pints tomato passata
Pinch of sugar
Salt and freshly ground black pepper, to taste
225–325g/8–12 oz ricotta cheese
225g/8 oz mozzarella cheese, thinly sliced
100g/4 oz Parmesan cheese, freshly grated, plus extra to serve

2 eggplants, sliced
Olive oil for sautéeing
1 lb small pasta such as little seashells or anellini (little rings)
4 cloves garlic, chopped
1/4–1/2 teaspoon fennel seeds
Large pinch of dried oregano
3½ cups tomato passata or tomato sauce
Pinch of sugar
Salt and freshly ground black pepper, to taste
1–1½ cups ricotta cheese
½ lb mozzarella cheese, thinly sliced
½ cup freshly grated Parmesan cheese, plus extra to serve

1. Fry or sauté the aubergine (eggplant) slices in a single layer in a small amount of oil until browned and tender. Cook in batches if necessary. Set aside.
2. Cook the pasta until *al dente* then drain. Rinse with cold water and set aside.
3. Sauté the garlic and fennel seeds in about 2 tablespoons of olive oil, then add the oregano and tomato passata and season with the sugar, salt and black pepper. Simmer for about 10 minutes.
4. Layer half the aubergine (eggplant) in a baking dish.
5. Mix the pasta with three-quarters of the tomato sauce, then spoon into the baking dish. Top with the remaining aubergine (eggplant).
6. Dot with the ricotta cheese, then cover with the mozzarella cheese, remaining tomato sauce and a final sprinkling of Parmesan cheese.
7. Bake in the oven at 190°C/375°F/gas mark 5 until cheese is bubbling and lightly browned, about 35 minutes.

Gratin of Mustard-Scented Macaroni and Cheese with Mexican Flavours

SERVES 4

This is as distinctive in its seasoning of roasted green (bell) pepper, Mexican spicing and tangy yogurt as it is deliciously satisfying. A wonderful main course for a winter's evening, preceded by a light and spicy tomato broth and accompanied by a crisp green salad, and maybe some buttery garlic bread.

1 green pepper
325g/12 oz macaroni or other medium to large pasta
15g/½ oz butter
1 tablespoon flour
250ml/8 fl oz hot, but not boiling, milk
3 tablespoons Greek yogurt or sour cream
2 teaspoons mustard of choice or a combination, e.g. wholegrain, a mild Dijon
Tabasco or other hot sauce to taste
½ teaspoon cumin, or to taste
Pinch of turmeric
2–3 cloves garlic, chopped
325g/12 oz sharp Cheddar cheese, coarsely grated
Salt and freshly ground black pepper and nutmeg, to taste
1 teaspoon paprika

1 green bell pepper
12 oz macaroni of choice
1 tablespoon butter or oil
1 tablespoon flour
1 cup hot, but not boiling, milk
¼ cup sour cream or half yogurt and half sour cream
2 teaspoons mustard of choice or a combination, e.g. wholeseed mustard and Dijon
Tabasco or other hot sauce to taste
½ teaspoon cumin, or to taste
Pinch of turmeric
2–3 cloves garlic, chopped
¾ lb sharp Cheddar cheese, coarsely grated
Salt and freshly ground black pepper and nutmeg, to taste
1 teaspoon paprika

1. Roast the pepper as described on page 262. Slice the peeled flesh into thin strips and set aside.
2. Cook the pasta until *al dente*. Drain.
3. Heat the butter in a pan, sprinkle in the flour, and cook for a minute or so. Remove from the heat and stir in the hot milk, then return to the heat and cook, stirring, until the mixture thickens.
4. Combine the green (bell) pepper strips, pasta, white sauce, yogurt and/or sour cream, mustard, Tabasco or other hot sauce, cumin, turmeric, garlic, cheese, salt, black pepper and nutmeg.
5. Pour into a casserole dish, sprinkle with the paprika, then bake in the oven at 190°C/375°F/gas mark 5 until golden brown in spots on top, about 40 minutes. Serve immediately.

Soufflé-Like Pasta Casserole
with Greek Flavours

SERVES 4–6

It is difficult to come up with an accurate name for this dish: it evolved from both the pastitsio and moussaka, but eliminates a tomato sauce and instead combines aubergine (eggplant) with a savoury cheese custard. A shot of dusky-flavoured cumin enhances the flavours in a surprisingly bright way.

Because of the eggs, the top puffs up as it bakes, giving a soufflé-like appearance. It falls quickly however, and is not meant for real soufflé-like heights. It is rustic and sturdy rather than airy and delicate. If you want a soufflé you could whip the egg whites separately, but I like it the way it is.

Though I don't always salt my aubergine (eggplant), in this dish I think it is necessary as it prevents the vegetable absorbing too much oil and making the dish oily and heavy.

1 medium to large aubergine	1 medium to large eggplant
3 tablespoons vegetable oil and olive oil, mixed	3 tablespoons vegetable oil and olive oil, mixed
325g/12 oz pasta such as elbows, small shells, etc.	12 oz pasta such as elbows, small shells, etc.
25g/1 oz butter	2 tablespoons butter
2 tablespoons flour	2 tablespoons flour
250ml/16 fl oz hot, but not boiling, milk	2 cups hot, but not boiling, milk
Salt and freshly ground black pepper and nutmeg, to taste	Salt and freshly ground black pepper and nutmeg, to taste
4 eggs, lightly beaten	4 eggs, lightly beaten
325g/12 oz cheese such as Cheddar or Havarti, or a combination of grated cheeses	¾ lb cheese such as sharp Cheddar, Havarti, Monterey Jack, or a combination of cheeses, grated
¾ teaspoon cumin	¾ teaspoon cumin

1. Slice the aubergine (eggplant) and sprinkle liberally with salt. Leave to drain for at least 30 minutes, then rinse well and dry.
2. Sauté the aubergine (eggplant) in the olive oil until lightly browned and just tender. Cut into strips or bite-sized pieces and set aside.
3. Cook the pasta until *al dente*. Drain and rinse with cold water. Set aside.

4. Heat the butter in a pan and sprinkle with the flour. Cook for a few minutes over medium heat until golden, then remove from the heat and gradually stir in the hot milk. Return to the heat and cook, stirring, until the sauce thickens. Season with salt, black pepper and nutmeg, then leave to cool.

5. Mix the eggs into the sauce with the cheese and cumin. Gently mix with the pasta and aubergine (eggplant) and pour into a casserole dish, preferably a rustic ceramic one of the sort you find in Spain.

6. Bake in the oven at 190°C/375°F/gas mark 5 until the top puffs up and browns in spots, about 35–40 minutes. Serve hot, though leftovers at room temperature are pretty good, too.

Baked Penne or Farfalle with Asparagus and Fontina

SERVES 4–6

When asparagus is out of season, replace with sugar snap peas or slices of blanched artichoke hearts.

450g/1 lb penne or farfalle
450g/1 lb asparagus, tough ends broken off and discarded, the spears cut into bite-sized lengths
50g/2 oz butter
2 tablespoons flour
250ml/8 fl oz hot, but not boiling, milk
250 ml/8 fl oz hot vegetable stock
Salt and freshly ground black pepper and nutmeg, to taste
325g/12 oz fontina cheese, grated
100g/4 oz Parmesan cheese, freshly grated
2 cloves garlic, chopped (optional)

1 lb penne or farfalle
1 lb asparagus, tough ends broken off and discarded, the spears cut into bite-sized lengths
4 tablespoons butter
2 tablespoons flour
1 cup hot, but not boiling, milk
1 cup hot vegetable stock
Salt and freshly ground black pepper and nutmeg, to taste
¾ lb fontina cheese, grated
½ cup freshly grated Parmesan cheese
2 cloves garlic, chopped (optional)

1. Cook the pasta until half done, then add the asparagus and continue cooking until both are *al dente*. Drain, toss with a quarter of the butter, and set aside.

2. Heat 25g/1 oz (2 tablespoons) of the butter in a pan, then sprinkle in the flour and cook for a few minutes until lightly golden. Remove from the heat, gradually stir in the milk, then the stock. Return to a medium heat and cook, stirring, until thickened, about 2 minutes. Season with salt, black pepper, and nutmeg.

3. Combine the pasta and asparagus with the sauce, then add two-thirds of the fontina cheese and several spoonfuls of the Parmesan cheese (and garlic, if using). Pour into a baking dish and cover with remaining fontina cheese, then sprinkle with the remaining Parmesan and dot with the remaining butter.

4. Bake in the oven at 190°C/375°F/gas mark 5 for 30 minutes or until the cheese topping is melted and golden.

Baked Pasta with Mushrooms, Green Beans, Gorgonzola and Tomatoes

SERVES 4–6

Quite rich, deliciously sloppy, elegant in a very unpretentious way. Nice with a salad of frisée or other young greens and mixed herbs.

325g/12 oz penne, rigatoni, farfalle, seashells, or similar pasta

175g/6 oz green beans, cut into bite-sized lengths

50g/2 oz butter

2 tablespoons flour

500ml/16 fl oz hot, but not boiling, milk

Pinch of freshly grated nutmeg

Salt and freshly ground black pepper, to taste

250g/8 oz mushrooms, chopped

1 onion, chopped

4 cloves garlic, chopped

8 ripe fresh or tinned tomatoes, diced

1 tablespoon chopped fresh parsley

3 tablespoons tomato paste

100–150g/4–5 oz Gorgonzola cheese, crumbled

225g/8 oz mozzarella cheese, diced or thinly sliced

Several tablespoons of freshly grated Parmesan cheese

12 oz penne, rigatoni, farfalle, seashells or similar pasta

2 cups green beans, cut into bite-sized lengths

4 tablespoons butter

2 tablespoons flour

2 cups hot, but not boiling, milk

Pinch of freshly grated nutmeg

Salt and freshly ground black pepper, to taste

½ lb mushrooms, chopped

1 onion, chopped

4 cloves garlic, chopped

8 ripe fresh or canned tomatoes, diced

1 tablespoon chopped fresh parsley

3 tablespoons tomato paste

⅔ cup crumbled blue cheese or Gorgonzola

½ lb mozzarella cheese, diced or thinly sliced

Several tablespoons of freshly grated Parmesan cheese

1. Cook the pasta until half done, then add the green beans and continue cooking until both are *al dente*. Drain.

2. Melt half the butter in a pan then sprinkle in the flour and cook for a few minutes until lightly golden. Remove from the heat, gradually stir in milk, then return to the heat and cook, stirring, until slightly thickened. Season with nutmeg, salt and black pepper and set aside.

3. Brown the mushrooms in half the remaining butter with half the garlic. Season with salt and black pepper and set aside.

4. Sauté the tomatoes, the rest of the garlic and the parsley in the remaining butter for about 5 minutes. When tender, add to the béchamel sauce with the tomato paste, reserved mushrooms, blue or Gorgonzola cheese, and half the mozzarella cheese.

5. Mix this with the pasta and green beans then pour into a baking dish. Top with the remaining mozzarella cheese and the Parmesan cheese then bake in the oven at 190°C/375°F/gas mark 5 for 20 minutes or until the top is melting and lightly browned.

Baked Ravioli with Fresh Rosemary and Tomatoes

SERVES 4

This casserole is amazingly light and clear-flavoured, and very easy to prepare. Fresh rosemary makes it special, and if you are able to find Italian fontina cheese, you will be impressed indeed.

325g/12 oz cheese- or spinach-filled ravioli
325g/12 oz ripe fresh or tinned tomatoes, diced and drained
3 cloves garlic, chopped
1–2 tablespoons chopped fresh rosemary
Salt and freshly ground black pepper, to taste
225g/8 oz fontina or mature Cheddar cheese, diced or coarsely shredded
1 tablespoon olive oil
Freshly grated Parmesan cheese to taste

12 oz cheese- or spinach-filled ravioli
1½–2 cups ripe fresh or canned diced tomatoes, drained
3 cloves garlic, chopped
1–2 tablespoons chopped fresh rosemary
Salt and freshly ground black pepper, to taste
½ lb fontina or young Asiago cheese or Monterey Jack, diced or coarsely grated
1 tablespoon olive oil
Freshly grated Parmesan cheese to taste

1. Cook the ravioli until *al dente*; drain.
2. Toss with the tomatoes, garlic, and rosemary, then season with salt and pepper. Layer in a casserole dish with the fontina, Cheddar, Asiago or Monterey Jack cheese, making 2 or 3 layers and ending with a layer of cheese.

3. Sprinkle with the olive oil and Parmesan cheese and bake in the oven at 190°C/375°F/gas mark 5 until the cheese is melted and lightly golden brown in spots. Serve immediately.

Rachel's Homely and Comforting Macaroni and Spinach Dish

SERVES 4

This casserole was prepared for me by my friend Rachel Wight at a time when she knew I needed something comforting and cosy. It is not innovative or glamorous, rather it is enormously comforting, the sort of dish that makes you feel extremely well cared for.

You can vary the cheese used as desired; I've eaten similar dishes in Italy made with fontina cheese, and in America where the cheese was Monterey Jack. The important thing is that the spinach is fresh, and that you are in the proper mood. If you feel like making a richer dish, top the casserole with buttered breadcrumbs before baking. And if you feel like something spicy, add hot pepper sauce or Tabasco.

325g/12 oz elbow or other small macaroni
1–2 bunches fresh spinach
40g/1½ oz butter
1 tablespoon flour
250ml/8 fl oz hot, but not boiling, milk
Salt, cayenne pepper and freshly grated nutmeg, to taste
2 hard-boiled eggs, diced
225g/8 oz Cheddar or other sharp cheese, shredded
75g/3 oz Parmesan cheese, freshly grated
A little paprika to serve (optional)

12 oz elbow or other small macaroni
1–2 bunches fresh spinach
3 tablespoons butter
1 tablespoon flour
1 cup hot, but not boiling, milk
Salt, cayenne pepper and freshly grated nutmeg, to taste
2 hard-cooked eggs, diced
½ lb sharp Cheddar or other sharp cheese such as a young Asiago or Pecorino
⅓–½ cup freshly grated Parmesan cheese
A little paprika to serve (optional)

1. Cook the pasta until *al dente*; drain.
2. Cook the spinach until just tender, then drain and squeeze dry.
3. Make a béchamel sauce by melting a third of the butter in a pan then sprinkling in the flour. Cook for a few minutes, then remove from the heat and gradually stir in the milk. Return to the heat and cook, stirring, until the mixture thickens. Season with salt, cayenne pepper, and nutmeg. Set aside.
4. Dot the bottom of a baking dish with a little of the remaining butter, then cover with half the macaroni. Top with the spinach, half the béchamel sauce, half the cheeses and half the hard-boiled egg, then the remaining macaroni, butter, hard-boiled egg, béchamel sauce and cheeses. Bake in the oven at 200°C/400°F/gas mark 6, until the top is golden brown. Serve immediately, sprinkled with a little paprika.

Fideos

MEXICAN-STYLE THIN PASTA WITH TOMATOES AND CHEESE

SERVES 5

This delicious, rather sloppy, messy pasta is very homy, and was taught to me by an exuberant little woman from northern Mexico. Thin capellini is cooked in a savoury souplike mixture of tomatoes, stock and vegetables, enlivened with sliced olives and capers, then layered with cheese in a casserole and baked.

2 onions, chopped
1 green pepper, sliced
1 red pepper, sliced
3 cloves garlic, chopped
2 bay leaves
3 tablespoons vegetable oil
1 teaspoon cumin
1–2 teaspoons mild chilli powder, or to taste
½ teaspoon dried oregano
½ teaspoon ground coriander
2 teaspoons paprika
225g/8 oz green beans, cut into bite-sized lengths
225g/8 oz fresh or frozen peas
1 carrot, diced
400g/14 oz diced ripe fresh or tinned tomatoes
900ml/1½ pints vegetable stock
325g/12 oz capellini
About 15 pimiento-stuffed green olives, sliced
1 tablespoon capers
Several generous shakes of Tabasco sauce
225g/8 oz Cheddar cheese or other sharp cheese, coarsely grated or sliced

2 onions, chopped
1 green bell pepper, sliced
1 red bell pepper, sliced
3 cloves garlic, chopped
2 bay leaves
3 tablespoons vegetable oil
1 teaspoon cumin
1–2 teaspoons chilli powder, or to taste
½ teaspoon dried oregano
½ teaspoon ground coriander
2 teaspoons paprika
½ lb/2 cups green beans, cut into bite-sized lengths
1 cup fresh or frozen peas
1 carrot, diced
1½ cups diced fresh or canned tomatoes
3 cups vegetable stock
12 oz capellini
About 15 pimiento-stuffed green olives, sliced
1 tablespoon capers
Several generous shakes of Tabasco sauce
½ lb sharp or creamy cheese such as Cheddar or Jack, coarsely grated

1. Sauté the onions, green and red (bell) peppers, garlic and bay leaves in the vegetable oil until the onions are softened. Sprinkle with the cumin, chilli powder, oregano, coriander and paprika and cook for a few minutes.
2. Add the green beans, peas, carrot, tomatoes and vegetable stock and bring to the boil.
3. Add the capellini and stir in, then cover the pan and cook over low to medium heat for about 6 minutes, or until the capellini is just tender and the liquid has been absorbed.
4. Mix in the olives, capers and Tabasco sauce. Layer in a casserole dish with about half the cheese, then top with the remaining cheese.
5. Bake in the oven at 190°C/375°F/gas mark 5 for about 30 minutes or until the cheese is bubbly and golden brown. Serve immediately.

Note: If I have an avocado, I mash it with lemon juice, chopped onion, chopped tomato, chopped chilli and and fresh coriander leaves (cilantro) to make guacamole, then serve a spoonful or two as a side relish for the baked pasta.

Spinach and Ricotta Lasagne

SERVES 4–6

The filling for this lasagne also makes excellent cannelloni, easily thrown together with egg-roll wrappers, which do not need to be precooked, and are tender and delicate.

2 onions, chopped
3 cloves garlic, chopped
2 tablespoons chopped fresh parsley
3 tablespoons olive oil
½ teaspoon fennel seeds
½ teaspoon dried thyme or mixed herbs
1 litre/1¾ pints tomato passata
3–4 tablespoons tomato paste
½ teaspoon sugar (optional)
Salt and freshly ground black pepper, to taste
325g/12 oz cooked spinach, squeezed dry (weigh after cooking)
675g/1½ lb ricotta cheese
1 egg, lightly beaten
100g/4 oz Parmesan cheese, freshly grated
225g/8 oz lasagne
175–225g/6–8 oz mozzarella cheese, thinly sliced or grated

2 onions, chopped
3 cloves garlic, chopped
2 tablespoons chopped fresh parsley
3 tablespoons olive oil
½ teaspoon fennel seeds
½ teaspoon dried thyme or mixed Italian herbs
4 cups tomato passata or tomato sauce
3–4 tablespoons tomato paste
½ teaspoon sugar (optional)
Salt and freshly ground black pepper, to taste
2 bunches fresh spinach, cooked and squeezed dry; 1½ cups cooked and chopped
1½–2 cups ricotta cheese
1 egg, lightly beaten
½ cup freshly grated Parmesan cheese
½ lb lasagne
½ lb mozzarella cheese, thinly sliced or grated

1. Sauté the onions, half the garlic and the parsley in 2 tablespoons of the olive oil until softened. Add the fennel seeds, dried herbs, tomato passata and tomato paste, bring to the boil, then reduce the heat and simmer for about 5 minutes or until thickened and full-flavoured. Season with sugar, if needed, and salt and black pepper, then set aside.
2. Sauté the remaining garlic in the remaining oil, then add the cooked spinach and cook for a minute or two. Mix with the ricotta cheese, egg, and about three-quarters of the Parmesan cheese and season with salt and pepper. Set aside.
3. Cook the lasagne in plenty of boiling water until al dente, then drain carefully so that the pasta sheets do not stick together.
4. Layer about a third of the pasta in a shallow baking dish, then top with about half the tomato sauce, then another layer of pasta, then the spinach and cheese mixture. Place the final layer of pasta on top of this, then spoon on the remaining tomato sauce. Top with the mozzarella cheese, sprinkle with the remaining Parmesan cheese, then bake in the oven at 190°C/375°F/gas mark 5 for about 45 minutes or until the top is browned.

Variations

Lasagne con Broccoli: Substitute 2 bunches broccoli, blanched, coarsely chopped, for the spinach.

Cannelloni: Prepare with egg-roll wrappers instead of lasagne. Since they are fresh and pliable they do not need to be precooked. Spread several spoonfuls of the spinach and cheese filling in the centre of each wrapper, then roll up. Arrange in a baking dish, then pour over the tomato sauce and 125ml/4 fl oz (½ cup) water, then top with the mozzarella cheese and sprinkle with Parmesan. Bake in the oven at 190°C/375°F/gas mark 5 for about 20 minutes, or long enough to cook the cannelloni through and melt the cheese.

Lasagne al Fungi

MUSHROOM LASAGNE

SERVES 4–6

Layers of pasta with a creamy béchamel and sautéed mushrooms and tomatoes form the basis of this lasagne. A small amount of porcini mushrooms are included for added flavour, but if they are unavailable or too costly, omit.

25g/1 oz dried porcini (optional)
250ml/8 fl oz hot, but not boiling, vegetable stock
450g/1 lb mushrooms, diced
1 onion, chopped
4 cloves garlic, chopped
3 tablespoons olive oil
Salt and freshly ground black pepper
3 tablespoons flour
2 tablespoons tomato paste
2 tablespoons chopped fresh parsley
1 oz/25g butter
500ml/16 fl oz hot, but not boiling, milk
Grating of fresh nutmeg
225g/8 oz green or white lasagne
100g/4 oz Parmesan cheese, freshly grated
225g/8 oz Mozzarella cheese, thinly sliced or grated

1 oz dried porcini (optional)
1 cup hot, but not boiling, vegetable stock
1 lb mushrooms, diced
1 onion, chopped
4 cloves garlic, chopped
3 tablespoons olive oil
Salt and freshly ground black pepper
3 tablespoons flour
2 tablespoons tomato paste
2 tablespoons chopped fresh parsley
2 tablespoons butter
2 cups hot, but not boiling, milk
Grating of fresh nutmeg
½ lb green or white lasagne
½ cup freshly grated Parmesan cheese, or to taste
½ lb mozzarella cheese, thinly sliced or grated

1. If using porcini mushrooms, rehydrate in the stock as described on page 262. Dice and set aside, reserving the soaking liquid.
2. Sauté the fresh mushrooms and the porcini, if using, with the onions and garlic in the olive oil until browned and reduced in volume. Season with salt and black pepper, then sprinkle in 1 tablespoon of the flour and cook for a few moments. Pour in the vegetable stock and cook until it forms a thickish sauce. Stir in the tomato paste and parsley and set aside.
3. Melt the butter and sprinkle in the remaining flour. Cook for a few minutes until lightly golden, then remove from the heat and gradually stir in the milk. Return to the heat and cook, stirring, until thickened. Remove from the heat again and season with nutmeg, salt and black pepper.
4. Cook the pasta until *al dente* and drain carefully so that the sheets of noodles do not break.
5. To assemble, first put about a third of the lasagne sheets in an oiled baking dish, letting

the noodles fall over the edge of the dish, so that you will be able to fold them over to enclose the filling. Top with about a third of the mushroom filling, then more pasta, then half the béchamel sauce and a generous sprinkling of Parmesan cheese. Add another layer of pasta, more mushroom filling, and close up the top with the sheets of pasta that hang over the edge of the baking dish. Top with the remaining béchamel, the remaining mushroom filling, then the mozzarella and Parmesan cheeses. Bake in the oven at 190°C/375°F/gas mark 5 for 45 minutes or until the top is golden brown. Leave to stand for about 5–10 minutes before serving, as it tends to fall apart when extremely hot.

Lasagne Verde, Venice-Style

SERVES 6–8

Anything with peas is a speciality in Venice, so it was no surprise when I found myself face to face not only with St Mark's Square, but with the following delectable lasagne.

Either white or green pasta may be used: I tend to use green lasagne as a contrast to the red tomato sauce and the white béchamel. The colours are reminiscent of the Italian flag.

For the béchamel
25g/1 oz butter
2 tablespoons flour
500ml/16 fl oz hot, but not boiling, milk
Salt, freshly ground black pepper and freshly grated nutmeg, to taste

For the tomato sauce
1 onion, chopped
3 cloves garlic, chopped
1 carrot, chopped
2 tablespoons chopped fresh parsley
2 tablespoons olive oil
½ teaspoon each: fennel seeds, dried basil, dried mixed herbs
900g/2 lbs ripe, fresh, chopped tomatoes or 2 400g/14 oz tins chopped tomatoes
2 tablespoons tomato paste
Pinch of sugar (optional)
Salt and freshly ground black pepper, to taste

For the béchamel
2 tablespoons butter
2 tablespoons flour
2 cups hot, but not boiling, milk
Salt, freshly ground black pepper and freshly grated nutmeg, to taste

For the tomato sauce
1 onion, chopped
3 cloves garlic, chopped
1 carrot, chopped
2 tablespoons chopped fresh parsley
2 tablespoons olive oil
½ teaspoon each: fennel seeds, dried basil, dried mixed herbs
2 lbs fresh ripe tomatoes, chopped, or 3 cups canned chopped tomatoes
2 tablespoons tomato paste
Pinch of sugar (optional)
Salt and freshly ground black pepper, to taste

To assemble and cook

450g/1 lb dried or fresh green lasagne

275g/10 oz fresh and blanched or
frozen peas

50–75g/2–3 oz Parmesan cheese, freshly
grated

325g/12 oz mozzarella or other mild
white cheese, thinly sliced or grated

1 tablespoon olive oil

½ teaspoon dried thyme

To assemble and cook

1 lb dried or fresh green lasagne

1½ cups fresh and blanched or frozen
peas ⅓–½ cup freshly grated
Parmesan cheese

¾ lb mozzarella, Jack, fontina, or
other mild cheese, thinly sliced or
grated

1 tablespoon olive oil

½ teaspoon dried thyme

1. To make the béchamel sauce, melt the butter in a heavy saucepan over medium heat then sprinkle in the flour. Cook for a few minutes until lightly coloured, then remove from the heat and gradually stir in the milk. Return to the heat and cook, stirring, over medium heat until thickened. Season with salt, black pepper and nutmeg. Set aside.

2. To make the tomato sauce, sauté the onion, garlic, carrot, and parsley in the olive oil for a few minutes until the onion is softened, then add the fennel seeds, basil, dried mixed herbs, tomatoes, tomato paste, sugar, if needed, and salt and black pepper. Simmer for 10 minutes or until well flavoured. Set aside.

3. Cook the pasta until *al dente*, then drain carefully so as not to break up the sheets. If using fresh pasta, do not cook, but pour a little water over the top of the prepared dish and bake 20 minutes longer.

4. To assemble, ladle several spoonfuls of the tomato sauce into the bottom of a baking dish then top with a quarter of the lasagne, letting the sheets rise up the side of the dish.

Top with half the béchamel sauce, half the peas, and a generous amount of the Parmesan cheese. Next add another layer of the pasta, another layer of tomato sauce and half the mozzarella cheese. Top with another layer of pasta, the remaining béchamel and peas, then the final layer of pasta. Top with the last of the tomato sauce, the remaining mozzarella and Parmesan cheeses. Drizzle the olive oil over and add a sprinkling of thyme. Bake in the oven at 200°C/400°F/gas mark 6 (lower the heat if it shows signs of burning) for 45 minutes or until the top is browned and melting.

Variation

Jenny's Aubergine (Eggplant) and Red (Bell) Pepper Lasagne Verde: Our young family friend, Jenny Wight, is as keen a cook and pasta-eater as we are. Recently she served us a delicious lasagne filled with aubergine (eggplant) and red (bell) peppers. To prepare: follow the recipe above, but substitute a layer of sliced sautéed aubergine (eggplant) and a layer of sautéed or roasted and peeled red (bell) peppers for the peas.

Esther's Apple-Cheese Kugel

SERVES 4

Sweet with apple and raisins, and fragrant with cinnamon, this kugel is courtesy of Dr Esther Novak, whose father brought the recipe from Russia. In a lifetime of kugel eating, this is the best I have tasted.

Though sweet, it is traditionally served as part of the main course rather than as a pudding.

325g/12 oz flat noodles, preferably egg noodles, or thin vermicelli
75g/3 oz unsalted butter
100g/4 oz cottage cheese
3 large eggs, lightly beaten
2 apples, coarsely grated (do not peel)
2 teaspoons ground cinnamon
225g/8 oz sugar
175–225g/6–8 oz raisins or sultanas
½ teaspoon baking powder
Tiny pinch of salt

12 oz flat noodles, preferably egg noodles, or thin vermicelli
¼–⅓ cup/⅔ stick butter
½ cup cottage cheese
3 large eggs, lightly beaten
2 apples, coarsely grated (do not peel)
2 teaspoons ground cinnamon
1 cup sugar
½ cup raisins or golden raisins
½ teaspoon baking soda
Tiny pinch of salt

1. Cook the noodles until *al dente*; drain.
2. Melt the butter, then combine with the noodles.
3. Add all the remaining ingredients and pour into a rectangular baking dish.
4. Bake in the oven at 180°C/350°F/gas mark 4 until brown and crusty, 1–1½ hours. Serve hot or at room temperature.

STUFFED PASTA AND DUMPLINGS

Delicatessens, speciality shops and even supermarkets abound these days with vegetable- and cheese-stuffed pasta. Even the tiniest corner shop seems to boast a selection of either fresh or dried stuffed pastas: ravioli, tortellini, and the like. The pasta used is often plain egg dough, but might also be green from spinach or chopped herbs, pink from tomato or red (bell) pepper, dusty brown from mushrooms, or yellow from saffron. The fillings range from simple ricotta cheese to spinach, asparagus, artichoke, mushrooms, even spiced mashed potato. (However, I've seen some alarming ones, filled with baked beans. Give these a miss.)

Stuffed pasta needs simpler saucing than plain pasta and the sauce you choose should complement its filling. For a simple and superb starter, simply cook a handful of stuffed pasta and float it in a simple broth. Or toss the *al dente* stuffed pasta with melted butter and lots of fragrant chopped fresh herbs, or grated cheese.

Stuffed pasta makes a good main course, too, as it is more substantial than plain pasta. Mix and match vegetable-stuffed pasta with vegetable sauces: mushroom-filled tortellini in asparagus cream; or reverse the flavours for asparagus-stuffed ravioli in mushroom cream. Or prepare both and serve for a festive meal, garnished with both sautéed mushrooms and asparagus. Or combine different types of stuffed pasta into one dish to make the meal a sort of treasure hunt; this is most easily done by buying the pasta loose.

Try creating your own stuffed pastas, too, either from your homemade pasta dough (see page 14), or using wonton wrappers. Then there is a whole range of dumpling-like pastas, unusual and worth making since they are seldom available in supermarkets, and they taste wonderful. I have included only a few of my favourites here; I am constantly discovering more.

Tortelloni in Broth with Green Vegetables and Herbs

SERVES 6

325g/12 oz fresh tortelloni, such as
    green pasta filled with ricotta cheese
1 litre/1¾ pints vegetable stock
Either 1 bunch broccoli, cut into
    florets, or 2 courgettes, diced, or a
    large handful of green beans, cut
    into bite-sized pieces, or a handful
    of peas, or choose any combination
    of green vegetables
2 tablespoons olive oil
2 tablespoons chopped fresh chives
1 tablespoon chopped fresh mixed
    herbs such as marjoram, sage,
    oregano, etc.

12 oz fresh tortelloni, such as cheese-
    stuffed green tortelloni
1 quart vegetable stock
Either 1 bunch broccoli, cut into
    florets, or 2 zucchini, diced, or a
    large handful of green beans, in
    bite-sized pieces, or a handful of
    peas, or any combination of green
    vegetables
2 tablespoons olive oil
2 tablespoon chopped fresh chives
1 tablespoon chopped fresh mixed
    herbs, such as marjoram, sage,
    oregano, etc.

1. Cook the tortelloni until *al dente*. Drain and set aside.
2. Combine the stock with the vegetables in a pan and bring to the boil. Cook until the vegetables are bright green and just tender.
3. Mix the olive oil, chives and mixed herbs together.
4. Add the tortelloni to the broth and serve immediately, each portion garnished with a spoonful of the herby oil.

Mushroom Ravioli with Summer Squash, Mushrooms and Sun-Dried Tomato-Garlic Broth

SERVES 4–6

6 cloves garlic, 5 coarsely cut up and
1 finely chopped
250ml/8 fl oz vegetable stock
2 summer squash, preferably yellow
courgettes or crookneck, or
ordinary green courgettes, diced
About 8 sun-dried tomatoes, cut into
strips
175g/6 oz mushrooms, thinly sliced
15g/½ oz butter or 1 tablespoon oil
325–450g/12–16 oz mushroom-stuffed
pasta
225g/8 oz mild white cheese such as a
mild Cheddar, mozzarella or
fontina, diced
1 tablespoon finely chopped fresh
parsley

6 cloves garlic, 5 coarsely cut up and
1 finely chopped
1 cup vegetable stock
2 yellow crookneck squash or
zucchini, diced
About 8 sun-dried tomatoes, cut into
strips
6 oz mushrooms, thinly sliced
1 tablespoon butter or oil
12–16 oz mushroom-stuffed pasta
½ lb mild white cheese such as Jack,
fontina, young Asiago or mozzarella,
diced
1 tablespoon finely chopped fresh
parsley

1. Combine the coarsely cut up garlic with the stock and bring to the boil. Cook over high heat until the garlic is tender and the liquid is reduced by at least half. Add the squash (or courgettes or zucchini) and sun-dried tomatoes and continue cooking until the squash is tender and the liquid even further reduced and intensified in flavour.
2. Quickly brown the mushrooms in the butter or oil and set aside.
3. Cook the pasta until *al dente*. Drain and combine with the reserved vegetable mixture, sautéed mushrooms, cheese, and finely chopped garlic. Toss together until the cheese melts, heating it over a medium flame if necessary.
4. Serve immediately, sprinkled with the parsley.

Ravioli with Sugar Snap Peas, Summer Squash, Chard and Basil

SERVES 4–6

75–100g/3–4 oz sugar snap peas

2 summer squash, preferably golden
courgettes or yellow crookneck, or
ordinary green courgettes, cut into
bite-sized pieces

10–15 leaves chard, cut into thin
ribbons

5–8 sun-dried tomatoes, cut into strips
(optional)

3–5 cloves garlic, chopped

4–5 tablespoons olive oil or 50g/2 oz
butter

Handful of fresh basil leaves, thinly
sliced

325g/12 oz fresh ravioli, preferably
stuffed with ricotta cheese

50g/2 oz Parmesan cheese, freshly
grated, or to taste

Salt and freshly ground black pepper,
to taste

¼ lb sugar snap peas

2 yellow crookneck or zucchini, cut
into bite-sized pieces

10–15 leaves chard, cut into thin
ribbons

5–8 sun-dried tomatoes, cut into strips
(optional)

3–5 cloves garlic, chopped

4–5 tablespoons olive oil or butter

¼ cup fresh basil leaves, thinly sliced

12 oz fresh ravioli, preferably stuffed
with ricotta cheese

½ cup freshly grated Parmesan cheese,
or to taste

Salt and freshly ground black pepper,
to taste

1. Blanch the vegetables, including the tomatoes if using, until crisp-tender; this may be done in one pan and should take about 4 minutes. Drain and set aside, reserving the water for cooking the pasta.
2. Heat the garlic in the olive oil or butter until golden. Add the blanched vegetables and toss briefly, then add the basil and set aside. Keep warm.
3. Meanwhile boil the pasta in the water you cooked the vegetables in until *al dente*. Drain and toss with the vegetables. Add the Parmesan cheese, salt and black pepper. Serve immediately.

Mushroom Ravioli with Beetroot (Beet) and Tomato Purée

SERVES 4

This sauce is Fauvist pink, the colour of hot neon. Fascinating and slightly intimidating. But the taste is lovely, with the delicate sweetness of beetroot (beets) paired with slightly acidic tomatoes, all smoothed out with a little cream. Splash it on to mushroom ravioli or, even simpler, toss it with little elbow shapes.

1 large beetroot, cooked but not pickled
8 ripe fresh tomatoes, peeled and diced, or 225g/8 oz tinned
1 small onion, chopped
150ml/5 fl oz single cream
Squeeze of lemon juice
Salt and freshly ground black pepper, to taste
325g/12 oz mushroom-stuffed ravioli
25g/1 oz butter
100g/4 oz dolcelatte cheese, crumbled, or a combination of crumbled Gorgonzola and mascarpone
8–10 fresh basil leaves, thinly sliced

1 large beet, cooked but not pickled
1 cup chopped ripe fresh or canned tomatoes
½ onion, chopped
½–⅔ cup whipping cream
Squeeze of lemon juice
Salt and freshly ground black pepper, to taste
12 oz mushroom-stuffed ravioli
2 tablespoons butter
4 oz/¼ lb Gorgonzola or blue cheese, crumbled, or a combination of Gorgonzola and mascarpone
8–10 fresh basil leaves, thinly sliced

1. Dice the beetroot (beet) and combine with the tomatoes and onion in a liquidizer (blender). Blend until smooth, then add the cream and continue to blend until well mixed. Season well with lemon juice, salt and black pepper and pour into a saucepan or frying pan (skillet).
2. Heat the sauce for just a few minutes, or until it darkens slightly in colour. Remove from the heat.
3. Meanwhile cook the pasta until *al dente*.

Drain and toss with the butter, then with the hot sauce. Serve immediately, sprinkled with the cheese and basil.

Variation

For a slightly different flavour, don't cook the sauce, but toss directly with the hot buttered pasta. It will be slightly sweeter, with the uncooked onion showing through in a more pronounced way.

Filling Your Own Ravioli Using Wonton Skins

RAVIOLI STUFFED WITH RICOTTA, HERBS AND BLACK OLIVES

SERVES ABOUT 6

Ricotta cheese is creamy but not rich. Here its blandness is balanced by pungent and salty black olives and fragrant herbs.

450g/1 lb ricotta cheese
25g/1 oz Parmesan cheese, freshly grated
3 cloves garlic, finely chopped
2 teaspoons fresh chopped thyme or rosemary
About 25 Kalamata olives, pitted and diced
2 eggs, lightly beaten
1 packet wonton wrappers, or 1 quantity fresh pasta dough (see page 14), rolled and cut into squares
25g/1 oz butter
Several thinly sliced fresh basil leaves, or large pinches of fresh thyme leaves

1 lb/2 cups ricotta cheese
¼ cup freshly grated Parmesan cheese
3 cloves garlic, finely chopped
2 teaspoons chopped fresh thyme or rosemary
About 25 Kalamata olives, pitted and diced
2 eggs, lightly beaten
1 package wonton wrappers, or 1 quantity fresh pasta dough (see page 14), rolled and cut into squares
2 tablespoons butter
Several thinly sliced leaves of fresh basil or large pinch of fresh thyme leaves

1. Mix the ricotta cheese with the Parmesan cheese, garlic, thyme or rosemary, olives and eggs.
2. Place a tablespoon or so of this filling into the centre of each wonton wrapper or pasta square, then brush the edges with water. Top with another wonton wrapper or pasta square, then press well to seal. Leave on a lightly floured plate or baking sheet for about 30 minutes.
3. Boil gently until *al dente*, about 3–4 minutes (you may want to add the pasta several at a time, wait a moment then add several more; this will help keep the pasta from cooking into one large lump). Drain carefully, removing the pasta from the pan using a slotted spoon so the pasta does not break apart.
4. Serve immediately, tossed in the butter and basil or thyme.

Broccoli- and Goat Cheese-Stuffed Ravioli

SERVES 4–6

*While these plump little parcels could be simply tossed with butter or cream, or a little
tomato sauce, I like garlic butter and fresh rosemary.*

5 cloves garlic, 2 coarsely chopped,
   3 finely chopped
1 tablespoon olive oil
Small pinch of hot red pepper flakes
175g/6 oz broccoli, cooked and
   coarsely chopped
225–350g/8–12 oz goat cheese,
   crumbled
25g/1 oz Parmesan cheese, freshly
   grated
Pinch of nutmeg
2 eggs, lightly beaten
Salt to taste
1 packet wonton wrappers, or 1
   quantity fresh pasta dough (see page
   14), rolled and cut into squares
25g/1 oz butter
3 tablespoons chopped fresh rosemary

5 cloves garlic, 2 coarsely chopped,
   3 finely chopped
1 tablespoon olive oil
Small pinch of hot red pepper flakes
¾ cup cooked coarsely chopped
   broccoli
8–12 oz goat cheese, crumbled
¼ cup freshly grated Parmesan cheese
Pinch of nutmeg
2 eggs, lightly beaten
Salt to taste
1 package wonton wrappers, or 1
   quantity fresh pasta dough (see page
   14), rolled and cut into squares
2 tablespoons butter
3 tablespoons chopped fresh rosemary

1. Lightly sauté the coarsely chopped garlic in the olive oil with the hot red pepper flakes until the garlic turns golden.
2. Toss the cooked broccoli with the garlic and oil, then mix in the goat cheese, Parmesan cheese, nutmeg, eggs and salt.
3. Place a tablespoon or so of this mixture in the centre of each wonton wrapper or pasta square. Brush the edges with water, top with another piece of pasta, seal the edges well, then leave on a floured board to dry and stick the edges together, for about 30 minutes. If chilling for later use, reflour the plate and check occasionally that the moisture from the filling has not soaked through. Flour again as needed.
4. Boil gently until *al dente*, about 3–4 minutes (you may want to add the pasta several at a time, wait a moment then add several more; this will help keep the pasta from cooking into one large lump). Drain carefully, removing the pasta from the pan using a slotted spoon so the pasta does not break apart.
5. Melt the butter in a pan, then remove from the heat and add the finely chopped garlic. Pour over the ravioli and serve immediately, sprinkled with the rosemary.

Potato Ravioli with Tomatoes and Thyme

SERVES 4

It might sound unlikely, but potato-filled ravioli are sublime. The bright nuggets of diced fresh tomatoes and lashing of thyme-flavoured butter give it spark.

450g/1 lb baking potatoes, peeled and diced
2 oz/50g Parmesan cheese, freshly grated
1 egg, lightly beaten
A little milk (optional)
Salt and freshly ground black pepper, to taste
5 spring onions, thinly sliced
1 packet wonton wrappers, or 1 quantity fresh pasta dough (see page 14), cut into squares or circles
75g/3 oz butter
2 teaspoons fresh thyme, or ½ teaspoon crumbled dried thyme
450g/1 lb ripe fresh tomatoes, peeled, seeded and diced

1 lb baking potatoes, peeled and diced
½ cup freshly grated Parmesan cheese
1 egg, lightly beaten
A little milk (optional)
Salt and freshly ground black pepper, to taste
5 green onions, thinly sliced
1 package wonton wrappers, or 1 quantity fresh pasta dough (see page 14) cut into squares or circles
⅔ stick butter
2 teaspoons fresh thyme or ½ teaspoon crumbled dried thyme
1 lb fresh ripe tomatoes, peeled, seeded and diced

1. Boil the potatoes until tender. Drain and mash.
2. Mix in the Parmesan cheese and the egg, then thin slightly with milk as needed. Season with salt and black pepper, then add the spring onions (green onions). Set aside to cool.
3. Place 1 heaped tablespoon of the potato mixture into the centre of each wonton wrapper or noodle. Brush the edges with water, then top with another wrapper or noodle. Dust lightly with flour and set aside on a floured board or baking sheet for about 30 minutes. (These can be made up to two months in advance and frozen. Place in single layer on waxed-paper lined baking sheets and freeze. Do not thaw before cooking.)
4. Cook in several batches in a large pan of boiling water until just tender, about 2 minutes if fresh and 5 minutes if frozen. Transfer to plates using a slotted spoon. Keep warm by lightly covering with foil.
5. Meanwhile, melt the butter in a small heavy frying pan (skillet) over medium heat. Mix in the thyme and spoon over the ravioli. Garnish with the diced tomatoes.

Variations

New York Lower East Side Pierogi: Pierogi are fat little ravioli-like dumplings, which are boiled until tender then slathered with butter and sour cream. Though they may be filled with other ingredients such as diced browned cabbage or even smoked fish, I like this straight-from-Poland Lower East Side version filled with mashed potatoes and masses of onions that have been browned until soft and savoury. Hearty pierogi are meant to be eaten in winter's biting cold.

Not light streamlined fare, to be sure, but worth every rich forkfull.

Prepare the potatoes as above but omit the Parmesan cheese and substitute 3 onions, sliced or chopped, then browned in butter or vegetable oil, for the spring onions (green onions). Prepare and cook as above, and when just tender, drain and drizzle with melted butter. Serve hot, each portion topped with a dollop of sour cream and a sprinkling of sliced spring onions (green onions).

Wholewheat pierogi: Chewy, nutty wholewheat pasta makes wonderful pierogi. Follow the preceding recipe but use fresh wholewheat pasta.

Cheese Ravioli with Crisp Fried Sage Leaves and Tomato Coulis

SERVES 4–6

25–30 fresh sage leaves (they must be fresh)
5 tablespoons olive oil
450g/1 lb fresh cheese-stuffed ravioli
Salt and freshly ground black pepper, to taste
4–6 ripe fresh tomatoes, diced
2–3 tablespoons freshly grated Parmesan cheese

¼ cup fresh sage leaves (they must be fresh)
¼–⅓ cup olive oil
1 lb cheese-stuffed ravioli
Salt and freshly ground black pepper, to taste
4–6 ripe fresh tomatoes, diced
2–3 tablespoons freshly grated Parmesan cheese

1. Fry the sage leaves in the olive oil until just crisp. Remove from the heat and set aside.
2. Cook the ravioli until *al dente*; drain.
3. Drizzle the oil and sage leaves over the hot ravioli, season with salt and black pepper, then sprinkle over the diced tomatoes. Serve immediately with the Parmesan cheese.

Fresh Herb and Edible Flower Pasta

Sandwich a layer of whole herb leaves and/or flower petals between two pieces of pasta dough or wonton wrappers and you have a delicate pasta that is not only beautiful and unusual, but deliciously flavoured too.

The pasta shapes – they can be triangles, rectangles, diamond shapes or circles – look opaque and starchy when raw, but when cooked they are transformed into little gems, almost like stained glass.

Any herb leaves and unsprayed edible flowers will do: coriander leaves (cilantro), fennel sprigs, tiny thyme, oregano or marjoram leaves, flat parsley, even a selection of herbs, coarsely chopped, are all beautiful once trapped between the sheets of translucent pasta. The addition of edible flower petals adds a colourful note; try sage leaves combined with purple sage blossom petals or chives and their lavender-hued blossoms. Nasturtiums are particularly fetching with their vivid colours, but their strong flavour makes them more than a colourful accent, to be prepared with an assortment of other herbs rather than on their own. Follow the basic recipe below and invent your own herb or flower fillings.

Admittedly they take a bit of time to assemble, but these stunning pastas are easily made, and are particularly convenient if you use wonton or egg-roll wrappers, purchased from Chinese grocers.

Fresh herbs such as flat-leaf parsley, coriander, sage, marjoram, oregano, thyme, fennel or dill sprigs, tarragon leaves, rosemary needles, etc. and/or edible blossom petals
2 teaspoons cornflour
2 tablespoons water
About 325g/12 oz wonton or egg roll wrappers

Fresh herbs such as flat-leaf parsley, cilantro, sage, marjoram, oregano, thyme, fennel, dill, tarragon, rosemary, etc., and/or edible blossom petals
2 teaspoons cornstarch
2 tablespoons water
About 12 oz wonton or egg roll wrappers

1. Cut the leaves from the stems and remove the petals from any blossoms. Rinse and dry both.
2. Mix the cornflour (cornstarch) with the water. Take 1 piece of dough and brush it with this mixture, then quickly arrange a single layer of a few herbs and/or flower petals on it, taking care to leave at least a 6mm/¼ inch border. Cover quickly with another equal-size piece of pasta and press together well to eliminate any trapped air.

For best results roll over the filled dough with a rolling pin.
3. Place on a board that you have dusted well with cornflour (cornstarch) or flour and repeat. When you have prepared a complete layer of filled pasta, cover with a piece of cling film (plastic wrap) and do another layer. They are delicate and beautiful rather than hearty and filling: allow 5 filled ravioli per person as a first course.

4. Cook carefully in gently boiling salted water, doing them in several batches to keep them from sticking together. They cook in about 2 to 3 minutes. Lift them out with a slotted spoon. Place on a hot platter and toss with melted butter or follow one of the serving suggestions below.

Sage and Sage-Blossom Pasta

SERVES ABOUT 6

Choose about 40 young and tender sage leaves and an equal number of the tiny purple blossoms for aproximately 40 wonton wrappers. Cook according to the recipe above and serve tossed in butter, with an optional garnish of sautéed coarsely chopped pumpkin.

Mixed Herb Pasta in Broth

SERVES ABOUT 6

Choose a combination of aromatic herbs: about 10 basil leaves, 15 oregano leaves, 20 rosemary leaves, and 1–2 teaspoons fresh thyme for 40 wonton or 20 egg-roll wrappers. Sprinkle over the pasta and brush with the cornflour (cornstarch) and water mixture and seal well; make either squares, by using wonton wrappers and covering with a second noodle, or triangles, by using egg-roll wrappers and folding on the diagonal. Serve the pasta, cooked as in the basic recipe, floating in a light vegetable broth.

Mixed Herb Pasta with Goat Cheese

Serve Mixed Herb Pasta (above) drained and tossed in butter, then topped with dollops of light and creamy goat cheese, especially the kind seasoned with garlic and herbs.

Coriander (Cilantro) and/or Spring Onion (Green Onion) Pasta with Red Chilli Powder

Choose about 40 coriander leaves (cilantro) and 3 chopped spring onions (green onions), if using both. If just using one, double the amount. Follow the basic recipe above and serve tossed in butter and sprinkled with salt, mild red chilli powder, and chopped spring onions (green onions).

Rosemary Pasta with Parmesan Cheese

Use several tablespoons of fresh rosemary leaves and proceed as in the basic recipe above. Serve tossed in butter and sprinkled with freshly grated Parmesan (or Pecorino) cheese. Any blossom whose flavour will not interfere with the rosemary could be included.

Spätzle

SERVES 4

These tiny dumplings are hearty yet delicate, and very versatile - warm them in garlic butter, season with saffron, toss with spring or autumn vegetables; and they are so easy to prepare it is ridiculous.

225-275g/8-10 oz plain flour
1 teaspoon salt
2 large eggs
100ml/4 fl oz milk
A little butter or olive oil
Chopped garlic or fresh herbs to serve

1-1½ cups all purpose flour
1 teaspoon salt
2 large eggs
½ cup milk
A little butter or olive oil
Chopped garlic or fresh herbs to serve

1. Combine the flour and salt in a bowl and set aside.
2. In another bowl, beat the eggs with the milk then stir into the flour. Combine well into a sticky, doughy batter.
3. Bring a large pan of salted water to the boil, then set a colander - the type with very large holes - over the boiling pot, pour in the dough and, using a large spoon, force it through the holes. They will form squiggly dumpling shapes eventually; at the point when you are forcing it through, however, it will fall like straggling lumps and seem more a mess than a prospective dinner.
4. Cover the pan, and ignoring the fact that it looks very messy, boil over medium to high heat for 5 minutes. Release the lid if it threatens to boil over.
5. Drain carefully and place the tiny dumplings in a bowl of cold water to firm up. Leave for 15-20 minutes; do not be tempted to omit this step or they will be gummy.
6. To serve, reheat the spätzle in a small amount of hot butter or olive oil, seasoned with a little chopped garlic and/or herbs.

Spätzle with Browned Onions, Dried Mushrooms, and Rosemary

SERVES 4

15–25g/½–1 oz dried mushrooms, such as porcini, shiitake, etc.
325ml/12 fl oz hot, but not boiling, water or vegetable stock
2 onions, chopped
3 cloves garlic, coarsely chopped (optional)
Butter or oil for sautéeing
Spätzle (see page 244), cooked, soaked and drained
Salt and freshly ground black pepper, to taste
2 tablespoons chopped fresh rosemary leaves

½–1 oz dried mushrooms such as porcini, shiitake, etc.
1½ cup hot, but not boiling, water or vegetable stock
2 onions, chopped
3 cloves garlic, coarsely chopped (optional)
Butter or oil for sautéeing
Spätzle (see page 244), cooked, soaked and drained
Salt and freshly ground black pepper, to taste
2 tablespoons chopped fresh rosemary leaves

1. Rehydrate the dried mushrooms in the hot water or stock as described on page 262, reserving the liquid. Cut into fairly small pieces.
2. Sauté the onions and garlic, if using, in butter or oil until golden, then add the mushrooms. Heat through, then add the spätzle, adding extra butter or oil if needed to keep the dumplings from falling apart. Season with salt and black pepper.
3. Pour 75–150ml/3–5 fl oz (⅓–⅔ cup) of the mushroom-soaking liquid into the pan and cook over medium to high heat until it has reduced.
4. Serve immediately, each portion sprinkled with fresh rosemary.

Herbed Broccoli Spätzle with Garlic and Diced Tomatoes

SERVES 4–6

Add 50–75g/2–3 oz (¼–½ cup) cooked and finely chopped broccoli and 1 teaspoon finely chopped fresh rosemary to the basic spätzle recipe. When pushing the dough into the boiling water, make sure that you use a colander with holes that are large enough for the bits of broccoli to fall through. Broccoli spätzle are a bit more delicate to prepare; take care when draining or they will appear more like broccoli-dough mush and be completely unredeemable.

To serve, heat several cloves of chopped garlic in a tablespoon or two of butter or olive oil over medium heat, then toss in the drained spätzle and cook for a few moments to heat through.

Remove from the pan, then swirl 8–10 diced peeled tomatoes or 200ml/6 fl oz (¾ cup) tomato passata through the hot pan, heat through, and serve tossed with the broccoli spätzle. Serve sprinkled with fresh coriander leaves (cilantro) and coarsely grated Parmesan cheese if liked.

Potato Gnocchi

SERVES 4–6

While you can purchase potato gnocchi imported from Italy, they are easy and inexpensive to make yourself. And when you do, you will be rewarded with gnocchi that are light and delicate.

The finest potato gnocchi I have ever tasted were made with yellow Finnish potatoes whose flesh was dry and mealy. I find that the vagaries of water content in potatoes available in our markets make preparing predictable gnocchi virtually impossible. If the potatoes are too moist, the dumplings will be leaden and gummy; too dry and you might have heavy dumplings.

The problem comes from the added water needed to boil the potatoes for mashing. You can eliminate this by baking rather than boiling your potatoes. The second method for excellent gnocchi is a surprising one: dehydrated instant mashed potatoes. It is surprising how well the dumplings turn out, considering that instant mashed potatoes are not at all appetizing on their own.

Serve these luscious little dumplings with a light garlicky tomato sauce such as the one for Tricolour Conchiglie with Garlic and Tomato Sauce (page 105), Lusty Tomato and Pea Sauce (page 112) or Creamy Porcini sauce (page 149).

If you do want to use fresh potatoes, use 900g/2 lb yellow Finnish or 450g/1 lb each of baking potatoes and waxy red or white ones.

900g/2 lb baking potatoes or 1 90g/3
   oz packet dehydrated mashed
   potatoes
1 egg, lightly beaten
About 450g/16 oz plain unbleached
   flour

To serve
A little butter
Sauce of choice (see above)
Freshly grated Parmesan cheese

2 lb baking potatoes or 1 3 oz package
   dehydrated mashed potatoes
1 egg, lightly beaten
About 2 cups all-purpose unbleached
   flour

To serve
A little butter
Sauce of choice (see above)
Freshly grated Parmesan cheese

1. Bake the potatoes until tender. Cool until you are able to handle them, then remove and mash their soft flesh. If using dehydrated potatoes, rehydrate with boiling water according to the directions on the packet. Stir well and leave to cool to room temperature.
2. Add the egg and half the flour and mix well, kneading as you would bread. But take care, because too much kneading will make the gnocchi tough. The batter should be soft yet hold its shape. Add the remaining flour as needed to achieve the correct consistency.
3. Break off chunks about the size of an apricot. With floured hands, gently roll them out into cylinders about 2cm/¾ inch thick, then with a sharp knife cut off short, squat lengths. Carefully lay the finished dumplings out on a floured board while you finish cutting the rest. Leave to dry for at least 15 minutes.
4. To cook, bring a large pan of water to the boil, then add the gnocchi, in several batches so that they don't stick together. Immediately turn the heat down to a simmer (too violent a boil will break apart the tender dumplings). When they are ready, after about 4–6 minutes, they will float to the surface.
5. Remove the gnocchi, using a slotted spoon; drain thoroughly then place on a baking sheet or serving platter. Either serve now, tossed in butter and splashed with a sauce, or leave them for 30–60 minutes to settle and firm up. I like the gnocchi best when they have had a chance to settle.
6. When ready to serve, heat the sauce and layer with the gnocchi in a baking dish. Top with grated Parmesan cheese and heat in a hot oven until the cheese melts. Serve immediately.

Khote and Achar

TIBETAN VEGETABLE DUMPLINGS WITH CURRIED TOMATO SAUCE

SERVES 4–6

These are chewy dumplings of freshly made pasta filled with curried potatoes and other vegetables, then steamed on a bed of leafy greens and eaten with a spicy, curried tomato sauce.

225g/8 oz plain flour
175ml/6 fl oz hot water (bring to the boil, then leave to cool for a moment)
900g/2 lb potatoes, preferably baking type, peeled and diced
1 onion, coarsely chopped
3 cloves garlic, chopped
25g/1 oz butter
¾ teaspoon cumin
¾ teaspoon curry powder
¾ teaspoon chopped fresh ginger root
½ teaspoon turmeric
1 small to medium broccoli stalk, coarsely chopped
½ carrot, coarsely chopped
¼ red pepper, coarsely chopped
1½ tablespoons lemon juice
1–2 tablespoons yogurt
1 tablespoon chopped fresh coriander leaves
Salt and cayenne pepper, to taste
1–2 bunches kale, cabbage leaves, dandelion, or other sturdy greens
Achar (see below)

1 cup all purpose unbleached flour
¾ cup hot water (bring to the boil, then leave to cool for a moment)
2 lb potatoes, preferably baking type, peeled and diced
1 onion, coarsely chopped
3 cloves garlic, chopped
2 tablespoons butter
¾ teaspoon cumin
¾ teaspoon curry powder
¾ teaspoon chopped fresh ginger root
½ teaspoon turmeric
1 small to medium broccoli stalk, coarsely chopped
½ carrot, coarsely chopped
¼ red bell pepper, coarsely chopped
1½ tablespoons lemon juice
1–2 tablespoons yogurt
1 tablespoon chopped fresh cilantro
Salt and cayenne pepper, to taste
1–2 bunches kale, dandelion, outer cabbage leaves, or other sturdy greens
Achar (see below)

1. Place the flour in a bowl. Pour in the hot water then mix with a fork. After a few moments, when cool enough to handle, finish mixing with your hands until it holds together. Wrap in plastic and chill.
2. Meanwhile make the filling: boil the potatoes until tender, then drain and mash.
3. Sauté the onion and garlic in the butter until softened, then add the cumin, curry powder, ginger root, turmeric, broccoli, carrot and red (bell) pepper and cook for a few minutes. Add to the mashed potatoes, along with the

lemon juice, yogurt, and coriander leaves (cilantro). Season to taste with salt and cayenne pepper, then set aside.

4. Working one piece at a time, pinch off walnut-sized pieces of the flour-and-water dough, then shape each into a ball and knead several times. Roll flat on a floured board into small discs.

5. Place a disc in your hand, one at a time, and place 1 tablespoon of the potato filling in the centre. Bring up the edges and seal at the top with little gathers. Leave a tiny hole at the top for steam to escape.

6. Line a steamer with the greens. Top with a layer of dumplings and steam over boiling water for 15–20 minutes.

7. Serve immediately with the Achar.

Achar

2 onions, chopped
3 cloves garlic, chopped
1 tablespoon vegetable oil (or mustard oil –
   a spicy oil fragrant with the scent of
   mustard and available in Asian and Indian
   groceries)
1 teaspoon curry powder
1 fresh hot chilli pepper, or more to taste,
   thinly sliced
6–8 ripe fresh or tinned (canned) tomatoes,
   chopped
Salt and lime juice to taste

1. Lightly sauté the onions and garlic in the oil until softened, then sprinkle with the curry powder and stir in the chilli.

2. Add the tomatoes and cook for a minute until saucelike and flavourful. Season with salt and lime juice.

Crisp-Fried Tofu and Shiitake Wonton with Ginger Sweet-Sour Sauce

MAKES ABOUT 50 WONTON, TO SERVE 6–8

Tofu, shiitake mushrooms and cloud ear fungus make a light wonton filling, served with a classic sweet-sour sauce. You could also make a sauce with soy sauce, vinegar and hot chilli oil, thinned out with a little of the mushroom soaking liquid and seasoned with finely chopped fresh coriander leaves (cilantro).

6–8 dried shiitake
2 large cloud ear or tree cloud fungus
225g/8 oz tofu, either regular or firm
3 spring onions, thinly sliced
2 tablespoons chopped fresh coriander
  leaves
8–10 fresh and blanched or tinned
  water chestnuts, chopped
1 tablespoon soy sauce
1 tablespoon sesame oil
1 packet wonton wrappers or similar
  fresh noodle dough
1 egg, beaten
Oil for deep frying

6–8 dried shiitake
2 large cloud ear or tree cloud fungus
8 oz regular or firm tofu
3 green onions, thinly sliced
2 tablespoons chopped fresh cilantro
8–10 fresh and blanched or canned
  water chestnuts, chopped
1 tablespoon soy sauce
1 tablespoon sesame oil
1 package wonton wrappers or similar
  fresh noodle dough
1 egg, beaten
Oil for deep frying

1. Rehydrate the shiitake and cloud ear or tree cloud fungus in hot water to cover, as described on page 262 (reserving the liquid for other dishes). Remove the stems and tough bits from the mushrooms and fungus, then chop finely.
2. Mash the tofu, then mix with the chopped mushrooms and fungus, spring onions (green onions), water chestnuts, soy sauce and sesame oil.
3. Place about a teaspoon of this filling in the centre of each wonton. Brush a little egg round the edges of each noodle, then fold the corners over and press to seal. You will now have a triangle shape; take the two corners and wet with a dab of water, then bring them together to seal and form the traditional wonton shape. Set aside for at least 10 minutes.
4. Deep fry until golden, about 2 minutes, then remove and drain on absorbent paper. Serve immediately, with Ginger Sweet-Sour Sauce.

Ginger Sweet-Sour Sauce

50g/2 oz dark brown demerara sugar
1 tablespoon cornflour
175ml/6 fl oz pineapple juice
2 tablespoons tomato ketchup
1 tablespoon chopped fresh ginger root
½ teaspoon salt, or to taste
50–75ml/2-3 fl oz white wine vinegar,
   or to taste

¼ cup dark brown sugar
1 tablespoon cornstarch
¾ cup pineapple juice
2 tablespoons catsup
1 tablespoon chopped fresh ginger root
½ teaspoon salt, or to taste
¼–⅓ cup white wine vinegar, or to
   taste

1. Put the sugar, cornflour (cornstarch), pineapple juice, ketchup (catsup), ginger root and salt in a pan. Cook over medium heat until the mixture thickens.
2. Add the vinegar and taste for seasoning, adjusting the sweet-sour balance if necessary.
3. Serve at room temperature with the fried wonton.

Variation

Instead of frying, boil the wonton and serve in a simple Chinese broth such as Black Mushroom Broth with Tofu, Tree Cloud Fungus, Broccoli and Cellophane Noodles (see page 190).

BASIC RECIPES

LEFTOVERS

Leftover pasta is different from freshly cooked pasta. Indeed many Italians claim it is good only to feed to the animals. (In Italy you will often see little piles of leftover pasta lying on the ground on a piece of newspaper, a crowd of mewing felines gathered around, pawing at the strands of spaghetti, chewing at whatever they are lucky enough to get a mouthful of.)

However, others, myself included, find leftover pasta can be quite tempting, especially as a solitary snack or late-night supper. Some pasta dishes with sauce are fine just reheated in a few spoonfuls of water, tossed quickly through over a medium to high heat, and forked up as a midnight feast.

But for more social eating experiences, omelettes or frittatas make an excellent way of using up leftover pasta.

Pasta Frittata

SERVES 2–4

I vary this frittata every time I make it, especially with toppings of basil pesto or red sun-dried tomato pesto, or spicy Mexican-style salsas.

2 cloves garlic, chopped
About 1 tablespoon olive oil
About 2 portions leftover sauced pasta
  with vegetables
4 eggs, lightly beaten
Salt and freshly ground black pepper
  to taste
100g/4 oz cheese such as Cheddar,
  Mozzarella, fontina, etc. or a
  combination that includes Parmesan,
  grated
Several large pinches of dried herbs
  such as oregano or mixed herbs, or
  chopped fresh herbs such as basil or
  rosemary

2 cloves garlic, chopped
About 1 tablespoon olive oil
About 2 portions leftover sauced pasta
  with vegetables
4 eggs, lightly beaten
Salt and freshly ground black pepper
  to taste
½–⅔ cup grated cheese such as Jack,
  Cheddar, Asiago, or a combination
  that includes Parmesan
Several large pinches of dried herbs
  such as oregano or mixed Italian
  herbs, or chopped fresh herbs such
  as basil or rosemary

1. Warm the garlic in the olive oil in a large frying pan (skillet).
2. Meanwhile, combine the pasta and vegetables with the eggs, first cutting up the vegetables into bite-sized pieces if necessary; season with salt and black pepper.
3. Pour this mixture into the pan, then cook over low to medium heat until the underneath is a golden colour and the top is more or less set.
4. Arrange the cheese on top and grill (broil) until melted. Serve immediately, sprinkled with herbs of choice.

Variations

Pasta Frittata Topped with Basil or Sun-Dried Tomato Pesto: Spread a thin layer of either basil or sun-dried tomato pesto over the frittata just before serving. Omit the herbs.

With Mexican Salsa: Spread a layer of Mexican style salsa over the melted cheese topping. The salsa can be as simple as diced tomato and fresh chilli, combined with garlic, cumin and fresh coriander (cilantro) to taste.

Pasta e Fagioli

HEARTY SOUP-STEW WITH BEANS

SERVES ABOUT 4, DEPENDING ON THE LEFTOVERS

Leftover tomato-and-vegetable-sauced pasta tossed into a pot with some garlic-flavoured oil, a little stock and some beans makes a hearty soup-stew, perfect for supper or midnight feasting.

3 cloves garlic, coarsely chopped
1 small carrot, finely diced
2–3 tablespoons olive oil
Any leftover plain blanched vegetables, if available: courgettes, chard, etc.
3 portions leftover sauced pasta, with vegetables such as peas, etc.
225g/8 oz cooked or drained, tinned beans, such as kidney, borlotti, cannellini, or chickpeas
500ml/16 fl oz vegetable stock, or as needed
Salt and freshly ground black pepper to taste
Generous handful of fresh herbs or pinches of dried herbs: fresh rosemary, crumbled mixed herbs, basil, pesto, whatever is available
Freshly grated Parmesan cheese to serve

3 cloves garlic, coarsely chopped
1 small carrot, finely chopped
2–3 tablespoons olive oil
Any leftover plain blanched vegetables, if available: zucchini, chard, etc.
3 portions leftover sauced pasta with vegetables such as peas, etc.
1 cup cooked or drained canned beans, such as kidney, borlotti, cannellini (white kidney), garbanzos
2 cups vegetable stock, or as needed
Salt and freshly ground black pepper to taste
Fresh herbs to taste: rosemary, basil, oregano, or dried herbs such as mixed Italian herbs, oregano, or a few spoonfuls of pesto
Freshly grated Parmesan cheese to taste

1. Lightly cook the garlic and carrot in the olive oil until the garlic is golden and the carrot softened, then add the vegetables, if using, and pasta and toss in the oil together with the beans, letting it all cook for a few minutes to absorb the garlic-scented oil.
2. Add the stock, then cook uncovered over medium to high heat until soupy, adding more stock if needed. Do not stir, merely turn once or twice. Season with salt and black pepper.
3. Serve hot, sprinkled with herbs of choice or with spoonfuls of pesto, and with grated cheese.

BASIC SAUCES

Pesto alla Genovese

MAKES ABOUT 350ML/12 FL OZ

This garlicky, herby balm from Genoa is delicious spooned into soups, spread on crusty bread for sandwiches, and of course, as a topping for a wide variety of pasta dishes.

4–6 cloves garlic, finely chopped
40g/1½ oz pine nuts
225g/8 oz basil leaves
100ml/4 fl oz olive oil
50g/2 oz Parmesan, Pecorino, or other similar cheese, freshly grated
Pinch of salt

4–6 cloves garlic, finely chopped
¼ cup pine nuts
3–4 cups basil leaves, packed tightly
½ cup olive oil
½ cup freshly grated Parmesan or similar cheese, freshly grated
Pinch of salt

1. Process the garlic in a liquidizer (blender) or food processor, or pound in a mortar and pestle. Add the pine nuts, crush, then add the basil leaves and either process or pound, then slowly add the olive oil, working it into a thick and pungent paste.
2. Add the cheese and salt to taste. Use immediately or refrigerate for up to 2 weeks. It also freezes extremely well.

Variations

Pesto Without Nuts: While the classic pesto is prepared with pine nuts or walnuts in Liguria, or with almonds in Sicily, my favourite version is made without any nuts at all. It is all basil and garlic essence, herbal and delicious. If I am in the mood for nuts, I toast them lightly and scatter them on top of the fragrant pesto-sauced pasta for a pure and crisp nutty accent. Offer extra cheese as desired.

Fred Barclay's Basil and Parsley Pesto: When our neighbour, physicist Fred Barclay, is fed up with solving the world's problems of energy and desalination, he retreats to the kitchen and deals with the physics involved in puréeing basil and parsley into a deep green and very refreshing pesto.

Follow the basic recipe, using half parsley and half basil. Whether or not you add nuts is up to you.

Red Pesto

MAKES ABOUT 350ML/12 FL OZ

A zesty, relish-like sauce, halfway between classic pesto and an Italian salsa. This recipe comes from my book The Flavour of California *(Thorsons). Enjoy red pesto as a sauce for nearly any pasta, either on its own or in conjunction with other sauces.*

4 cloves garlic, finely chopped

15 oil-marinated sun-dried tomatoes, diced

6–8 ripe fresh or tinned tomatoes, chopped

75ml/3 fl oz oil from the jar of sun-dried tomatoes (make up with olive oil if necessary)

15–30g/½–1 oz fresh basil, coarsely chopped

4 cloves garlic, finely chopped

15 oil-marinated sun-dried tomatoes, diced

6–8 ripe fresh or canned tomatoes, chopped

⅓ cup oil from the jar of sun-dried tomatoes (make up with olive oil if necessary)

½ cup fresh basil leaves, coarsely chopped

1. Combine all the ingredients in a liquidizer (blender) or food processor or by hand, and mix well until you have a saucelike consistency with a chunky texture.

2. Use immediately or keep in the refrigerator for up to 3 days.

Olio Santo

OLIVE OIL SEASONED WITH HOT PEPPERS AND HERBS

MAKES ABOUT 500ML/16 FL OZ

Olio Santo is the Tuscan preparation of dried hot peppers and basil steeped in olive oil. Traditionally used as a last-minute seasoning drizzled on to pasta and robust soups, I find it is also good on salads and pizza.

500ml/16 fl oz olive oil
5 small dried hot red chilli peppers
About 20 fresh basil leaves

2 cups olive oil
5 small dried hot red chilli peppers
About 20 fresh basil leaves

1. Pour the olive oil into a clean jar or bottle.
2. Add the hot peppers and basil and leave in a dark place. It develops flavour with time, but is good after only a few days.

Variations

Chillied Olive Oil: Omit the herbs and use only chillies and oil.

With Mint: Substitute about 10 fresh mint leaves and 1–2 teaspoons dried mixed herbs for the basil.

Garlic Olive Oil: Chopped or sliced garlic steeped in olive oil makes a delicious Tuscan flavouring for pasta, roasted (bell) peppers, salads, pizza, and so on. Be careful, though, not to leave the garlic in the oil for longer than 2 weeks as garlic sitting in oil can breed dangerous toxins. It is so delicious, however, that it will probably not last long enough to be a consideration.

Béchamel Sauce

25g/1 oz butter
2 tablespoons flour
500ml/16 fl oz hot, but not boiling,
  milk
Salt and freshly ground black pepper
  to taste
Freshly grated nutmeg to taste

2 tablespoons butter
2 tablespoons flour
2 cups hot, but not boiling, milk
Salt and freshly ground black pepper
  to taste
Freshly grated nutmeg to taste

1. Melt the butter in a pan and sprinkle in the flour. Cook for a few moments until golden, then remove from the heat and gradually stir in the milk, a little at a time.

2. Return to medium heat and bring to the boil, then cook, stirring, until it thickens. Season with salt, black pepper and nutmeg.

Quick Garlicky Tomato Sauce

4 cloves garlic, chopped
2 tablespoons olive oil
500ml/16 fl oz tomato passata
Large pinch of fennel seeds
Large pinch of dried mixed herbs
Salt and freshly ground black pepper
  to taste
Pinch of sugar (optional)

4 cloves garlic, chopped
2 tablespoons olive oil
2 cups tomato passata or tomato sauce
Large pinch of fennel seeds
Large pinch of dried mixed Italian
  herbs
Salt and freshly ground black pepper
  to taste
Pinch of sugar (optional)

1. Lightly sauté the garlic in the olive oil until fragrant, then pour in the tomato passata (or sauce).

2. Simmer for 5–10 minutes, then season with the fennel seeds and dried herbs, salt and black pepper, and sugar, if needed.

LEFTOVER UNSAUCED PASTA

If cooked slightly underdone, pasta may be reheated by briefly submerging it in boiling water and heating it through for just a few moments.

LEFTOVER SAUCES

Leftover sauces make wonderful fillings for omelettes – French rolled ones or Italian- or Spanish-style flat ones. Tuck a few spoonfuls of sauce into the centre of a rolled omelette, add a sprinkling of gruyère or other mild cheese and let it melt in. For a flat omelette, frittata-style, combine a few spoonfuls of the sauce with some diced vegetables, and add the beaten eggs. Leave to stand so the eggs absorb the flavours of the sauce and vegetables, then pour into a pan containing a small amount of hot olive oil and cook as you would any frittata or tortilla.

Many vegetable sauces make a delicious basis for soups. A small amount of a smooth purée, for instance, can be stretched into a savoury soup by adding a pint or two of vegetable stock. Ditto for chunky vegetable sauces, though you might like to add more vegetables.

Pizza is another grateful recipient of leftover pasta sauces: a few tablespoons of a chunky vegetable sauce is delicious spread on to French bread or a pizza dough base, then topped with cheese and baked until golden brown and melting.

Vegetable Stock 1

The most frugal of vegetable stocks are also the most delicious, since they consist of using vegetable trimmings and/or leftover vegetable cooking liquid together with a handful of aromatics. A vegetable stock cube or two in lieu of salt makes the stock rich and flavourful rather than listless as vegetable stocks can sometimes be.

The water left from spinach, carrots, potatoes, peas, green beans, courgettes (zucchini), and other fresh-tasting vegetables makes the best stock. Do not use the water from cabbage or other strong-smelling vegetables.

Adding whole cloves of garlic makes a gently fragrant stock, as garlic loses its strong scent as it simmers.

1 litre/2 pints liquid (leftover water from cooking vegetables, plus enough water to make up a litre)

Trimmings from vegetables: celery, carrot, leeks, turnips, tomatoes, parsley, courgettes (zucchini), red (bell) pepper, potato peelings, etc.

6 whole cloves garlic, unpeeled (or less, to taste) or 1 small onion, cut into quarters

A few sprigs of parsley or other fresh herbs

2–3 vegetable stock cubes

1 quart liquid (leftover water from cooking vegetables, plus enough water to make up the difference)

Trimmings from vegetables: celery, carrots, leeks, turnips, tomatoes, zucchini, bell peppers, parsley, potato peelings, etc.

6 whole cloves garlic, unpeeled (or less, to taste) or 1 small onion, cut into quarters

A few sprigs of parsley or other fresh herbs

2–3 vegetable bouillon cubes

1. Combine all the ingredients, bring to the boil, then reduce the heat and simmer for 15–20 minutes or until the garlic is tender.
2. Strain and use as desired.

Vegetable Stock 2

1 litre/2 pints water
1 onion, quartered
2 celery stalks, cut into bite-sized
   pieces
2 carrots, cut into bite-sized pieces
Handful of parsley, dill, or other herb
2–3 vegetable stock cubes

1 quart water
1 onion, quartered
2 celery stalks, cut into bite-sized
   pieces
2 carrots, cut into bite-sized pieces
Handful of parsley, dill, or other herb
2–3 vegetable bouillon cubes

1. Combine all the ingredients.
2. Bring to the boil, then reduce the heat and simmer for 20 minutes or until the carrots and celery are tender. Strain or keep the vegetables in the stock, as you wish.

Roasted Tomatoes

Roasting intensifies the flavour of tomatoes and caramelizes the juices. They make an almost instant sauce for pasta, combined with other simple seasonings such as olive oil, garlic, capers, hot pepper, etc. They also make a delicious basis for sauces and soups.

Tomatoes may be roasted in advance and kept in the refrigerator, well covered, for up to 5 days.

1. Place enough small to medium tomatoes in a heavy casserole or baking dish to cover the base in a single layer, leaving enough room to turn the tomatoes.
2. Place under the grill (broiler) and grill (broil) until their tops char a bit and their skins begin to split.
3. Remove from the grill and gently turn each tomato over so that its charred side is down.
4. Bake in the oven at 200°C/400°F/gas mark 6 until the tomatoes are charred all over and some of the juices have trickled out and caramelized a little – about 40 minutes.
5. Remove from the oven and leave to cool (the juices will be thin at first and thicken as they cool). Before using, remove the skins, which will just slip off, and dice the tomato flesh, then combine with the thickened juices from the roasting.

Roasted (Bell) Peppers

Roasting or grilling transforms the crunchy fresh (bell) pepper into a completely different vegetable: tender and almost silky in texture, with a smoky nuance. Red, yellow and green (bell) peppers all roast to distinctly different flavours: red and yellow become sweet, green peppers strong-flavoured and very vegetal.

Roasted (bell) peppers make the basis of wonderful salads, soups, sandwich fillings, sauces and the like, and seem to be at their best when combined with pasta.

1. Roast the (bell) peppers over an open flame on top of the cooker (stove) or under a hot grill (broiler) until they are charred in spots and the flesh has softened, about 6 minutes on each side.
2. Place in a paper or plastic bag and seal, or place in a bowl and cover. This creates steam, which helps to loosen the skin. Leave for about 20 minutes.
3. Peel away and discard the skin. Clean and deseed the peppers, then proceed as directed in the recipe.

Dried Mushrooms

Dried mushrooms provide a delicious, strong and versatile flavour addition in the pasta kitchen. There are a wide variety of mushrooms (and other fungi) available, but the most easily found are the shiitake or Chinese black mushroom, the utterly delicious Italian porcini, delicate French cèpe, or the pungent, almost smoky-flavoured morel.

Dried mushrooms are often more flavourful than their fresh counterparts as their flavours and aromas have been intensified by the drying process; when rehydrated they still seem to have more flavour than the originals, and you have the added bonus of their soaking liquid, which gives delicious flavour to any recipe.

Other fungi, such as the Chinese tree cloud fungus or wood ears, may be rehydrated by the same method as below, but their soaking liquid is not as flavourful as the mushrooms.

1. Place the dried mushrooms in a bowl and pour hot but not boiling stock or water over. Cover and leave for about 30 minutes.
2. When cool enough to handle, squeeze the mushrooms over the soaking bowl, then strain all the liquid, discarding the sandy debris. The liquid can be kept (it freezes well) and used for soups or sauces if it is not needed in the recipe.
3. Soak the mushrooms for a few minutes in cold water, swishing them around a bit to dislodge any grit still clinging to them, then squeeze again. Discard this liquid, which is not as flavourful as the liquid from the first soaking. Proceed as directed in the recipe.

Preparing Fresh Artichokes

Artichokes are often served whole, simply boiled or steamed, and the spiky leaves are pulled off one by one, dipped into melted butter or a mayonnaise-type sauce, then scraped with the teeth to eat the tiny bit of delicate artichoke flesh at the base. The inner heart is then exposed (its fuzzy choke removed) and the essence of artichoke flavour is yours to enjoy. The whole process is messy and utterly delicious. But for recipes such as soups, stews and pasta sauces that use fresh artichokes you must rid each vegetable of its sharp tough leaves and pare it down to its tender heart.

While tinned (canned) and frozen artichoke hearts are readily available, it is worth knowing how to prepare fresh ones: their subtle, rich and distinctive flavour is incomparable.

1. Cut off the stem of each artichoke and peel to remove the stringy fibres. Often the stems are delicious, sometimes they are not. Cook them anyway and decide later.
2. Trim the bottom of the artichoke, again just paring away the tough outer covering of the vegetable, then begin removing the leaves by pulling each back until it snaps off. The edible portion, or most of it, will remain behind. Discard the tough leaves as you snap them off.
3. When you reach the more tender inner leaves, cut off their sharp tops but leave the edible bottom part. Trim the edges where you have pulled the leaves off. You now have an artichoke heart.
4. Some artichoke hearts do not have much of an inner fuzzy choke and may be eaten whole, but others have large inedible chokes which need to be removed. Do this by cutting each heart in half or quarters and with a sharp paring knife just cut out the choke.
5. Place in a saucepan of acidulated water, that is, water to which you've added either the juice of half a lemon or a spoonful of flour. This is to prevent the artichokes discolouring. Bring to the boil and cook until just tender. Cooking time will depend upon the size and age of the artichokes, but halves or quarters should take 10–15 minutes. Drain and use as directed by the recipe.

Sun-Dried Tomatoes

In parts of Italy's South you will see the sweet fruit halved and set in the midday sun to dry on wire beds. Sun-dried tomatoes are originally Italian, but have become a staple in the cuisine of California as well, and are to be found in much contemporary Mediterranean-inspired fare. They are little nuggets of concentrated tomato flavour.

Once dry they are chewy and slightly cardboard-like; if you nibble one in this state you will wonder what all the fuss is about. To bring out their special flavour they must be rehydrated and either marinated with garlic and olive oil and enjoyed as an appetizer, or cooked as a savoury accent to other ingredients.

Alternatively, sun-dried tomatoes may be purchased ready-marinated in olive oil and they are delicious, with the added bonus of their seasoned oil for sauces, pasta, salads, etc. Storebought marinated sun-dried tomatoes will last quite a while in the refrigerator while homemade ones will not – I'm not sure why, but I suspect that the salt content of the commercially produced ones has something to do with it.

To rehydrate dried tomatoes: Place in a saucepan with water to cover and bring to the boil. Reduce the heat and simmer for about 15 minutes or until the tomatoes plump up. Drain, reserve the water for another use, if liked, and add the tomatoes to pasta sauces, stews, soups, etc.

To marinate: Place the rehydrated and drained tomatoes in a bowl with chopped garlic and fresh basil or thyme to taste, a generous sprinkling of salt (unless they have already been salted before drying), a splash of balsamic or red wine vinegar and olive oil to cover. Leave to stand for at least an hour and serve as an antipasto or snack with bread. They will keep for several days in the refrigerator.

INDEX

Achar 249
acini de pepe, in tomato and garlic broth 28
African Spicy Peanut Soup-Stew with Noodles 35
artichokes, preparing fresh 263
artichoke sauce, with fettuccine 111
arugula (rocket), with pasta and spicy tomato sauce 90
asparagus, with pasta and light creamy pesto 107
    and tomato sauce with fettuccine 108
    and capellini with creamy purée of hazelnuts, porcini and mascarpone 150
    baked with penne or farfalle, with fontina 221
    with spicy pasta and red pesto 79
Aubergine (Eggplant)
    and small pasta with ricotta and mozzarella 218
    casserole with small pasta with Ricotta and Mozzarella cheese 218
    simmered with red wine and tomato sauce, with pasta and cheese 139
    sliced and browned, with spaghetti and tomato sauce 142
    Syracusan-style sauce, with peppers, tomatoes, olives, capers, garlic, and basil-scented tomato sauce 140
    with Capellini, Cumin and Roasted Garlic 56
Auntie Estelle's Chinese Leaf Salad with Crunchy Noodles and Nuts 60
Autumn-Day Capellini with Roasted Garlic, Mushrooms and Tomatoes 152
Autumn Vegetable Ragu 160

Baked Pasta with Mushrooms, Green Beans, Gorgonzola and

Tomatoes 222
Baked Penne or Farfalle with Asparagus and Fontina 221
Baked Ravioli with Fresh Rosemary and Tomatoes 223
baked tomato sauce, with pasta 100
Béchamel sauce 230, 258
Beetroot (beets) relish, with capellini, broccoli and blue cheese 59
Black Bean Chow Mein with Vegetables and Tofu 209
Black Mushroom Broth with Tofu, Tree Cloud Fungus, Broccoli and Cellophane Noodles 190
Braised Onions with Red Wine and Tomato 136
breadcrumbs, garlic-buttered with spaghetti 76
broad beans, with pasta, goat cheese and black olives 96
Broccoli
    in black mushroom broth with tofu and cellophane noodles 190
    curried, with spaghetti and chickpeas 185
    in curried yogurt soup 41
    and ditalini with creamy blue cheese sauce 182
    and goat cheese-stuffed ravioli 239
    and pastina in garlic broth 24
    in salad with pasta shells and tahini dressing 49
    salad with pasta, sesame and soy 53
    spätzle, with garlic and diced tomatoes 246
    spinach, with fettuccine and carrot-butter 133
    with papardelle and red beans 183
    with tomato-sauced pasta and ricotta cheese 132
    with wholewheat spaghetti, hot pepper and garlic 75
Broccoli Carbonara 78
Broccoli Chow Fun 203
Broccoli and Pastina in Garlic

Broth 24
Broth-Cooked Orzo with Lemon and Parsley 94
Broth-Cooked Pasta Tossed with Olives and Parsley 81
Brown Lentil, Red Bean, Broccoli, and Pasta Shell Stew 42
Buckwheat or Wholewheat Noodles with Cabbage and Blue Cheese 179
Buckwheat Soba with Peas and Cream 80
Burmese Noodles with Curry Sauce and Assorted Toppings 210
Buttered Bay-Scented Capellini 98

Cabbage
    and tomato soup, Goan Style 22
    and tomato soup, spicy Spanish style, with capellini 31
    with buckwheat noodles and blue cheese 179
    with leeks, tomatoes, pasta and cheese 178
Cal-Asian Salad 205
Cannelloni 227
Capellini
    cooked with bay leaves and buttered 98
    with roasted garlic and cumin-aubergine (eggplant) 56
Capellini, in spicy Cabbage and Tomato Soup 31
Capellini or Fettuccine with Asparagus and a Creamy Purée of Hazelnuts, Porcini and Mascarpone Cheese 150
Capellini with Beetroot (Beets) Relish, Broccoli and Blue Cheese 59
Capellini with Peas, Porcini and Tomatoes 148
carrot butter 133
Casserole of Aubergine (Eggplant) and Small Pasta with Ricotta and Mozzarella Cheese 218
cauliflower and farfalle gratin 173

Cellophane Noodles 16
  in black mushroom broth, with
    broccoli, tofu, and tree cloud
    fungus 190
Cheese Ravioli with Crisp Fried Sage
  Leaves and Tomato Coulis 241
Chickpea and Tagliatelle Soup 43
Chilli-Spiked Tomato Sauce with
  Pasta 62
Chinese Breakfast Noodles 197
Chinese Egg Noodles
  in coconut soup, with green beans
    and waterchestnuts 192
Chinese Noodles with Spicy Peanut
  Butter Sauce and Salad 215
Chinese Peanut Butter-Dressed
  Noodle Salad with Red Cabbage
  and Bean Sprouts 63
Chorreadas Sauce 176
chow mein, with spicy black bean
  sauce, cabbage and shiitake 208
Coconut Curry with Rice Noodles,
  Chinese Black Mushrooms
  (Shiitake) and Water
  Chestnuts 195
Cold Buckwheat Soba with
  Mangetout (Snow Peas) and
  Water Chestnuts 202
Cold Pasta
  Auntie Estelle's Chinese Leaf Salad
    with Crunchy Noodles and
    Nuts 60
  broccoli with sesame and soy
    dressing 53
  broccoli and pasta shells with
    tahini dressing 49
  buckwheat soba, with mangetout
    (snow peas) and water
    chestnuts 202
  Cal-Asian Salad 205
  capellini with beetroot (beet)
    relish, broccoli and blue
    cheese 59
  capellini, with roasted garlic and
    cumin-aubergine (eggplant) 56
  Chinese noodles with peanut
    butter dressing, red cabbage and
    beansprouts 63
  with coriander (cilantro)-mint raita
    and cucumber 52
  with courgettes (zucchini), sun-
    dried tomatoes and rosemary 54
  farfalle, with multicoloured tomato
    salad 55
  Fourth of July macaroni salad 50
  garlic-scented macaroni with
    tomatoes, goat cheese, and
    basil 45
  penne alla malefemmina (with
    spicy tomatoes, capers, olives
    and basil) 48
  penne with red peppers, feta and
    mint 46
  rice noodles with tomatoes, black
    olive and herb relish 61
  rice noodles with shredded lettuce,
    cucumber, mint, onion, peanuts
    and chilli 205
  with roasted tomatoes, and red
    (bell) peppers 58
  with tomatoes, mozzarella and
    basil 51
  shells, with courgettes (zucchini),
    and tomato-olive relish 57
  spicy East-West noodles 47
Cold Pasta with Broccoli, Sesame and
  Soy 53
Conchiglie (shells) Tricolore with
  Garlic and Tomato Sauce 105
Conchiglie (shells) with Yellow (Bell)
  Peppers and Aubergine
  (Eggplant) Sauce 162
confetti of vegetables, with fettuccine
  and garlic-mint sauce 68
Coriander (Cilantro) and Spring
  Onion (Green Onion) Pasta with
  Red Chilli Powder 243
corn, courgettes (zucchini) and
  peppers with gingered fusilli 117
cottage cheese, with pasta 75
Courgettes (zucchini)
  with orzo and tomatoes 121
  with pasta, beaten egg and
    cheese 120
  with pasta, red (bell) peppers and
    tomatoes 58
  pasta salad, with sun-dried
    tomatoes and rosemary 54
  sautéed, with pasta, mozzarella and
    egg 120
  shredded with cream and
    spaghetti 119
  with tomato sauce and pasta 125
couscous, lemon-scented with
  artichokes, olives and sun-dried
  tomatoes 110
Couscous Pilaff with Shiitake 151
couscous, with roasted tomatoes,
  green beans and ginger 163
Cream of Garlic Soup with Tri-
  Coloured Pasta 23
Creamy Onion Soup with Tiny
  Pasta 32
Crisp-Fried Rice Noodle Cloud Over
  Spicy-Sweet Mixed Vegetable
  Stir-Fry 198
Crisp-Fried Tofu and Shiitake
  Wonton with Ginger Sweet-Sour
  Sauce 250
Curly Pasta with Curried Soya Mince
  (Textured Soy Protein), Browned
  Garlic Oil, and Minted
  Yogurt 186
Curried Yogurt Soup with Broccoli,
  Chickpeas (Garbanzos) and
  Lumachine 41

Ditalini and Broccoli with Creamy
  Blue Cheese Sauce 182
Ditalini with Fennel-Scented Peas 116
Ditalini with Flageolets and Pesto 73
Ditalini, Spaghetti, Green Beans and
  Peas with Garlic and Tomato
  Sauce 105
Don Don Mein (Sichuan Noodles
  with Spicy Sauce) 201
Dried Mushrooms 262
dumplings, Tibetan vegetable, with
  curried tomato sauce 248

East-West Pasta Primavera 204
egg-lemon soup with courgettes
  (zucchini) and thin pasta 29
Eggplant, see Aubergine
endive, curly, with spaghetti and
  balsamic vinegar 70
Esther's Apple-Cheese Kugel 232

Far Eastern Pasta 16–17, 189–215
  cold noodle salad with Chinese
    leaf, crunchy noodles, and
    nuts 60
  cold pasta with broccoli, sesame
    and soy 53
  noodles with coriander (cilantro)-
    mint raita and cucumber 52
  rice noodles with tomato-chilli
    salsa 62
  salad, with peanut-butter dressed

noodles, red cabbage and bean
   sprouts 63
spicy fragrant East-West noodles 47
Farfalle (butterflies)
   and cauliflower gratin 173
   in Italian-inspired soup with
      vegetables 30
Farfalle or Penne with Sun-Dried
   Tomato and Goat Cheese
   Purée 174
Farfalle with Creamy Tarragon and
   Shredded Mushroom Sauce 145
Farfalle with Multicoloured Tomato
   Salad 55
Farfalle with Pumpkin and Mild Red
   Chilli 127
Fazzoletti di Seta con Pesto 72
Fettuccine alla Perugina 108
Fettuccine or Tagliatelle with Creamy
   Onion Sauce 134
Fettuccine with asparagus and tomato
   sauce 108
Fettuccine with Broccoli and Spinach
   and Carrot-Butter 133
Fettuccine with a Confetti of
   Vegetables and Garlic-Mint
   Sauce 68
Fettuccine with Creamy Pumpkin
   and Red (Bell) Pepper Sauce 126
Fettuccine with Creamy Diced
   Artichoke Sauce 111
Fettuccine with Green Olives, Goat
   Cheese and Thyme 88
Fettuccine with Mascarpone, Pine
   Nuts and Basil 71
Fettuccine with Spicy Tequila-Spiked
   Creamy Tomato Sauce 103
Fettuccine with Tarragon-Scented
   Mushroom Sauce Aurora 144
Fettuccine with Truffle Sauce 93
   and strands of multicoloured
   vegetables 93
Fettuccine with Yellow and Red (Bell)
   Peppers in Garlicky Cream
   Sauce 131
fideos 225
flageolets with ditalini and pesto 73
flowers, fresh, in pasta 242
Fourth of July Macaroni Salad 50
Fred Barclay's Basil and Parsley
   Pesto 255
Fresh Herb and Edible Flower
   Pasta 242

Fresh Pasta 14
fresh pasta squares with pesto 72
frittata, pasta 253
   leftovers 252
   with basil or sun-dried
      tomatoes 253
   with Mexican salsa 253
Fusilli (twists) Salad with Courgettes
   (Zucchini), Sun-Dried Tomatoes,
   and Rosemary 54
Fusilli (twists) Siracusani 140
Fusilli (twists) Verde with Broccoli
   and Red (Bell) Peppers in Spicy
   Tomato Sauce 89
Fusilli (twists) with Diced Autumn
   Vegetables 160

Garlic, Cream and Tri-Coloured
   Pasta Soup 23
Garlic-and-Olive-Oil-Scented
   Macaroni Salad with Tomatoes,
   Goat Cheese and Basil 45
Garlic-Parsley Macaroni with
   Cauliflower, Courgettes
   (Zucchini) and Red (Bell)
   Peppers 129
garlic pasta variations, with:
   basil leaves 65
   cabbage, Italian style 65
   capers 65
   cayenne pepper, parsley and
      lime 65
   hot pepper and parsley 65
Garlic, Provençal Soup 27
garlic, roasted
   with aubergine (eggplant) and
      capellini 56
Garlic Soup, with Cream and Tri-
   Coloured Pasta 23
Garlicky Pasta with Fresh Green
   Herbs 67
ginger and garlic pasta with hot
   pepper, mint and basil 104
Ginger Sweet-Sour Sauce 251
Gingered Fusilli Lunghi with Corn,
   Courgettes (Zucchini) and
   Peppers 117
Gnocchi with Artichokes, Porcini
   and Carrot 109
Gnocchi with Truffle Sauce 93
Gnocchi, potato 246
Goan Ginger-Scented Tomato and
   Cabbage Soup with Small Pasta

and Fresh Mint 22
Goat Cheese
   and broccoli-filled ravioli 239
   with fettuccine, green olives and
      thyme 88
   with fresh pasta squares and
      pesto 72
   with green beans, garlic, basil and
      spaghetti 96
   with macaroni, roasted green (bell)
      peppers and tomatoes 130
   with pasta and rustic baked
      tomatoes 100
   in pasta salad with tomatoes and
      basil 45
   with spaghetti or penne and sun-
      dried tomatoes 84
   with wholewheat spaghetti,
      tomatoes, green beans, and
      pesto 69
   with wholewheat spaghetti,
      tomatoes and olives 87
Goat Cheese and Sun-Dried Tomato
   Purée 174
Gorgonzola, baked with pasta,
   mushrooms, green beans and
   tomatoes 222
Gratin of Mustard-Scented Macaroni
   with Cheese with Mexican
   Flavours 219
Greek-Flavour Lemon Orzo with
   Yogurt-Vegetable Topping 153
Green Vegetable Soup with Pesto 19
Greens
   with pasta and cherry
      tomatoes 157
   spinach, in creamy sauce 224
   spinach, with macaroni and
      cheese 224
   turnip tops, with orecchiette 159
Grilled Summer Vegetable Pasta 166

hazelnuts, puréed with porcini and
   mascarpone 150
Hazelnut Pesto 168
Herbed Broccoli Spätzle with Garlic
   and Diced Tomatoes 246
herbs, fresh with garlicky pasta 67
Hot Pepper and Garlic Spaghetti 91
Hot and Sour Soup 191

Italian-Inspired Soup of Tomatoes,
   Vegetables and Farfalle 30

Italian Soup of Pumpkin, Beans and Orzo 40

Japanese-Style Noodles in Broth Topped with Savoury Custard 194
Jenny's Aubergine (Eggplant) and Red (Bell) Pepper Lasagne Verde 231

Khote and Achar 248
kugel, apple and cheese 232

Lasagne al Funghi 228
Lasagne con Broccoli 227
lasagne, spinach and ricotta 226
Lasagne Verde, Venice-Style 230
Lemon-Scented Couscous with Artichokes, Olives and Sun-Dried Tomatoes 110
Leslie Forbes' Last-Minute Spicy Pasta with Red Pesto and Asparagus 79
Linguine with Roasted Tomatoes, Basil, Garlic and Pine Nuts 167
Linguine alla Pizzaiola (Linguine with Tomatoes, Mozzarella and Basil) 172
Lockshen and Cheese 74
Lo Mein, with mu shu vegetables 214
Lumache or Penne with Creamy Spinach and Ricotta Sauce 155
Lumache or Penne with Ricotta Cheese and Black Olives 181
lumachine, in broccoli carbonara 78
lumachine, in curried yogurt soup with broccoli and chickpeas 41
lumachine, in pasta salad 57
Lumachine with Sun-Dried Tomatoes 83
and yellow squash (golden courgettes, yellow crookneck, etc.) 83

Macaroni
  basil, parsley and lime 66
  comforting, with spinach 224
  with mustard-flavoured cheese sauce and Mexican flavours 219
Macaroni and Cheddar Cheese Gratin with Tangy Beetroot Relish 217
Macaroni with Peas and Ricotta 112
Macaroni with Red Beans and Tomatoes 38
Macaroni with Roasted Green (Bell) Peppers, Tomatoes and Goat Cheese 130
Macaroni Salad 45
Marlena's Cottage Cheese and Pasta 75
Mascarpone
  and breadcrumb sauce 173
  with fettuccine, pine nuts and basil 71
  with fresh pasta squares and pesto 72
Mee Goreng 206
Melissa's Spaghetti 154
Mexican-Style Thin Pasta with Tomatoes and Cheese 225
Middle Eastern Cinnamon-Scented Egg and Lemon Soup with Courgettes (Zucchini) and Thin Pasta 29
Mixed Fresh Herb Pasta
  in broth 243
  with goat cheese 243
morel mushrooms, see mushrooms
Mozzarella, fresh
  with ricotta, small pasta, and aubergine (eggplant) 218
  with spaghetti and double-tomato relish 95
  with tomatoes, basil and linguine 172
Mushrooms
  Chinese black mushrooms, in broth with cellophane noodles and broccoli 190
  dried 262
  with hazelnuts, asparagus, mascarpone and pasta 150
  lasagne 228
  pesto, with black olives 141
  porcini 109
  porcini, with capellini, peas, and tomatoes 148
  puréed with porcini and cream, with pasta 149
  with roasted garlic and tomatoes, over capellini 152
  sauce aurora, tarragon-scented 144
  shiitake, with couscous 151
  shiitake, with rice noodles, tree cloud fungus, greens and sesame oil 196
shredded in a creamy tarragon sauce with farfalle 145
tree cloud fungus with tofu, broccoli, and cellophane noodles in black mushroom broth 190
Mushroom Ravioli with Beetroot (Beet) and Tomato Purée 237
Mushroom Ravioli with Summer Squash, Mushrooms and Sun-Dried Tomato-Garlic Broth 235
Mu Shu Vegetables Lo Mein 214

noodle-lettuce parcels, with spicy sauce, herbs, and nuts, Vietnamese-style 212
Noodles with Coriander (Cilantro)-Mint Raita and Cucumber 52

Olio Santo 257
  chillied 257
  garlic olive oil 257
  with mint 257
Onions
  braised, three sauces made from 135
  browned, with spaghetti, spinach and blue cheese 175
  creamy sauce of 134
  sautéed with pasta and vignottes cheese 171
Orange-Scented Tomato Sauce 102
Orecchiette (little ears) with Cherry Tomatoes, Celery and Garlic Croûtons 157
Orrechiette (little ears) with Turnip Tops 159
Orzo
  cooked in broth, with lemon and parsley 94
  with peas, asparagus or courgette (zucchini) blossoms in saffron-garlic cream 113
  lemon-flavoured with yogurt vegetable topping 153
  with radicchio 170
  in soup with pumpkin and beans 40
  with tomatoes and diced courgettes (zucchini) 121
Orzo with Greek Island Flavours 156
Orzo with Peas in Saffron and Garlic Cream 113
Orzo Pilaff with Tomatoes and Diced

Courgettes (Zucchini) 121

Pacific Rim Pasta: Rice Noodles with
    Tomato-Chilli Salsa 62
Paglia e Fieno al Aurora 114
Panthe Kaukswe 210
Pappardelle with Broccoli and Red
    Beans 183
Pasta Aglio e Olio 65
Pasta al Ceci 187
Pasta alla Giardino 161
Pasta Arrabbiata 104
    with Coriander (Cilantro)
        Pesto 104
    with Ginger-Garlic Butter 104
Pasta with Beans
    brown lentil, red bean, broccoli,
        and pasta shell stew 42
    with cannellini beans and curly
        endive 70
    with chickpeas and garlic-rosemary
        sauce 184
    with chickpeas and tomato
        sauce 187
    curried yogurt soup with broccoli,
        chickpeas, and lumachine (pasta
        shells) 41
    Italian soup of pumpkin, beans and
        orzo 40
    macaroni with red beans and
        tomatoes 38
    pappardelle and broccoli and red
        beans 183
    rigatoni with white beans and red
        pesto 188
    spaghetti with curried broccoli and
        chickpeas (garbanzos) 185
Pasta e Fagioli a la Toscana 37
Pasta e Fagioli, with leftovers 254
Pasta Frittata 253
Pasta From the Garden 161
Pasta Soufflé 145, 220
Pasta Stew with White Beans and
    Black Olive Sauce 39
Pasta Types
    chive 15
    coriander (cilantro) 243
    corn 15
    Far Eastern 16–17, 189–215
    fresh 14
    ginger 15
    hot pepper 15
    mixed herb 243

pesto 15
ragtag 16
rosemary 15, 243
saffron 15
sage and sage blossom 243
white wine 14
Pasta with Asparagus and Creamy
    Light Pesto Sauce 107
Pasta with Aubergine (Eggplant) and
    Tomato Sauce 139
Pasta with Basil-Scented Walnut
    Pesto 169
Pasta with Black Olive and Rosemary
    Cream 82
Pasta with Broccoli and Spicy-Tangy
    Tahini Dressing 49
Pasta with Cabbage, Leeks and
    Tomatoes Topped with
    Cheese 178
Pasta with Cannellini Beans and
    Curly Endive 70
Pasta with Chickpeas (garbanzos) and
    Garlic-Rosemary-Lemon
    Sauce 184
Pasta with Courgettes (Zucchini),
    Beaten Egg and Cheese 120
Pasta with Courgettes (Zucchini),
    Red (Bell) Peppers and
    Tomatoes 128
Pasta with courgettes (zucchini) and
    tomato-olive relish 57
Pasta with Creamy Pesto and Blue
    Cheese Sauce 92
Pasta with Creamy Porcini Sauce 146
Pasta with Creamy Sauce of Puréed
    Mushrooms and Porcini 149
Pasta with East-West Pesto 207
Pasta and Green Beans (or Asparagus)
    with Mascarpone and
    Breadcrumb Sauce 173
Pasta with Green Beans, Red (Bell)
    Peppers, Olives, Basil and Pine
    Nuts 118
Pasta with Grilled Summer
    Vegetables, Northern California
    Style 166
Pasta with Mushroom and Black
    Olive Pesto 141
Pasta with Pissaladière-Style Sauce of
    Onions and Olives 138
Pasta with Provençal Flavours 124
Pasta with Pungent Greens and
    Cherry Tomatoes 157

Pasta with Puréed Red (Bell) Pepper
    Sauce 122
Pasta with Radicchio 70
Pasta with Red, Yellow and Green
    (Bell) Peppers and Black
    Olives 123
Pasta with Roasted Tomatoes and Red
    (Bell) Peppers 58
Pasta with Sage Sauce 147
Pasta with a Sauce of Rustic Baked
    Tomatoes 100
Pasta with a Sauce of Spinach, Peas,
    and Rosemary Cream 158
Pasta with Sautéed Onions and
    Vignottes Cheese 171
Pasta with Tomato Sauce, Beaten
    Egg, Cheese and Basil 106
Pasta with Tomato and Courgette
    (Zucchini) Sauce 125
Pasta with Truffle Cream 93
pastina, with broccoli in garlic
    broth 24
peanut soup-stew, African style 35
pea and tomato sauce, with
    spaghetti 112
Penne (quills); _see also_ listings for
    lumache or lumachine, macaroni
    with black olives, feta and
        parsley 46
    green vegetables 158
    with red (bell) peppers, feta and
        mint 46
    with spicy tomatoes, capers, olives
        and basil 48
Penne or Gnocchetti alla
    Boscaiola 141
Penne alla Malefemmina 48
Penne alla Puttanesca 101
Pesto
    alla Genovese 255
    basil and parsley pesto 255
    in creamy blue cheese sauce with
        pasta 92
    creamy light sauce with pasta and
        asparagus 107
    East-West, with chillies, peanuts,
        coriander (cilantro) and mint 207
    in green vegetable soup 19
    with flageolets and ditalini 73
    with fresh pasta squares (fazzoletti
        di seta) and goat cheese 72
    with fresh pasta squares (fazzoletti
        di seta) and mascarpone 72

hazelnut pesto 168
red 79, 188, 256
walnut and basil 169
with wholewheat spaghetti,
   tomatoes, green beans and goat
   cheese 69
without nuts 255
Pierogi, New York Lower East
   Side 240
Piperade Pasta 123
Porcini (see also mushrooms)
creamy sauce of 146
Potato Gnocchi 246
Potato Ravioli with Tomatoes and
   Thyme 240
Provençal Garlic Soup 27
Pumpkin
creamy sauce with red (bell)
   peppers, with fettuccine 126
and farfalle, with mild red
   chilli 127
Italian soup with beans and
   orzo 40
spicy soup with thin pasta 25

Quick Garlicky Tomato Sauce 258

Rachel's Homely and Comforting
   Macaroni and Spinach Dish 224
Radiatore with Tomato Sauce and
   multicoloured (Bell) Peppers 112
Radicchio, with pasta 70
Ragtag Pasta 16
ramen 16
in salad with Chinese leaves and
   nuts 60
Ravioli
baked with rosemary and
   tomatoes 223
broccoli and goat cheese-
   stuffed 239
with crisp fried sage leaves and
   tomato coulis 241
mushroom, with beetroot (beets)
   and tomato purée 237
mushroom, with summer squash
   and sun-dried tomatoes 235
potato, with tomatoes and
   thyme 240
stuffed with ricotta, herbs and
   black olives 238
made with won-ton skins 238
Ravioli con salsa de Noci (with

walnut cream) 97
Ravioli with Sugar Snap Peas,
   Summer Squash, Chard and
   Basil 236
Red (Bell) Pepper Purée Sauce 122
Red Pesto 79, 188, 256
Rice Noodles, also known as rice
   sticks 17
crisp-fried, with spicy-sweet
   vegetable stir-fry 198
cold, with lettuce shreds, mint,
   peanuts, red bell pepper,
   cucumber, and chilli 205
with ginger-garlic green beans and
   peanut sauce 200
with shiitake and tomatoes 195
with shiitake, tree cloud fungus,
   greens and sesame oil 196
in Southeast Asian broth, with
   lime, chillies, salad and
   peanuts 191
spicy, Hong Kong-style 199
Rigatoni and Green Beans with
   Chorreadas Sauce 176
Rigatoni with White Beans, Tomato-
   Parsley Sauce and Red
   Pesto 188
Roasted Garlic with Cumin-
   Aubergine (Eggplant) and
   Capellini 56
Roasted (Bell) Peppers 262
Roasted Tomatoes 261
with cold pasta and red (bell)
   peppers 58
with couscous, green beans, and
   ginger 163
and garlic broth with green beans
   and stelline 34
with linguine, basil, garlic and pine
   nuts 167
with spaghetti and raw garlic 165
roasted vegetable soup-stew,
   Mediterranean style 20
roasted vegetables, puréed 164
Roman-style spaghetti with garlic,
   mint and a whiff of lemon 86
Rosemary-and-Garlic Buttered
   Pasta 74
Rosemary Pasta with Parmesan
   Cheese 243
Rotelle, Penne or Rigatoni, with
   Tomato Sauce, Broccoli and
   Ricotta Cheese 132

Sage, crisp-fried, with ravioli and
   tomato coulis 241
sage sauce for pasta 147
Sage and Sage-Blossom Pasta 243
Sardinian-Inspired Pasta with Tomato
   Sauce and Mint-Seasoned
   Ricotta Cheese 177
Sichuan Noodles with Spicy
   Sauce 201
Sicilian Aubergine (Eggplant)
   Pasta 140
Soba, buckwheat 16
cold, with mangetout (snow peas)
   and water chestnuts 202
with peas and cream 80
Somen 16
Soufflé-Like Pasta Casserole with
   Greek Flavours 220
Soups
African Spicy Peanut Soup-Stew
   with Noodles 35
Broccoli and Pastina in Garlic
   Broth 24
Chickpea (Garbanzo) and
   Tagliatelle Soup 43
Cream of Garlic, with Tri-
   Coloured Pasta 23
Creamy Onion Soup with Tiny
   Pasta 32
Creamy Red (Bell) Pepper
   Bisque 122
Curried Yogurt Soup with Broccoli,
   Chickpeas (garbanzos), and
   Lumachine (pasta shells) 41
Goan Ginger-Scented Tomato and
   Cabbage Soup with Small Pasta
   and Fresh Mint 22
Green Vegetable Soup with
   Pesto 19
Italian-Inspired Soup of Tomatoes,
   Vegetables and Farfalle 30
Italian Soup of Pumpkin, Beans and
   Orzo 40
Japanese Noodles in Broth with
   Savoury Custard 194
Middle Eastern Cinnamon-Scented
   Egg and Lemon Soup with
   Courgettes (Zucchini) and Thin
   Pasta 29
Provençal Garlic Soup 27
Roasted Tomato and Garlic Broth
   with Green Beans and Stelline
   (tiny stars) 34

Southeast Asian Rice Noodle Broth with Lime, Chillies, Salad and Peanuts 191
South Pacific-East Asian Coconut Soup with Chinese Egg Noodles, Green Beans and Water Chestnuts 192
Spicy Lemon-Scented Tomato and Onion Broth with Spaghetti 26
Spicy Pumpkin Soup with Thin Pasta 25
Spicy Spinach Cabbage and Tomato Soup with Capellini 31
Tomato and Garlic Broth with Acini di Pepe, from an Italian Countryside Summer 28
Tomato and Pea Soup with Nidi 33
Tortelloni in Broth with Green Vegetables and Herbs 234
Tuscan Soup of Puréed Beans with Pasta 37
Vietnamese-style Tomato Broth with Cellophane Noodles and Bean Sprouts 193
Southeast Asian Rice Noodles with Ginger-Garlic Green Beans and Peanut Sauce 200
soya mince (textured vegetable protein), curried with pasta, garlic oil and mint yogurt 186
Spätzle 244
with browned onions, dried mushrooms, and rosemary 245
herbed broccoli, with garlic and diced tomatoes 246
Spaghetti
with aubergine (eggplant) 142
with celery 154
cooked in hot pepper and garlic-seasoned water 91
courgette (zucchini) shreds and cream 119
with garlic and ginger 86
Spaghetti alla Norma 142
Spaghetti al Zenzero 86
Spaghetti o Cavatieddi with Tomatoes and Rocket (Arugula) 90
Spaghetti with Basil-Scented Courgette (Zucchini) Shreds and Cream 119
Spaghetti with Browned Onions,

Spinach and Blue Cheese 175
Spaghetti with Curried Broccoli and Chickpeas (Garbanzos) 185
Spaghetti with Double Tomato Relish and Fresh Mozzarella 95
Spaghetti with Garlic-Buttered Breadcrumbs 76
Spaghetti with Garlic Butter and Walnuts 97
Spaghetti with Green Beans, Goat Cheese, Garlic and Basil 96
Spaghetti with Green Beans, Tomatoes and Olives 115
Spaghetti with Hazelnut Pesto 168
Spaghetti with Lusty Tomato and Pea Sauce 112
Spaghetti with Orange-Scented Tomato Sacue 102
Spaghetti with Roasted Vegetable Purée 164
Spaghetti with Sautéed Curly Endive and Balsamic Vinegar 70
Spaghetti or Penne with Sun-Dried Tomatoes and Goat Cheese 84
Spaghetti with Toasted Cumin and Simmered Garlic in Tangy Cheese Sauce 180
Spaghettini with Provençal Onion Sauce, Seasoned with Capers and Tomatoes 137
Spaghettini with Roasted Tomatoes and Raw Garlic 165
Spagettini con Whisky, Porcini, e Panna 146
Spicy Black Bean Chow Mein with Stir-Fried Cabbage and Shiitake 208
Spicy Fragrant East-West Noodles 47
Spicy Lemon-Scented Tomato and Onion Broth with Spaghetti 26
Spicy Penne with Green Beans, Chinese Style 53
Spicy Pumpkin Soup with Thin Pasta 25
Spicy Rice Noodle Snack from the Streets of Hong Kong 199
Spicy Spanish Cabbage and Tomato Soup with Capellini 31
Spinach, see greens
Spinach and Ricotta Lasagne 226
Stelline (tiny stars) with White Beans and Black Olive Sauce 39
Stews

African Spicy Soup-Stew with Noodles 35
Brown Lentil, Red Bean, Broccoli and Pasta Shell Stew 42
Macaroni with Red Beans and Tomatoes 38
Mediterranean Roasted Vegetable Soup-Stew 20
pasta e fagioli, Tuscan style 37
pasta e fagioli, with leftovers 254
Summer-Afternoon Pasta with Tomatoes, Mozzarella and Basil 51
Sun-Dried Tomatoes 264
with cold fusilli, courgettes (zucchini) and rosemary 54
and garlic broth, with mushroom ravioli and summer squash 235
puréed with goat cheese 174
rehydrating and marinating 264
with couscous, artichokes and olives 110
with lumachine pasta 83
with penne or spaghetti, and goat cheese 84

Tagliatelle, with chickpeas in soup 43
Tagliatelle with Mushrooms and Tomatoes 143
Tarragon and Lemon Pasta with Sharp Cheese 85
Tender Rice Noodles with Tomato, Black Olive and Herb Relish 61
Tequila-Spiked Creamy Tomato Sauce 103
Three Spaghettini Dishes Made with Braised Onions 135
Tibetan Vegetable Dumplings with Curried Tomato Sauce 248
Tiny Elbow Pasta with Basil, Parsley and Lime 66
Tiny Seashells or Orzo with Radicchio 170
Tofu, in Black Mushroom Broth with Cellophane Noodles and Broccoli 190
Tomato Broth with Peas and Ditalini 116
Tomato and Garlic Broth with Acini de Pepe 28
Tomato and Pea Soup with Nidi 33
Tortelloni in Broth with Green Vegetables and Herbs 234

Tri-Coloured Pasta, in Cream of
    Garlic Soup 23
Truffle Sauce 93
Tuscan Soup of Puréed Beans with
    Pasta 37

Udon 16

Vegetable Stock 1 260
Vegetable Stock 2 261
Vietnamese Noodle-Lettuce
    Parcels 212
Vietnamese-Style Tomato Broth with
    Cellophane Noodles and Bean
    Sprouts 193

walnuts, with spaghetti and garlic
    butter 97
Wholewheat Pasta with Broccoli

Tops 90
Wholewheat Spaghetti with Goat
    Cheese, Fresh Tomatoes, and
    Olives 87
Wholewheat Spaghetti with Green
    Beans, Black Olive Paste and
    Goat Cheese 69
Wholewheat Spaghetti with Green
    Beans and Pesto 69
Wholewheat Spaghetti with Toasted
    Garlic, Hot Pepper and
    Broccoli 75
Wholewheat Spaghetti with
    Tomatoes, Green Beans, Pesto
    and Goat Cheese 69
Whore's Style Pasta (with olives,
    capers, and tomatoes) 101
Wide Noodles with Garlic Butter,
    Fresh Sage and Black Wrinkled

Olives 87
Wonton noodles
    ravioli 238
    with fresh herbs and edible
        flowers 242
    with soy sauce and sesame oil,
        green onions and peanuts 197

Yellow and Green Pasta in a Creamy
    Tomato Sauce with Mushrooms
    and Peas 114
    with thin green and yellow wax
        beans 114
yellow wax beans with spaghetti,
    green beans, tomatoes and
    olives 115

Zucchini, *see* Courgettes